Praise for *Touched by the Extraordinary*

As a child I had a near-death experience and as an adult
rienced a past-life. I am grateful for what they taught me
life. *Touched By The Extraordinary* gives us all the ch
share this experience and the wisdom it provides, as it he'
understand. Read on and open your mind to life and creation.

> — BERNIE SIEGEL, MD,
> Author of *365 Prescriptions For The Soul*
> and *Help Me To Heal*

"*Touched by the Extraordinary* is a gift of love and wisdom from
Susan for all us who are seeking new spiritual understandings
. . . remarkable stories of premonitions of death, after-death
communications, extraordinary encounters with angels and of
the healing power of prayer . . .

    . . . I personally was stunned and amazed by *Touched by
the Extraordinary.* It is itself an extraordinary book. This book
is an essential step in catalyzing a new spiritual paradigm in our
society. Read this book. It can change your life."

> — MELVIN MORSE, M.D.,
> Near-Death Researcher and Author of
> *Closer to the Light* and *Where God Lives*

"Superbly written and thoroughly accessible from beginning
to end . . . informed and informative reading strongly recom-
mended for dedicated students of Metaphysical Studies . . . "

> — JIM COX,
> Small Press Bookwatch, Midwest Book Review

"*Touched by the Extraordinary* is full of true stories about the
power of spirit that will inspire and uplift everyone. Most of all,
this book affirms beyond all doubt that our true essence is not
limited by time or space—and that life and death are far more
magnificent and meaningful than we've dreamed possible."

> — CHRISTIANE NORTHRUP, M.D.
> author of *Mother-Daughter Wisdom, The Wisdom of
> Menopause,* and *Women's Bodies, Women's Wisdom*

"*Touched by the Extraordinary* was written with such warmth and love. I felt Susan was talking directly to me, sharing her all that she has learned over the years. Susan takes a difficult subject and presents it in an easy to understand manner."

— JOSEY ROSENTHAL,
Cancer Survivor

"If you have had inexplicable nonordinary experiences and wondered what they meant, *Touched by the Extraordinary* will serve you well. Apollon's book will help each reader to discover and learn to live more fully from his or her greater self in a more meaningful and connected manner."

— RHEA A. WHITE,
Founder and Director of
Exceptional Human Experience Network, Inc.

"For anyone who has ever struggled with self-doubts and feelings of helplessness, this is an important book. It explains how the power of healing prayer and the compassion for all living things can create miracles, both medical and spiritual."

— KIM KURZ,
Singer and Writer

"*Touched by the Extraordinary* . . . escorts the reader inward to an assured, settled, knowing place. Once there, one reconnects, refocuses and remembers the capacity to see, sense, feel, and joyfully experience the eternal life and love of another."

— JOSI FEIT,
Metastatic Cancer Survivor

In a world in which phenomena elude the human eye, and the rational and cynical mind casts aside that which cannot be explained, yet the heart is moved and the soul yearns for embracing, Susan has compassionately and courageously brought her wealth of experience as a therapist, and her many personal encounters with the extraordinary to the reader. She is a healer who has touched a myriad of lives in her travels, and her extraordinary work lovingly offers her credo that we can bring forth the Divine and create miracles in our own lives.

— RABBI ANDREW R. SKLARZ, MA, MSW

"Susan beautifully illustrates that the 'Energy of Love' is the key component to the wisdom of intuition. Through dozens of personally related experiences, Susan guides the reader to the realization that Love can break through the barriers of time and space . . . and it is Love which allows miracles to happen.

By the time the reader finishes this book he or she will not only 'believe' in the possibilities of miracles . . . but will 'expect' a miracle."

— SUSAN DELORENZO,
Reiki Master/Teacher

"I believe that if anything is to turn the tide of humankind to a better way of living in this miraculous world, it is the power of story. More than science, religion, philosophy, or history, it is story that speaks to us and changes us, and opens us to all the other realms of being that can only be touched in this manner. Susan Apollon has crafted a beautiful collection of stories that offer a wealth of reflective soul food for those who wonder about our connection with the afterlife—and who doesn't?"

— SUSAN CHERNAK MCELROY,
Author of *Animals as Teachers and Healers*

"Susan Apollon's book renews, re-establishes, and, most importantly, re-spiritualizes our lives. Losing, first, a husband and, then, my only child, is pain too incomprehensible for most people. Without her understanding of a greater spiritual world, I would still be drowning in darkness and despair."

— SANDRA ESNER,
President of Angels Without Wings

"*Touched by the Extraordinary* gives compelling and comforting evidence of the continuation and expansion of individuated life force. Her work comes from many years of service to humanity and through careful and exhaustive investigation, she leads the reader towards acceptance of life as an eternal process. Susan's contributive work is part of our collective journey of understanding the mystery of life."

— REVEREND BRUCE KELLOGG,
Pastoral Care Minister,
Christ Unity Church, Sacramento, CA

"*Touched* . . . was not only interesting but also very touching. I don't feel so alone on my path of grieving. It validates my feelings, dreams and visions. I now know I am not crazy.

I hope people will open their minds to what Susan has written . . . I don't want people rolling their eyes, thinking I am nuts . . . Perhaps my own stories won't seem so strange and bizarre."

— CAROL CONNELLY
Mom of Stephen (1985–2002)

"Combining her talents as a compassionate spiritual psychologist and healer/researcher, Susan eloquently guides you down a journey where there are no limits to experiences. With Susan I smiled and cried, learned and shared, experienced pain and healing . . . such a precious gift no one should let pass by."

—ELLEN SARACINI,
Wife of Victor Saracini, captain of United Airlines
Flight 175, hijacked by terrorists on 9/11/2001

Touched By The Extraordinary is a wonderful book that is a true guide through the synchronicities of the extraordinary. Susan Apollon has written a book that is a combination of instruction and uplifting stories so filled with light, love and hope that I found it difficult to put it down.

— FIONA HAVLISH,
Wife of Donald Havlish, 9/11/2001 World Trade
Center victim

"Susan provides her audience with a spiritual roadmap of the metaphysical world, sharing her own personal evolution and growth of consciousness. Her stories and experiences bestow great comfort to those in despair and can help each of us to boldly embrace our future and relinquish our fear of uncertainty."

— ROBERT SASSON, M.D.

"I found *Touched by the Extraordinary* to be beautiful, thoughtful, warm and stirring . . . This book is so personal that it reached within me to nudge me forward on my own journey . . . Readers needing comfort will find it through Susan's words and those that choose to read the book for pleasure will enjoy the ride."

— AMY DOHERTY
Mother and Teacher

Touched
by the
Extraordinary

Bonus Offer

In appreciation of your reading this book,
you are invited to receive an additional
special report online for free.

Visit my website:
www.touched-by-the-extraordinary.com/specialreport

register your name and
enter the password:

TBTEBook

Touched by the Extraordinary

An Intuitive Psychologist Shares Insights,
Lessons, and True Stories of Spirit and Love
to Transform and Heal the Soul

Susan Barbara Apollon

Yardley, Pennsylvania

Matters of the Soul, LLC
Box 403
Yardley, PA 19067

ISBN 0-9754036-4-8

Cover and Interior design by Desktop Miracles, Inc.

Publisher's Cataloging-in-Publication
(Provided by Quality Books, Inc.)

Apollon, Susan Barbara.
    Touched by the extraordinary : an intuitive
psychologist shares insights, lessons, and true stories of
spirit and love to transform and heal the soul / by Susan
Barbara Apollon. — 1st ed.
        p.   cm.
    Includes bibliographical references and index.
    LCCN: 2004105485
    ISBN 0975403648

    1. Spiritual life   2. Spiritual healing.   3. Soul.
4. Parapsychology.   I. Title.
BL624.A66   2005   204
                                    QBI04-700288

Printed in the United States of America

Dedication

With heartfelt gratitude and love I dedicate this book to the memory of two extraordinary women:

My Mother, Simmy Ginsburg

and

My Grandmother, Sarah Wodowsky

Your compassion, love and wisdom are forever with me.

Table of Contents

PART ONE

"The Extraordinary—101"

PART TWO

The Stories

Acknowledgements:
With Appreciation and Gratitude

Bringing this book to you, the reader, has truly been a labor of love. The original version of the book you are about to read was completed in 1999, after more than ten years of intensive research and writing. However, the book was put on hold for more than a year while I struggled to decide whether or not to simply make a few necessary changes, or to undertake a major revision of the manuscript. During that year, I realized that my task would be to completely rewrite the material. This was a significant decision that would require much time, energy and patience on both my part and that of my family and friends.

Because this book has been a work in progress for more than a decade, it represents the collaborative effort of many people in my life. My heart and soul feel only appreciation and love for those who have supported me during this time. For the past fifteen years, so many of you, including patients, family members, colleagues and others, have shared your special stories of encounters with loved ones who have died and other remarkable stories, including synchronicities, miracles, near-death experiences, healings and special animal encounters, all of which have transformed you on some level. Without these stories, which have so beautifully enriched my life, this book would not have come to be.

The stories included in this book represent a sampling of the myriad of experiences that may be considered extraordinary or remarkable. Please know that every story, precious memory, vision, dream and incident have contributed in some part to the research upon which this book is based. Your stories have led

to a deeper understanding of the extraordinary, or conscious-
ness, and to an awareness that all life is both connected and
eternal. To each of you, whether or not your story appears in
this volume, please know that taking the time to share your
story with me has been an integral part of the creation of this
book. For this, I shall forever be very, very grateful.

Also, be assured that my intention has been to protect the
identity of those whose stories are included in this book. To
maintain confidentiality (unless specifically given permission
to use a real name), names and various identifiable character-
istics have been changed. I have placed an asterisk following
the name to indicate this.

Jaime and Yanni Maniates, the universe blessed me with
the gift of having you in my life. You both have so much to
do with the creation of this book. I shall always be indebted
to you for your wisdom, trust and belief in my own untapped
potential, guidance, friendship and your love.

Mira Borodovsky, my dear, wonderful, intuitive friend of
several decades, this book would not be what it is without you.
You have been there for me with your gentle compassion and
kindness, your tender caring and your intuitive wisdom. You
have taught me so much. How blessed I have been to share the
journey of this lifetime with you. Thank you from the depths
of my soul.

Bob and Bobbie Schutter, thank you, thank you, thank
you for both trusting and encouraging me with this project,
especially in the midst of some difficult moments. Despite the
passage of many years, I have never forgotten your words of
support and belief in the value of this material. I shall also
never forget the hot chocolate our families shared in the wee
hours of the morning. Know that I shall always be grateful to
you and your family for all that you contributed to make this
book a reality.

Beverly Stoughton, I could not have accomplished this
without you and your many gifts. As an editor, poet and

writer, you are especially blessed with literary expertise, a strong editorial style and the most wonderful and endearing sense of humor. Your heartwarming enthusiasm, dear friendship and very special support have enabled me to bring order out of chaos and actually make this book happen. You have my deepest appreciation, gratitude and affection.

Heartfelt thanks to you, Barbara Ryalls, for your neverending support and guidance and for bringing Bev into my life. It is difficult to convey my feeling of gratitude for the gift of this connection. Clearly, you are an angel for me. You were in the right place at the right time.

Kim Peck, special thanks to you as well for laboring countless hours to type the first draft of this manuscript. Though many years have passed since the completion of the first book, I continue to be indebted to you for your invaluable encouragement, kind words, helpful suggestions and feedback. Thank you, Kim, for helping me to believe in myself and in the creation of this book.

Karen Fallon, I shall always appreciate your willingness to transcribe countless hours of interviews while you were balancing family responsibilities. Thanks to you and your assistance, I was better able to more accurately describe the stories shared with me. I am in awe of your strength and your determination. How lucky your children are to have you for their mom!

Linda Schival, what would I do without you? I could not ask for a more caring or more dedicated assistant and friend. Some of the attributes that make you so special include your capability, loyalty, supportiveness and compassion. You are both my right hand and my left! Not only do you bring order to my life and that of my patients and my family, but you also have the heart of an angel, always available and touching those in need. I appreciate you. I value you and treasure your gift of presence in my life.

Amy Doherty, JoAnn Baram and Kim Kurz, you gave so much of your time and energy to the editing of this book. I shall always be grateful for your carving out many hours to edit and proof various drafts of the manuscript. My heart is filled with gratitude and love for giving so selflessly and for your suggestions, as well as your tender words of encouragement.

Dan Newman, your special knowledge and expertise helped to make this book the reality that I had so long imagined. Know that I am very grateful to you for giving so generously of your time to assist me in this project.

Joyce Goodrich, you have my sincere appreciation and gratitude for providing me with needed names, phone numbers and your special wisdom whenever I would call upon you for assistance. You are not only a gifted teacher of healing but also a very dear and caring soul.

Rosalie Schack, Susan DeLorenzo, Bob Sasson, Josey Rosenthal, Judy Cantrell, Jewel McCabe, Sandra Esner and Josi Feit, my dear and faithful friends who have enveloped me in a cocoon of warm, loving support and encouragement, you have my heartfelt thanks, appreciation and affection for all that each of you have contributed to the development of this book. For the many hours you have donated to the reading of the various drafts of the manuscript, your invaluable suggestions and your words of encouragement and wisdom, know that you have each deeply touched my heart.

Rebecca and David, you have been such a source of strength for me during the many years involved in the creation of this book. I could not have made this happen without your belief in me and in my dream, your loving support and your availability at any hour of the day to see me through my many computer crises (which involved your tutoring me, doing damage control and protecting my manuscript). David, I do not have adequate words to convey how grateful I am for your coming to my side, literally and figuratively, always "saving the day" for me with your computer wisdom and your marketing expertise, in order to bring this manuscript to the public. Rebecca, how grateful I am to you for carving out time from your busy schedule to proof and edit material for me. I feel celestially blessed to have you both in my life. Know that you have been two of my greatest teachers and that my heart overflows with love for you, and for you, Toni, as well. Your love, precious support and encouragement have been special gifts for many years.

And finally, Warren, a book like this cannot become a reality unless it is allowed to be; that is, unless it is given room and time in which it can be developed. The evolution of this book parallels my own evolution. For this to happen, you needed to be there, nurturing me, supporting me, giving me room to grow and attempt to spread my wings and fly, and allowing me to fall down as I tried new ventures. Your quiet strength, your belief in my potential (long before I was aware of it) and your steadfast and enduring love have sustained me through the years, touched my heart and soul and have enabled me to give birth to this book. You are my grounding: you make everything worth something. I am genuinely blessed!

Foreword

BY MELVIN MORSE, M.D.

It is been over 25 years since the publication of Raymond Moody's classic *Life After Life,* and, yet, we are just starting to learn the true meaning of near-death experiences. Since that time there has been considerable research into the science of the experiences, who has the experiences, what sorts of experiences they have, and what we might expect about what the experience will bring in terms of transformations of the soul.

We have learned that NDE's are real. My own research has documented that not only are they real, but that there is an area in our brain, our right temporal lobe, which allows us to access the energetic patterns that make up the universe. We don't have to wait until we die to have these experiences. Science has now validated information that mystics and psychics have known for thousands of years; that is that we all have the ability to directly communicate and receive spiritual inspiration from a source outside our body.

There are many names for this source of spiritual information, and it presents itself in a variety of ways. For some it is a voice from "God," for others it is a "gut feeling" or a "knowing." Even my six-year-old son Cody once said in frustration to me "but what is God's real name?". Though there are many labels for this source of love and inspiration, the naming of the source, or the method of communication, is not important. What is important is that we can trust that this information is just as genuine and just as valid as any other information that our brain receives and uses to create its model of reality. Spiritual intuitions and perceptions are just as real as math, and just as authentic as the energy patterns our brain receives from our eyes to create a visual picture of reality.

The stereotype and popular misconception of these experiences is that they are beautiful visions of an unearthly realm. Those who have them are bathed in joy and light. All that is true, but misses the point of the experiences. These experiences empower those who have them by giving them the emotional strength to overcome fear in their lives. They learn that fear is the opposite of love, and that it is fear that is often what keeps us from our true potential as human beings.

Understanding spiritual experiences requires an act of faith and courage. Our scientific understanding of the experiences can only take us so far. These experiences speak to us deep within our own souls; they often involve a "knowing" or a sensing of powerful forces beyond our understanding. When properly understood, they have the potential to heal grief and give us the strength to overcome depression, fear and anxiety. If we have the courage and faith to embrace them, we can use them to generate new understandings and meaning in our lives. These new understandings have the power to allow us to find our ultimate potential as human beings and ultimate happiness.

Unfortunately, far too many of us dismiss our own spiritual intuitions as crazy dreams, weird thoughts or foolish ideas. As a pediatrician, I regularly counsel grieving parents. Frequently they dismiss the powerful after-death communications of their dead children, communications which contain seeds to heal grief, as "wish fulfilling fantasies" or hallucinations. As a medical scientist, I typically point out that science validates these experiences as real. Society does not agree, however, and far too often we have no support systems or cultural context to use to understand these experiences. Society has not caught up with the science of the twenty-first century. Our cultural myths trivialize our spiritual feelings and intuitions. Irrationally, they are considered the products of brain pathology instead of real communications with a "god" or a "loving light" or as one child told me "a light who told me who I am and where I was to go."

Susan Apollon's book *Touched by the Extraordinary* represents an essential handbook and guide to understanding our spiritual selves. It took extraordinary courage for her to publish it. Mainstream psychology specifically rejects using spiritual intuitions to heal the soul. "Intuitive psychologists" are immediately suspect as they represent a new way of understanding and healing the human spirit. Psychiatrists and psychologists are more comfortable using medications to treat the grief. Spiritual visions are regarded as products of brain pathology instead of sources of healing and understanding.

Our society is in desperate need of new ways of understanding our spiritual selves. *Touched by the Extraordinary* is an essential source material for anyone trying to have a deeper understanding of their spiritual selves. It is beautifully written, drawing on story after story to demonstrate spiritual truths. Susan writes in the great tradition of shamans and teachers throughout history, using stories to help us to reach greater spiritual insights.

Susan started to write her book to help patients to better understand grief. She quickly realized that she needed to address greater issues of the nature of mind and consciousness. Soon she recognized that she needed an understanding of modern quantum physics and the science of spirituality to continue in her own spiritual journey. Only after her own personal transformation of growth and learning was she able to see life from an important new perspective. Her own development of her intuition led to a deeper wisdom that she shares with us in her book.

Touched by the Extraordinary is a gift of love and wisdom from Susan for all of us who are seeking new spiritual understandings. She tells remarkable stories of premonitions of death, after-death communications, extraordinary encounters with angels and of the healing power of prayer. She devotes two powerful chapters to stories from women who lost loved ones in the events of 9/11. No one can fail to be touched by these stories of spiritual inspiration and compassion.

She uses these stories of extraordinary encounters to teach us how to develop our own intuitions and spiritual insights. *Touched by the Extraordinary* is a spiritual how-to manual; it is practical as well as deeply philosophical. Susan is not content to be just a story teller. She shows us how to develop our own intuition and spiritual wisdom. In scientific terms, I would describe her as a psychologist who teaches us how to use our right temporal lobe to communicate with a source of spiritual wisdom beyond our bodies. A more religious person might describe her as someone who teaches us how to pray effectively to find inspiration from the healing light that surrounds us all.

I personally was stunned and amazed by *Touched by the Extraordinary*. It is itself an extraordinary book. As a society, we are only just starting to learn how to fully use our brains to understand our spiritual selves. This book is an essential step in catalyzing a new spiritual paradigm in our society. Read this book. It can change your life.

Prologue

*The transformation of our lives now
is the urgent and essential point.*
Sᴏɢʏᴀʟ Rɪɴᴘᴏᴄʜᴇ, *Tibetan Book of Living and Dying*

It is with great excitement, enthusiasm and passion that I write this prologue. The book you are about to read has been a labor of love for more than ten years. My wish is that this material will serve the evolution of your soul as it has served mine. It is my gift to you. May it take you to a place that is filled with joy, peace and love, to a reconnection with your soul.

In my work as a psychologist, I have found that my questions are the same as those of so many others. Back in the late eighties, I found myself pondering such questions as, *Why am I here? What is the nature of the soul? What is my soul's purpose? What happens to the soul after one dies?* I also had thoughts and questions about death: *Is the dying process painful? Is there life after death? Do loved ones who have died know that they have died? Can they communicate with the living? If so, how does the communication take place?* It did not stop there. I also pondered other considerations: *What about angels, guides and Masters? Are meaningful coincidences just coincidences? Does prayer work? What accounts for remarkable healings and miracles?* Little did I know then that my research, clinical work and my life's personal journey were going to be roads that would lead me to the same exciting destination—the wonderful, joyful present.

In order to find answers to these questions, I began by looking at the research of my colleagues. As both a Pennsylvania and New Jersey-certified school psychologist and a Pennsylvania-licensed psychologist, specializing in work with children, bereavement and medical issues (especially oncology), many patients were referred to me for treatment. They shared stories of extraordinary events and circumstances which touched them, but which they felt uncomfortable discussing with others. And, yes, as you may have guessed, their stories were also providing answers to some of my questions.

Furthermore, I had begun my own evolution by engaging in several periods of research—each of which paralleled that of my clinical and personal life. Turning first to the work of fellow psychologists and psychiatrists which dealt with the work of past life regression material, including that of Ian Stevenson and Brian Weiss, I found myself deeply moved, more willing to accept the idea that we are immortal beings and more eager to move ahead with my own work.

Focusing next on near-death experiences provided me with valuable insight and answers regarding life-after-life questions. My mentors included physicians Raymond Moody, Melvin Morse and Elisabeth Kübler-Ross. Their work served to validate and confirm the anecdotes my patients were telling me of their sense of a visitation, presence, vision or communication with deceased loved ones—all of which they experienced as real and genuine occurrences. I was becoming more confident that life does not end with death and that we are eternal. There also began to appear in the early nineties published accounts of fascinating, detailed near-death experiences, including those of Betty Eadie and Dannion Brinkley. In addition, leading hospice physicians and nurses were writing remarkable stories regarding their own patients that further provided information, reinforcing the possibility that the soul does not die.

Before continuing, it is important for me to share the following piece of my story with you, in order that you understand how this has all come to be. In November 1991, my clinical work included a family that played a major role in supporting my research findings that we do not die and that there is life after life. I remember well the day the Simontons,* Richard and Beth, brought Kathy, their eight-year-old daughter, to see me for treatment of issues related to heart surgery which she had undergone during the previous year. Though the surgery had been successful, Kathy had begun to experience anxiety and fears about dying.

Since our first meeting, I have worked not only with Kathy, but also with her parents and siblings, for a variety of medically related matters, as well as bereavement concerns. Over the years of our working together, they have shared countless stories of unusual events occurring in their individual lives and in their home, including the manifestation of Richard's parents on several occasions. It almost seems that the Universe brought them into my life to help me explore the various dimensions of reality and of life and death. Also, thanks to their willingness to share with me their stories of times when they were touched by "the extraordinary," others with similar situations have been comforted and helped.

Specifically, my introduction to the extraordinary happenings of the Simonton family began when Kathy matter-of-factly told me the family story of how her brother Ricky, would have nightly conversations with his deceased grandmother when he was just 3½ years old. When I asked the family about this, Kathy's mother, Beth, explained that she and her husband had often heard Ricky talking in his crib during the night. However, she recalled one night when their youngest son, Tommy, about 1½ at the time, had come running into their bedroom, crying hysterically.

According to Tommy, who shared bunk beds with Ricky, he had been awakened by the sound of Ricky talking to someone. He also remembered having seen something white—perhaps a shadow. Tommy had become frightened and hysterical at that point and had run into his parents' bedroom. Evidently, Ricky had told his brother not to be afraid because the white shadow was their grandmother. This had not been much comfort for Tommy. By the time Beth and Richard had returned to their sons' bedroom, the white shadow had disappeared.

Kathy tied this incident to another powerful and remarkable event that took place nine months later, underscoring the importance of the earlier incident. According to Kathy and Beth, Richard's father, who was living with the Simontons, had shown the family photo album to Ricky, who loved to go through it and pick out pictures of the people he knew. As Ricky was going through the photos, he suddenly pointed at one and said, "This is Mom-Mom." This stunned Beth because her mother-in-law had died in 1972, and even Beth had never met her. Ricky hadn't been born until 1976. As for Ricky's grandfather, Beth said, "He was floored."

Incidentally, Ricky reported that even at the time of our interview, while he was a sophomore in college, he remembered being aware, as a very young child, of his grandmother's presence. He could still repeat conversations he had had with her. He went on to say that he had more recently experienced moments when he sensed a presence that he believed to be that of his grandmother. These occurrences, Ricky said, seemed to come at times of great stress and anxiety, such as during exams and finals. He said that feeling his grandmother's presence provided him with comfort, reassurance and a sense that he was going to be all right. (Other college students have reported similar experiences.)

Having shared this story with you, I return now to the next focus of my research: mind and consciousness. I had come to realize, from both my previous research and from the interviews I had been conducting, that there clearly is a part of us that continues *to be*, regardless of whether or not there is a physical body. I fine-tuned my questions and wondered, *What part of the mind lives on? What is mind? What is the relationship of the body to the brain, the mind and consciousness? What is the relationship of mind and consciousness to the soul? Is it mind— or soul—that allows for re-incarnation? When we talk about mind, are we talking about energy? What is healing? How does it happen? What is this thing called karma?*

Motivated by my work with patients who were dealing with cancer and life-threatening illness, I felt that I could be of greatest service if I had more information and more answers to both their questions and mine. My gut feeling was that if I could help my patients eliminate their fear of death, they might be able to have an improved quality of life.

I turned my attention to a new group of teachers, the quantum physicists (including Albert Einstein, David Bohm, Erwin Schrödinger and Henry Margenau), as well as other prominent scientists (Rubert Sheldrake, Russell Targ and Dean Radin). I studied works dealing with consciousness, healing, prayer, meditation and intuition, written by prominent psychiatrists, physicians and psychologists, such as Carl Jung, Judith Orloff, Joan Borysenko, Wayne Dyer, Larry LeShan, Larry Dossey and Mona Lisa Schulz. I explored the research of those who study spontaneous recoveries, including Caryle Hirshberg, Marc Barasch, Paul Pearsall and Paul Raud. In addition, I examined the work of spiritual leaders and teachers that included the Dalai Lama, Carolyn Myss, Sogyal Rinpoche, Eckhart Tolle, Don Miguel Ruiz and Rabbi David Cooper. Along with these sources, I turned also to those whose work includes connections with the soul, angels, guides and teachers. Among this group were Rosemary Altea, James Van Praagh, Edgar Cayce, Doreen Virtue, Stevan Thayer and Sophie Burnham.

It is impossible for anyone to undertake such a journey without a personal transformation involving growth and learning to see life from a different perspective. **The essential findings of all those I have studied include these basics:** there is no other time than the Now, the only place where there is peace and well being; life is meant to be lived in the Now.

Mind is nonlocal (meaning that it is detached from person, time and place), which helps to explain why prayer and healing are often quite effective. When we connect with the innermost part of ourselves, our core and our soul, we connect with a wisdom—our intuitive wisdom—which provides us with a knowing that extends beyond our five senses. We truly are multisensory beings (a term frequently used by Gary Zukav in his book, *The Seat of the Soul).*

There is one more piece that must be added to this story. I vividly recall a day during the mid-nineties thinking that it was time I should begin the formal study of intuitive development. Reading about mind, consciousness, remote viewing, energy work and healing was not enough for me. I had already begun to engage in various studies of energy, including reiki and therapeutic touch. But I felt the need to understand better the process of working with mind—or consciousness. I also wanted, on a first-hand basis, to explore the ability to use my mind to assist others to heal themselves.

And so I began the work of developing my intuition. The universe honored my request for outstanding teachers by sending me Yanni Maniates, Philip Burley and Joyce Goodrich. I have been attending classes and intuitive development circles, as well as practicing the breath, meditation, healing and mindfulness, for more than a decade. In addition, given that mind is nonlocal, detached from person, time and place, I have learned much from nonphysical teachers whose teachings have been channeled and intuited, including the *Emmanuel* material channeled by Pat Rodegast and Judith Stanton, as well as the wisdom of a group of nonphysical teachers who channel through Esther Hicks, using the name *Abraham.* (Please see Bibliography and Recommended Material for more information.)

Once you begin to honor and respect the wisdom of your intuition, your life is never the same. You move to the next level of the evolution of your soul, located fully in the present. You discover that life lived fully in the Now is filled with love, peace, joy, enthusiasm and vitality; that we really all are One; and that your increased exuberance permeates your relationships with others as well. Along with all this, you realize that what you once considered extraordinary now feels more normal and comfortable—less out of the ordinary. I still smile every time something unusual—and extraordinary—occurs, because I have learned that it is the universe speaking directly to me.

The overall result of this journey of more than a decade is that I know each of us is more than our thoughts, feelings and our body. We are eternal beings who are connected to God, Source, or whatever you feel comfortable labeling the Divine. What this means is that we are here for joy and for love.

My original intention, more than a decade ago, was to write a book that would provide comfort for those who grieve for loved ones. I believed that the sharing of stories about deceased family members and friends who appear after their death in some form or presence would not only validate the experiences of those who grieve, but would also expedite the healing process—especially for those who tend to bury, suppress, deny and negate experiences they believe others have not encountered. Validation is a powerful, therapeutic tool. When we learn that others have experiences similar to ours, we feel validated (a feeling which contributes to enhanced well-being). This book is also written as a validation for each of you who have undergone at least one or more extraordinary events during your lifetime.

Furthermore, the sharing of remarkable experiences reinforces the possibility that life may continue after death, and this, in turn, may contribute to not feeling so terribly frightened of death. Such thoughts also go a long way in easing pain over the loss of someone dearly loved—especially when you believe you will see him or her again.

I have also written this book in order to comfort those of you who have unexpectedly lost loved ones and who feel guilty that you have not yet felt a sense of connection with them. My research has validated several significant points which I believe may help you. First, the soul continues to live (with or without a physical body) as mind and/or consciousness. Furthermore, each of us is endowed with an exquisite intuitive network that develops and matures as we move through life and engage in experiences such as reading books of this type. Finally, love never dies. Deceased friends and family continue to shower us with their love. My hope is that this material will move or touch you in such a manner as to gently nudge you along your intuitive development. What is important for you to keep in mind is that deceased loved ones continue to love, care and be present for you, whether or not you intuit them.

Something wonderful and exciting emerged as this book was taking form. With the integration of the research, the stories and the experiences of my own personal journey, I found myself guiding the reader in ways to experience more fully the moment—and to understand better the meaning of the stories in the context of the evolving, intuitive soul. In doing this, I realized I was being guided to help you and others to discover the joy of reconnecting with your soul.

To accomplish this, I have divided the book into two major parts. Part One presents the bottom line information, intertwined with anecdotes from those I have interviewed and from material I have researched, which will help you understand the various types of unique events you may find yourself experiencing at times. Part Two represents a sampling of stories shared with me over the past decade. These are stories that I hope will serve to comfort you, validate your feelings and bring you closer to aligning with your own soul.

May the material you are about to read not only entertain you, but also enlighten you with a new awareness of who you truly are.

The secret is to go with the mystery. When the situation doesn't make sense, a larger overall message may appear if you let it unfold naturally.

JUDITH ORLOFF, M.D., *Second Sight*

Introduction to Part One

Whether you encounter a connection or communication with a deceased loved one via a dream, vision, olfactory, electrical and/or auditory experience, or you find yourself dealing with a near-death experience, precognition or psychic event, you are being touched, on some level, by something quite extraordinary. These unique experiences, which I often like to think of as *delicious and mystifying,* frequently fall into the "difficult-to-label-and-understand" category.

To assist you in making sense of all this, a synopsis of a course I call *The Extraordinary—101* is presented in the following pages. My intention is to familiarize you with three different points: those doing the talking (sometimes referred to as the key players); the various reasons or circumstances that may be responsible for the unusual event; and consideration of whether or not the situation is simply coincidental or a synchronistic coincidence.

Included in Part One are numerous references to notable researchers in the field of extraordinary (sometimes referred to as psychic) phenomena. I have also chosen to incorporate examples from their work, as well as their key findings, for several reasons. First, they validate the experiences of those who have contributed to this book. And, second, my hope is that their presence will both enlighten you and contribute to your willingness to challenge your long-standing beliefs regarding what is and what is not real, truthful and meaningful.

CHAPTER 1

Defining the
Extraordinary

*We forget that it isn't important how they happen
(spiritual experiences) as it is that they happen.*

MELVIN MORSE, M.D.

Have you ever had a strong hunch regarding someone, something or an event that is to occur that, indeed, becomes a reality? Have you found yourself thinking of someone and, shortly afterwards, received a phone call from him or her? Or awakened from a dream that seemed so real, clear and lucid that you were not sure what was reality and what was actually a dream? Have you ever had the strong sense of being touched by the presence of a loved one whom you know has died? Have you ever been in danger, as in a car accident, in which you were sure you were going to die—and should have—but, miraculously, did not? Planned an event, but felt a strong urge not to follow through which, in turn, saved your life?

Have you ever had a near-death experience in which you were described as "clinically dead" for a brief time, but continued to experience a conscious awareness of all that was going on around you? Found yourself in actual communication—through another person—with a loved one who has died? Or noticed that as you were speaking or thinking of a loved one who has died, an object or a picture connected with that person fell, moved or made its presence known?

Given that *Webster's College Dictionary (Random House)* defines **extraordinary** as "being beyond what is usual, regular or ordinary," and as "exceptional to a high degree," and "remarkable," any of the situations described in the previous paragraph may be appropriately considered to be extraordinary. Furthermore, these same types of events might also be considered by some to be paranormal, which, according to the *American Heritage Dictionary,* is defined as "not within the range of normal experience or scientifically explainable phenomena."

The experiences just described may also be regarded as mystical if one agrees with Webster that the definitions of mystical are "mysteries transcending ordinary human knowledge" and "spiritually symbolic." Those who view such experiences as mystical tend to view them also as spiritual moments—"pertaining to the spirit or soul as distinguished from the physical nature," according to *Webster's Dictionary*.

When events occur that are similar to those described in the preceding paragraph, an individual undergoing the event can honestly consider it to be an extraordinary experience that may or may not also be described as mystical or spiritual. These events may make one feel that there is something involved that is truly unique, special and perhaps connected to the Divine, the spirit or the soul. Extraordinary moments become, or should become, "wake up, listen and pay attention" moments in life. Having stated this, I must confess that there are many people whom I have interviewed who have experienced so many remarkable and often spiritually significant moments that they tend to view the extraordinary as almost ordinary!

CHAPTER 2

Extraordinary Connections and Communications

You are not enclosed within your bodies nor confined to houses and fields. That which is you dwells above the mountain and roves with the wind. It is not a thing that crawls into the sun for warmth or digs holes into darkness for safety. But a thing free, a spirit that envelops the earth and moves in ether.

KAHLIL GIBRAN, *The Prophet*

Extraordinary moments often involve a sense of connection, as well as communication, with something that we intuitively know goes well beyond this plane of reality. There are many ways in which we can experience and communicate with the extraordinary. In fact, I have been extremely impressed with the creativity displayed in the extraordinary and, sometimes, mystical encounters of those I have interviewed.

Visions

Visions represent a specific type of extraordinary encounter that takes many forms and which serves many purposes. Melvin Morse, M.D., a prominent pediatrician, author and researcher of the near-death experience (known as NDE), has written extensively in his work, *Parting Visions*, of the types of visionary events that typically occur. In fact, Morse finds it difficult to understand the public's unwillingness to accept the significance of death-related visions since more than ten percent of the population has experienced such visions.[1]

The Normalcy of Visions

Morse refers to research in which almost half of a sample of close to 300 widows and widowers reported visionary events involving their deceased loved ones. He expresses his frustration with critics who interpret the visions as hallucinations and as being caused by "derangements of brain chemistry." His retort to his critics who view visions as hallucinations is that every study has shown that the visions normally occur when individuals are in a healthy physical and mental state rather than when they are ill, highly medicated or experiencing dementia.[2]

Visions may occur during both the conscious (waking) and unconscious (sleep/dream) states. They can stand alone or may be part of other extraordinary moments, such as near-death experiences, a presence, enmeshments, dreams, precognitions and intuitive revelations. Visions may include not only deceased loved ones, but also great spiritual representatives, forces and leaders, including Buddha, Jesus, Moses, Mary, the Dalai Lama, archangels, masters and guides.

Physicians, who have been known to be uncomfortable dealing with stories of visions, have traditionally tended to dismiss such stories as hallucinations brought on by illness and/or medications. Larry Dossey, M.D., a renowned author and researcher of consciousness, including prayer, distant healing and spirituality in medicine, differs in thinking from these physicians. He writes in *Reinventing Medicine* that visionary experiences need to be recognized as a valuable component in the healing process, especially in the new era of medicine that he has named Era III medicine.[3]

Visions Come in Many Sizes, Shapes and Forms

So many people with whom I have spoken in interviews for this book shared stories that contained descriptions of experienced visions. For example, one woman described awakening several times during her first two pregnancies to the sight of a woman standing in her room, keeping watch over her. Though frightened initially, the woman came to sense that this vision was that of her grandmother. The mother of a young patient of mine reported seeing a gentleman at the top of her stairs that she believed to be the guardian angel of her young son. Another woman, a friend of mine, awoke in the early morning hours to discover her mother standing on the other side of the room. Her mother had come to reassure her that she was doing fine—many years after she had been killed by a hit-and-run driver. Another friend of mine, whose father had died when she was eighteen years old, awoke on two occasions to see her father standing at the foot of her bed. A number of stories include seeing the deceased loved one sitting in his or her favorite rocking chair or desk chair, as he or she had done so often while alive.

The Simontons, whose story I presented in the Prologue, have shared with me numerous anecdotes of seeing visions of deceased family members who had evidently come to be with them for a period of time, especially during holidays, anniversaries and special events. In some of the visionary experiences, the father/grandfather had actually manifested and joined his son and grandson while they watched Phillies games together, something he had held dear while alive. And, on top of manifesting, he shouted out with great enthusiasm in support of his favorite team, "Way to go, Phillies!", an action which really got the attention of stunned family members.

The Girl in the Mirror

My dear friend Rosalie has a passion for refinishing furniture. She had fallen in love with a large antique dressing table and mirror, imagining how perfect it would be to change her grand-babies on its handsome surface. Being intuitive, she noticed that as she began to work on the table she had a sense of a presence. Then, before she could really reflect much on that, she found herself looking at a young girl with long golden-brown hair who, while seated in front of the mirror, was having her hair brushed by a lovely woman. At first, Rosalie felt that the woman might have been her mother. She noticed that the young girl would toss her head back each time the woman ran the brush through her hair. However, according to Rosalie, both the young girl and her mother were dressed in clothes apparently from another era, perhaps the late nineteenth century.

Such experiences are relatively ordinary for Rosalie when she is around old pieces of furniture. She has told me that she is accustomed to picking up impressions of individuals who may be associated with the furniture on which she may be working. This experience, however, was much more vivid than a simple impression. Not frightened at all by what she was seeing, Rosalie felt that she was being presented with a gift, a glimpse of another time and other lives. She felt that she was truly connecting with the former owners of the antique dressing table, and she was delighted.

Other Types of Visionary Experiences

Visions may also be encountered in group settings. You may recall reading newspapers and hearing television bulletins describing visionary encounters throughout the world. Many of these, including the world-famous ones in Fátima, Portugal in 1917, and in Medjugorje, Yugoslavia in 1981, involved visions of the Virgin Mary. These visions were reported as appearing almost nightly to millions of pilgrims who traveled to the latter site. The sharing of the experience seems to reinforce the significance of the vision as well as validate the authenticity of such extraordinary moments.

Raymond Moody, M.D., considered by many to be the preeminent authority of the near-death experience (NDE), has done extensive research on visionary encounters with loved ones who have died. He presents his research findings in *Reunions,* in which he includes detailed descriptions of the techniques used to enable individuals to communicate with departed loved ones. Through the use of mirror gazing and other techniques employed in his Theater of the Mind (a research facility that he created to develop experiments to better comprehend the mind), he has engendered numerous visionary experiences.[4]

Edgar Cayce, known for his psychic gifts both in the sleeping and waking states, reported having numerous visions from the time he was a young child throughout his adult years. Cayce's visions served many purposes, most of which dealt with understanding the past, present and future. All of his readings have been recorded, along with additional material, which provide a wealth of validating documentation.[5]

Dreams

It is in our dreams that we so often experience a powerful and meaningful connection with the unusual. Dreams, I believe, are one of the wonderful ways we have of connecting with the wisdom of our soul. They serve as a major part of our intuitive network, guiding us ever so subtly to do what we need to do in order to develop our potential. It is through our dreams that we are given *ways of knowing*—about our own lives as well as those of others close to us.

Visions often appear in dreams. According to Joseph Campbell, in *A Portable Jung,* Swiss psychiatrist Carl Jung took the position that dreams may represent the fantasies we wish were real.[6] Keeping this in mind, it is not difficult to understand how people who have lost loved ones might experience an encounter with them while in a dream state.

Jung's research also revealed that the content of dreams of people of all cultures was strikingly similar. The same *archetypal* images, he found, appeared in the myths, religious stories, visions and fantasies of all individuals, whether they lived in China, Africa, the North Pole or the United States. The reason for this, he believed, is that these archetypal images exist in the *collective unconscious,* a sort of universal field with which one's mind interacts. Furthermore, Jung believed (and I agree) that the purpose of dreams is to heighten our awareness. In Jung's words, ". . . the dream is, properly speaking, a highly objective, natural product of the psyche, from which we might expect indications, or at least hints, about certain basic trends in the psychic process."[7] In other words, dreams assist us with ways to make the unconscious conscious, which, in turn, contributes to the fulfilling of our life's purpose.

Two Basic Kinds of Dreams

There are two basic kinds of dreams, according to Judith Orloff, M.D., author of *Second Sight*: those that are psychological and those that are psychic. The psychological dreams are the more common of the two types. These dreams are those that address the emotional issues with which we are dealing, such as anxiety, depression, rage or troublesome personality traits. The ego is highly adept at keeping disturbing feelings and thoughts from creeping into the conscious state but fails miserably once the individual moves into the sleep/dream state. A classic example of a psychological dream is one in which we arrive late for a final exam and find that we are either locked out or that we have forgotten our pen.[8]

The second kind of dream, according to Orloff, is the psychic dream. These dreams tend to be impersonal and exceptionally vivid and clear. They may provide us with information, guidance and counseling about personal problems with which we are dealing. Orloff writes in *Second Sight* of being given instructions in her dreams regarding the healing of her patients, friends and family.[9]

Psychic dreams may also be precognitive and involve visions of future life experience, as well as provide requested and needed guidance. Individuals in both my practice and personal life have often reported awakening in the morning with the solution to a problem with which they had been struggling. "Just sleeping on it" may indeed provide the answer. While I do not recall the source, I do remember reading that Jonas Salk's creation of the polio vaccine was used as an example of a solution which came following a period of sleep during the time in which he was seeking to solve a specific problem.

Time Is an Illusion in the Universal Mind

Einstein once said, "For us believing physicists the distinction between past, present and future is only an illusion, even if a stubborn one."[10] Time is not an issue for the majority of quantum physicists. They tend to believe that all time exists at the same time—the present. Thus, it is not surprising that a person, in an intuitive state, such as a dream, could have access to a field of information that includes all time.

Furthermore, there is the belief among many scientists, including many quantum physicists, Carl Jung[11] and world-renowned biologist Rupert Sheldrake,[12] that mind or consciousness exists as a sort of field or river that includes every thought ever thought. Some have named this field the Akashic records, which is thought of as something like a river into which we can intuitively tap. This consideration helps us to better conceive how it is possible that while dreaming (an intuitive state), we could experience a sense of events to come or be given needed problem-solving information.

I have often thought of dreams as being either direct or indirect. I believe that the wisdom of the soul speaks to us symbolically, or indirectly. Some dreams are so strange and bizarre, and yet seem so real, that they need to be interpreted symbolically. Other dreams appear to be so real and lucid that dreamers may feel they are being given a good look at either the present or the future. These dreams tend to be more direct and explicit regarding their meaning and purpose.

Many of my patients have described dreams about a loved one who is dying or has died, who appears to come to them almost as a vision. My patients do know the difference between the waking and sleeping or dreaming states. However, they still choose to describe these occurrences as extraordinary and they make every effort to understand the meaning of the encounter.

Meeting Our Higher Self in Our Dreams

The dream state is, I believe, as real as our waking state of consciousness. In fact, we are more likely to discover our true spiritual energetic self, inner being, or our higher self, when we take time to explore the content of our dreams. The reason for this is that *we are the creators of our dreams,* whether we are speaking of visions or psychological, psychic, direct or indirect kinds of dreams.

There is a two-way process involved between the dreaming and awake states. Keeping in mind that everything in the universe is energy, including our thoughts, our dreams are energetic manifestations of both our conscious and unconscious states. For example, when you are concerned or worried about various life stressors, be they financial, personal, occupational or academic, it is not uncommon to find yourself having dreams that reflect elements of such concerns. This is the wisdom of your soul, or your energetic higher self, guiding and speaking to you through the content of the dream experience. However, what your soul, or higher self, wishes you to know is that you can, if you choose, turn your dreams into your waking, conscious reality. In other words, your dreams have the potential to be a part of your waking, physical reality. This is especially important for those precognitive dreams that offer gems of possibilities.

One of my favorite authors, renowned psychologist and spiritual teacher Dr. Wayne Dyer, writes in his book, *Your*

Sacred Self, "Your dreams are created with the same body and the same brain as is the rest of your perceptual world. It is all yours—you do not leave every night and take on a new brain to experience your night-time reality. . . . Everything that you are capable of knowing and being convinced of in your dream has a potential for being experienced at all moments of your daily life. Everything! Yes, this is a radical notion, but it leads you to know the power of your energy body."[13]

I also am in complete agreement with Dr. Dyer's statement: "I believe that your dreams do not reveal things about you but that they are you. They are real and they can become highly effective in helping you to experience your highest spiritual self."[14]

The Communicative Power of Dreams

Before concluding this section, I wish to share the experience of a family with whom I am presently working that exemplifies the vision-like quality of a loved one who comes and speaks with family members through their dreams. The family has given me permission to share their story with you. Their seventeen-year old son, Steven, who recently died quite unexpectedly, has come to each member of the family. The dreams are often described as vivid, realistic scenes and can be explained from either the psychological or the psychic perspective.

It is becoming apparent that Steven is using the dream state and various kinds of symbolism to express the thoughts and feelings that he could not bring himself to share with family members before dying and which appear to have contributed to his death. Some of the dreams are silly, light-hearted, almost "tricksterish" and very much like the way Steven often presented himself to the world. But there was a very deep, sensitive side to Steven that also comes across in the dreams.

No matter what the content may be, the family members are grateful for each of their dream experiences. They feel Steven's love, as well as a deep sense of connection with him and are pleased that he is seeking to communicate with them, despite his being in a nonphysical state.

A Presence

A presence can take many forms—physical and nonphysical. According to Larry Dossey, M.D., in *Reinventing Medicine:* "Presences seem to precipitate from another dimension. They may be sensed as a person with a particular identity, as an ethereal 'being of light,' an angel, or as an 'immaterial something' that is impossible to describe.

No matter what form it takes, a presence can bring immense comfort to a dying person."[15]

The reason for the comfort? The presence may serve as an indication that perhaps the soul has survived, may be immortal and therefore continues to live. And, if that is the case, the implication is that we either may not be alone or we may be reunited with a loved one at some point in the future.

Given that the word 'presence' is rooted in Latin words meaning 'to be' and 'before,' the meaning of presence embodies our own essential, timeless, fundamental nature.[16] When we are genuinely present with someone, we extend him or her a helping hand, connecting the individual with the infinite— and in that, there is healing. Dossey and Kübler-Ross have written of individuals whose presences have been so comforting that they have been able to assist with the healing of their patients.

In the Presence of Love

Kübler-Ross, in several of her works, has described the actions of one of the hospital's janitorial women as being so helpful in touching the soul of her patient who was dying, that she hired the woman as her assistant.[17] The black woman, who Elisabeth describes as her "greatest teacher," eventually shared her story. She spoke to Dr. Ross without anger or resentment, talking about the poverty with which she grew up in New York and how she, with no money for medication, would wait with her infant son in her arms for hours for the arrival of a physician. She spoke of her desperation and of how one day her little one died in her arms as she waited.

This uneducated but immensely wise woman explained to Kübler-Ross, who did not initially understand why the woman was sharing her agonizing and painful story, the following: "You see, Dr. Ross, death is not a stranger to me anymore. He is like an old, old acquaintance. I am not afraid of him anymore. Sometimes when I walk into the room of your dying patients, they look so scared. I can't help but walk over to them and touch them and say, "It's not so terrible."[18]

Kübler-Ross was deeply moved by the woman's story. Only after hearing her words did Elisabeth understand how she had touched the lives of her patients. From the heart and soul of having experienced the deepest of losses, that of a child, this cleaning woman came to Kübler-Ross's patients as a presence with the greatest gift of all, loving compassion. She had been there and faced unflinchingly. Furthermore, she knew not only how horrific it was, but that it was survivable as well. In Kübler-Ross's words, "It does not matter what you do in life. The only thing that matters is that you do what you do with love."[19] Recognizing the gifts of her cleaning woman, Kübler-Ross promoted her to her first assistant, to the dismay of her fellow physicians.

Electrical, Olfactory and Auditory Encounters

In the course of interviewing patients and others over the years, many have shared stories of a sense of connection with a deceased loved one via the most extraordinary and, yet, ordinary means of communication. These experiences may or may not be accompanied by a vision. And, honestly, having a vision of a loved one is not considered a necessity for an individual to believe that their loved one is really present. What matters, I believe, is the timing of many of these events. Often it is reported to me that these encounters occur at just the moment one is thinking of their loved one, at a time when the person is in need of some assistance or when one is in some sort of danger.

Audible Connections

An audible occurrence that frequently takes place is hearing the voice of a deceased loved one suddenly calling out one's name. As you may imagine, the individual who hears this is usually quite startled and thinks that he or she is imagining the whole thing. For example, one man spoke of being awakened by hearing his mother's voice calling his name loudly and sternly. The purpose? To awaken him because he had, much to his surprise, overslept and was late for work.

Sophy Burnham, author of *A Book of Angels,* writes of a Connecticut woman who had been in a car accident. When knocked unconscious and unable to move, she not only heard a voice that warned her to "Get out!", but she also felt invisible hands pulling her from her car. As she crawled away from the car, she heard it exploding behind her. Had it not been for the voice, she would not have survived.[20]

My friend, Samantha, whose story appears further on in this book, has had several experiences while driving in which she has heard a voice directing her to quickly move away from a particular car or truck. Had she not done so, she and her passengers would have certainly resulted in either being injured or killed. Sometimes, her close calls have been "too close for comfort." She has admitted to me that these experiences have left her feeling very protected.

One of my patients whose husband was killed in the World Trade Center recently told me that her husband's oldest, dearest friend has experienced her husband's presence, as an actual vision and voice, speaking to him on several occasions. Just knowing this has brought her great comfort.

Other audible experiences also often occur. How many times have you heard individuals who have lost loved ones reporting sounds like someone going up and down the stairs and doors opening and closing in another part of their home? Others have told me that they have heard kitchen cabinets and refrigerators being opened, kitchen and desk chairs being moved, and have observed pictures and meaningful objects falling off the wall just as they were remembering their loved ones.

Wired Connections

Many of those I have interviewed have also shared with me stories in which at the moment they were especially missing their loved ones and feeling particularly hopeless, grief-stricken and alone, an electrical event would occur. Perhaps the electrical lights in the room would blink or their beeper would go off. Perhaps their phone would ring suddenly, revealing the phone number of the deceased loved one, or their television and/or VCR would go on automatically. These events would always bring some form of comfort to those experiencing them.

I recall an incident that occurred several years ago when I had been asked to speak to a group of parents and their children who were about to graduate from high school. One of the young women, dearly loved by all those present, had been killed just a few days before. As I spoke, I did not notice that the light next to me had blinked several times. Several days later, in speaking with the owner of the home, I was told that there was absolutely nothing wrong with the lamp. The bulb was fine, as was the electrical cord. It was her sense that this was the way the young woman who had died was trying to let her friends and family know that she was present.

The Scent of Love

I find that one of the most comforting experiences is that of breathing in the scent of a loved one. Extraordinary olfactory events involving the sense of connection with a deceased loved one have been described to me on several occasions. Some have described the surprise of suddenly and unexpectedly smelling a familiar floral scent, or sometimes that of a favorite perfume, cologne or toilet water—even that of a favorite flower—of their loved one. I am often told that these scents come quickly, linger only a few moments and then are gone. However, the sense of the presence of the loved one remains long after the scent has disappeared. Though these individuals try to find logical explanations for these times, there are none.

This, once again, was brought to my attention just recently, while speaking with my patient, Anna.* Anna, a mother whose seventeen-year-old daughter had died unexpectedly, described several recurring scenarios in which she had been in her daughter's room, going through her dresser and closet, trying to accept the reality of her death. While holding her daughter's favorite jeans, Anna suddenly picked up the scent of her daughter's favorite perfume. This happened again when she entered her daughter's closet. Anna told me that she knew, with absolutely no doubt, that her daughter was letting her know that she was still with her. To add further validation to the event, when her children entered the room to talk with her, the scent vanished. And when the children left the room, the scent reappeared. To go one step further, Anna picked up the scent in my office during the following session. The experience was enormously comforting for Anna, who used these moments of connection as opportunities to let her daughter know how much she missed and loved her.

I also was comforted by the experience, given that my work is directed towards the healing of not only those who are here physically, but those who may be in a nonphysical state and are still in need of healing as well. It was the scent of Anna's daughter's perfume that served to validate my own intuitive sense that her daughter had been present with both of us during the session.

The Animal Kingdom

So many people I have met are animal lovers. Consequently, I have had many stories shared with me of miraculous deeds concerning either pets or animals in people's lives. However, one does not have to be an animal lover to experience extraordinary events dealing with animals. Animals are extremely wise, intuitive and sensitive, probably more so than most individuals, to changes in the energy in their environment. It comes as no surprise then, that it is either before or after the death of a loved one that many of the stories shared with me occur. These include heartwarming, unusual and moving encounters with dogs, cats, butterflies, dolphins, cardinals and owls.

Thank goodness for the research of Rupert Sheldrake! Sheldrake, renowned British biologist and author, presents his research in his work, *Dogs That Know When Their Owners Are Coming Home,* which demonstrates the telepathic communication that appears to take place between animals and their owners.[21]

Telepathic Connections

Remember all those stories you have heard concerning animals who would wait by the door for their owners to return home, or those who would become separated from their owners while in the process of a move and who would somehow find their way home? And what of the stories of pet owners who would frequently engage in communication with a pet in another part of the house? Whether it is intuition or telepathy, animals often appear to have a sense of knowing what it is that we are thinking or what is about to happen.

In our own family, our two precious cats have demonstrated a sort of knowing when they are about to be groomed. Despite my efforts at neither thinking about having to get them ready for the groomer nor behaving in any way that would give away my intentions, they always seem to know beforehand my plans for them. They seek out places to hide, trying to be as discreet as possible, making it difficult for me to have them ready to be picked up by the groomer. I find myself feeling both frustrated and amused as I run around looking for them in our home.

Sensing Owner's Health Problems

If the reader is interested in reading more about the intuitive nature of animals, I strongly recommend reading Sheldrake's

Dogs That Know When Their Owners Are Coming Home. It is filled with touching and wonderful anecdotal stories regarding animals that are so connected with their masters that they are even able to sense their state of health and impending death. I recommend also the work of Penelope Smith, an intuitive who teaches us the perspective and the wisdom of animals, as well as ways in which we can improve our communication and understanding with all animals.[22]

Even as I write this, I am reminded of a story told to me recently by a good friend. His wife has been through a difficult year and a half. She had been diagnosed with a thyroid problem some eighteen months before our conversation. The problem contributed to significant and painful problems with her eyes, which, in turn, led to several tough surgeries. What is interesting here is that only recently did she realize that their dear cat, who is extremely attached to her, would follow her about everywhere in their home. Whenever she would sit or lie down, their cat would jump up on her and persistently knead her neck and throat area. She never understood this until she suddenly found herself putting the two pieces of information together. Apparently, her cat sensed a problem with her thyroid long before she or her doctors were aware that there was a problem! What a pity she and her cat were not able to have a direct one-on-one conversation while she was trying to find answers to her intuitive knowledge that something was not right!

Sheldrake, in *Dogs That Know When Their Owners Are Coming Home,* informs the reader of the research of Andrew Edney which dealt with the warning behavior of dogs. Edney studied the behavior of twenty-one dogs that were able to predict when their epileptic owners were about to have a seizure. What he learned was that all the dogs, which included the gamut of breeds and sizes, would behave in restless, agitated states, barking, whining and licking the hands and faces of their owners, as their way of both warning and protecting them. The dogs would then guide their owners to safety, where they could lie down while the dogs either stayed with them or went for help.[23]

What is impressive here is that the dogs were extremely accurate, even able to detect a fake seizure attempt. Sheldrake provides stories of cats and rabbits whose behavior has also served to warn their owners of epileptic seizures. The result of this research has led to the pioneering of training seizure-alert dogs both in England and in America.[24]

Dolphins are especially known for their intelligence and their intuitive ability to be aware of human beings who are either pregnant or ill. Stories have appeared both on television and in publications about individuals who, when swimming with the dolphins, would report that the dolphins would swim in close proximity to them, often very close to parts of the body which were later shown to have a medical diagnosis, such as a tumor or even a pregnancy (something of which the woman was not yet aware).

I have had several patients who, in their terminal stage of cancer, traveled to Florida in order to swim with the dolphins. Another patient who has had several significant losses has traveled to Hawaii several times to swim freely with the dolphins in the Pacific. They all have shared with me the pure joy of such an experience, always speaking of the comfort and sense of healing that they felt while with the dolphins.

Sensing the Death of a Loved One

One of the most touching stories shared with me by a patient dealt with the death of her dad and the reaction of her dog, Brownie*. Elisa* had been very close to her dad, so close that while he was gravely ill and actively fighting for his life, he had lived with Elisa in her living room, which she had converted into a makeshift bedroom. Being in her home had provided numerous opportunities for her dog, Brownie, a brown Labrador, to get to know her dad. In fact, they had become the closest of buddies by the time her dad had to go into the hospital for emergency treatment. Unfortunately, Elisa's father deteriorated significantly while in the hospital, despite lifesaving measures that had been taken.

According to Elisa, she clearly recalled one evening when she knew her dad was close to death. (Elisa was uncommonly intuitive.) She had said her goodbyes and expressed her love to him before returning home that night. Later in the evening, while sitting with her family and Brownie, the phone rang. As she got up to answer it, Brownie, obviously sensing something not right, lifted his head, and went over to be by her side. As she received the news that her father had just died, Brownie let out a howl, reflecting what could only be interpreted as feelings of great loss and pain. Without her saying a word, Brownie intuitively had known that her dad had died.

This became even more obvious when Elisa, who was also feeling both a sense of loss and relief for the end of her dad's pain, returned to the large brown leather chair in which she had been sitting. Brownie followed Elisa to the chair. As soon as she sat down, Brownie also sat down, just in front of her, and put his head on her lap, his large brown eyes staring up at Elisa while at the same time making a very quiet but audible whimpering sound. Brownie was crying and grieving for his friend who had just died—and all of this without Elisa verbally communicating anything to him regarding the nature of the phone call.

Intuitive Wisdom

How do you "just know" something sometimes? How familiar is that feeling of suddenly knowing what is happening to an individual who lives in another state or town? How often have you experienced the sense of knowing exactly what ailment a friend or loved one is suffering? Do you recall those times when you had a sense that you would shortly be seeing someone, and then found yourself face to face with the person only minutes or hours later? Each of these is an example of intuitive wisdom, a way of knowing unlike any other.

The Intuitive Network

Intuitive wisdom represents a type of knowing with which we are born. In fact, we are all born with a kind of intuitive network, succinctly described by Mona Lisa Schulz, M.D., Ph.D., renowned researcher of intuition, neuropsychiatrist and author. According to Schulz in *Awakening Intuition,* our intuitive network consists of the following: *our brain,* consisting of the right hemisphere which receives the intuition and the left hemisphere which translates and interprets what has been received, and where our memories and dreams are processed verbally; *our dreams,* which often guide us through the use of symbols; *our memories,* which have been verbally processed and encoded in our brains; and *our bodies,* which also non-verbally process and store memories throughout our physical being.[25]

Schulz emphasizes that we are always being intuitively guided by our own system. There is a communication taking place every time we have an intuitive sense of something. As I have so often explained to my own patients, every time we have a thought, feeling or sense of something, the information is immediately translated by the brain and sent to the body by means of chemicals called neurotransmitters. Whether we call these chemicals neurotransmitters, endorphins or neuropeptides, their job is to communicate with the rest of our being what we are experiencing. The heart, liver, intestines, lungs, blood vessels—everything—are totally aware of what is going on. This is instant communication in all its glory.

All of us, I believe, are born with the gift of intuition. Unfortunately, it seems to take many decades to develop our intuitive skills and to trust our own intuitive wisdom. It does not have to be this way. While some of us are born with the gift more highly developed than others, all of us, as human beings, have within us the capacity to develop our intuition.

The Uniqueness of Intuition

Having studied intuition for the past several years, what I have come to learn is that it is unique for each person. That is, every individual experiences intuition differently. For example, if two individuals were to focus on the same subject, the ultimate information they might end up with might very possibly be the same thing! However, the way they got to that information, or intuited it, would most likely be very different. What I am referring to is the difference in the symbols each would receive that, when interpreted, would convey the same meaning or, ultimately, the same message.

Some of us are intuitive empathically. That is, we are able to sense what another is feeling, either physically or emotionally. Author and teacher Carolyn Myss, Ph.D.[26] and Mona Lisa Schulz are both empathically gifted medical intuitives. This is an especially valuable skill for those who are in the medical field. It is my belief, and that of others, that this skill can be developed with practice.

I have come to think of intuitive wisdom as the wisdom of the soul. Like Gary Zukav, in *Seat of the Soul*,[27] I believe that the purpose of our intuition is to connect us with both our own internal wisdom, which is the wisdom of our soul, and also to connect us with other sources of wisdom, whether it be the wisdom of God, angels, teachers, masters, or deceased loved ones. The wisdom of the soul is divine wisdom. It belongs to our Higher Self. When we connect with this, we *know* with our entire being that we are on the right track

Sometimes intuition comes in the form of pictures created by the mind's eye, and is called **clairvoyance. Clairaudience** is a type of intuition that comes by way of sounds or a sense of what others may be saying, and which is created by the mind's ear. **Clairsentience** is frequently referred to as *"mother's intuition."* This is a form of intuition that involves the receiving of information via sensations in one's own physiology. It is not uncommon for individuals to experience intuition through more than one modality.[28]

Intuition in the form of clairvoyance—or remote viewing—has gained respectable recognition as a result of the research conducted by both the governments of the United States and Russia. Physicist Russell Targ, hired by the CIA, and spiritual healer Jane Katra co-authored *Miracles of Mind.* The book includes many of the remote viewing experiments he and others carried out at the Stanford Research Institute from 1972 to 1986. His descriptions are a testament to the belief that the CIA recognized the value of **nonlocal mind or consciousness** in protecting the national security of the United States. His writing indicates that Russia was, at the same time, conducting the same type of research. According to Targ, their research indicated that distance, electromagnetic shielding and size of the subject in no way impacted the accuracy and reliability of one's remote viewing.[29] In other words, there is nothing that can block what one intends to see intuitively. That, I believe, is rather impressive, and speaks to the power of using our inner knowing or intuition.

Intuitive wisdom has been the source of some of the world's greatest creations. Included among these are Thomas Edison's invention of the electric light and the polio vaccine of Jonas Salk. Think for a moment and recall how many times you have heard individuals say that their best inspirations, thoughts, solutions and answers to problems they have pondered for great periods of time have come to them shortly after awakening from a deep sleep. This is intuition at work while the body sleeps, a fact that supports the need for a good night's sleep.

One dear family member, my sister-in-law Rosemary, is a very successful attorney. She has shared with me that on the morning she starts a new trial, she often awakens at 2:00 A.M., her mind filled with overflowing inspiration regarding her trial presentation. It is these moments of inspiration that she feels have contributed to the success of her cases. My father, a physician for more than fifty years, has often shared stories with me of having a problem, thinking about it just before going to sleep, and awakening in the morning with the solution he had been seeking.

While recently speaking, in session, with Gabriella,* a highly intelligent and very respected woman whose husband died in the World Trade Center, I learned that she had been given the opportunity to speak with a gifted and esteemed medium through whom she was able to connect with her husband. The details provided by her husband were personal, indicating the genuineness of the exchange. It was during this time that her husband told her that he was the source of those many thoughts of inspiration that "just came out of the blue" to her. In other words, he validated her sense that the sudden thoughts and ideas she had in numerous situations were, indeed, coming from him. Gabriella had thought this to be the case. However, hearing him say this to her was incredibly reassuring, and, once again, very comforting.

A Mother's Intuition

Before concluding this topic, I would like to finish with a wonderful example of a type of intuition that is considered to be both clairsentience and a type of telesomatic event. Schulz, in *Awakening Intuition,* writes of her own mother's intuitive experience that occurred when Schulz was hit by a truck while jogging across a bridge in Oregon. At the very moment that Schulz was being hurled into the air by an oncoming truck, her mother suddenly stood up in her hometown historical meeting, three thousand miles away, and declared that something had just happened to Mona Lisa. The time of the incident was confirmed because it was recorded in the minutes of the historical meeting that her mother was attending.[30]

It comes as no surprise to me that Schulz is as intuitive as she is, given her mother's empathic intuitive sensitivity. Moms simply have a way of knowing. Once again, think how often you have heard stories of mothers who suddenly sensed a problem with their offspring. Mothers frequently know when their children are not doing well, when they are ill, when they have been injured, and when they are hurting emotionally. Somehow, using their empathic intuitive connection, they truly feel within their own bodies what their children are feeling. It is really a very impressive phenomenon.

Enmeshment

Can you imagine what it might be like to find yourself experiencing the energy of a loved one who has recently died, if even for just a few moments? Especially when you were in the throes of missing them enormously?

Probably the most fascinating stories shared with me, in over ten years of interviewing individuals regarding their extraordinary stories, have been those encounters that dealt with detailed descriptions of people who have had a strong sense that the energy of a loved one who has died has enmeshed, or merged, with their own bodies or that of someone close to them for a period of time. The incidents do not appear to last long, but those who have reported them to me have indicated that they found them to be incredibly comforting and soothing moments. In fact, every one of the stories has been a positive experience, unlike stories of individuals being possessed by spirits, which have always been uncomfortable and disturbing.

When Guardian Angels Merge with Love

The stories of enmeshment that I have gathered come from my patients, friends, family and myself. One special example of enmeshment will be described in a later chapter. However, at this time, I would like to share with you a story of enmeshment that has moved me deeply.

Anita,* the mother of one of my young patients, had been working as a nanny for a family in which the young mother had recently died, leaving behind two children, Darren, 6, and Krista, 8. Their dad, a physician, had a difficult work schedule and was finding it challenging to raise his two children without some additional assistance. Given that the children had already known Anita, they were comfortable having her in their home as a nanny.

As I came to know Anita over many months, it became obvious to me that she was intuitive. In fact, she shared numerous stories with me that indicated her sensitivity to nonphysical energy. She had experienced her own grandmother who had died and the energy of others, including the guardian angel of her first-born child. Anita also sensed those spirits who continue to dwell in Victorian homes. She had no difficulty experiencing the presence of nonphysical energy. It neither frightened her nor made her feel terribly uncomfortable.

According to Anita, there were often times when, seated at the kitchen table feeding the children their dinner, she would hear the front door bell-ring. She could see, from her seat at the table, through to the foyer and the front door. Anita told me that she would watch the door open and close, on its own, just after the bell would ring. There were times when she could actually see the children's mother enter the house. Neither Darren nor Krista were able to actually see their mom, though Anita would tell them that the bell might be their mom coming to make sure they were happy and being well cared for.

Anita explained that she had frequently seen a woman at the attic window on the third floor each morning as she walked Darren and Krista to the bus stop in front of their home. It was Anita's feeling that the children's mom watched over her children on a daily basis. Anita received confirmation of this from her own daughter, Renie,* who had come to spend a day with her. Having already demonstrated her intuitive abilities to her mom from a very young age, it came as little surprise to Anita when Renie asked her mom about the woman standing at the window on the third floor. Even she had caught the mother keeping watch over her children.

As Anita told me the story, on a warm fall afternoon, Darren, Krista and Anita were all seated in the living room, a room filled with the warmth and beauty of the afternoon sun. The children were excited about their day at school and were eagerly sharing all the details of the day's events with Anita.

Anita was seated on the comfortable rose and mauve sofa, listening to Darren talk to Krista with great gusto, when, quite suddenly, Anita noticed the face of Darren's mother appear from behind and merge with Darren's so that the child, for just a moment, fully resembled his mother. His mother then withdrew, and Darren was once again simply Darren. But for just a moment, mother and child had become one. This was enmeshment, in its purest form. Again, Darren had not appeared to be aware of this, at least not consciously aware. But Anita certainly had been! Indeed, Anita has never forgotten her sense of awe and amazement regarding this event.

The Gift of Hugs

Hugs are another great example of where enmeshment frequently occurs. For example, I recall that not long after my mom died, I had a visit with Samantha,* my friend who is a superbly gifted intuitive and medium. My mom often chose to come unexpectedly and speak with me through her. Given that my mom and I had an exceptionally close relationship, I grieved deeply for her after her death.

I recall that Samantha had made a distinct point of getting up from her seat to give me a huge, warm and poignant hug and kiss on the cheek on several occasions. What she eventually shared with me—and I had pretty much figured out—was that my mom's energy had merged with Samantha, and that somehow the hug was an embrace from my mom. No wonder I often left Samantha feeling warm all over and teary-eyed!

Gabriella, whose story has previously been described, also experienced a similar sense of connection with her husband. After finishing her session with the medium, Gabriella heard the medium say that her husband wanted her (the medium) to hug Gabriella. The hug was different from any that Gabriella had experienced with someone she did not know well. It was a deep, penetrating, touching hug, very much like that her husband had given her when he was alive. *This is my husband,* she thought to herself as she was embraced. *This is my husband.* And as she was saying this to herself, she heard the medium make a sound that she immediately recognized as an attempt by her husband to speak with her. Gabriella's eyes filled with tears as she conveyed to me the beauty of this extraordinary experience. She knew that, thanks to the efforts of her husband and those of the medium, she had been blessed with a deeper sense of connection with her husband than she had had since his death.

My own sense of this experience that I call enmeshment is that it provides the nonphysical with the capacity to reconnect with loved ones who are physical. At the same time, perhaps it provides their loved ones with a sense of protection, well-being, great love and energy.

Automatic Writing

Several years ago while teaching a class on the extraordinary at the Bucks County Community College in Newtown, Pennsylvania, I asked a couple to share with the class and me a remarkable story regarding how their daughter, who had died several years before, had chosen to come to them. With tears in their eyes, the couple explained that their other daughter had been writing one afternoon when she suddenly had the sensation that her hand was being guided. Much to her surprise, she discovered that the words she was forming were those of her sister. It was not very comfortable for her initially because of the awkwardness she experienced as she tried to make the needed letters and words to express the thoughts that came from her sister. However, with time, this improved and the fact that their loved one has chosen a manner to both be present and to convey her thoughts and feelings has brought immeasurable comfort and joy to all her family.

Out of the Mouths of Our Guides and Loved Ones

Since that experience, I have further explored and researched this phenomenon. Ruth Montgomery, best-selling author of more than fifteen books dealing with paranormal and psychic subjects and who has been honored for her journalism as an outstanding White House correspondent describes her own experience of automatic writing in *The World to Come*. Every day she sits and, before beginning to write, meditates, prays for protection and places her fingers in typing position. And that is it. When finished meditating and praying, she begins to write, often dialoguing with her guides. What I found particularly fascinating were the conversations she writes about in which she has dialogued with her deceased husband, her guides and her parents (who apologized for opposing her writing about psychic subject matter).[31] The writing is clearly one of collaboration, and something that she has obviously enjoyed having over the years.

James Van Praagh, a gifted medium and author, has also described automatic writing in *Heaven and Earth*. In his first experience, he describes a moment when, while doing a rather boring and monotonous activity, he felt a sudden sense of inspiration to jot down an idea for something he had been working on.

He states: "I sat with my eyes closed and tried not to control my hand. At first, my fingers felt light and airy . . . Then my hand began to move in circular motions . . . The longer I kept my hand on the page, the faster the circles came. Later I learned that this was spirit's method of aligning with my energy field and building up the energy in order to write."[32] Van Praagh continues to describe how the process became more refined over time, allowing him to easily read the messages he was receiving.

Van Praagh continued to practice this for about a year, connecting with various guides, teachers and spirits. Although he did not fully understand the meaning of the messages dealing with his life in the future, including his responsibilities as teacher and guide to others, he states, "Feelings of love, understanding, and joy were always apparent when they entered my space to communicate in this manner."[33]

What these experiences reveal to us, once again, is that we are blessed with guidance and that it is within our power to find ways to both express and listen to this wisdom. The choice is ours.

Precognition

Precognition is having a strong sense of what is going to happen at some point in the future. If you are feeling that there is an overlapping here with all that has so far been presented, you are absolutely correct.

Any time you have a strong feeling or thought of something that is about to take place, you are having a precognitive moment. So much of life is filled with these experiences. Consider this: aren't hunches, dreams, telepathy and intuition ways in which we have an awareness of what may take place? These are ways of knowing. As human beings, we go about our lives without truly appreciating how gifted we are regarding our ability to know what the future may hold for us. If we were to truly recognize and respect the ways we receive information, we could cope far more effectively with the challenges of life.

Nonlocal Mind—Intuition's Common Denominator

Larry Dossey, M.D., in *Reinventing Medicine,* states, "There are no absolute separations between premonition, insight, intuition, dreams, hunches, synchronicities, revelations, telepathy and clairvoyance. The common denominator is **nonlocal mind**—a way of knowing that operates outside of space and time."[34] Nonlocal mind describes mind as not being connected to any particular place (the brain), time (the present), and space (the body). Borrowed from the research of the quantum physicists, the idea that mind is nonlocal is a beautiful way of making sense of precognitive experiences. I promise that it will receive further discussion in this book.

Judith Orloff, M.D., an intuitive, psychic and author, describes in her first book, *Second Sight,* how her dreams have been powerful experiences of precognition which have served to guide her in treating her patients and which have also warned her of impending danger, such as earthquakes.[35] Orloff views all dreams, including the good and the not so good, as blessings or gifts because, for her, they represent a deep sense of connection between our world and us.

Rupert Sheldrake, renowned biologist and author whose theory of morphogenesis (regarding the evolution of form and structure of all organisms) may be one way to explain so much of the phenomena that is considered extraordinary, admits in his book, *Dogs That Know When Their Owners Are Coming Home,* that even his concept of morphogenetic fields cannot adequately explain it all. He writes, "For me, the most mysterious kinds of perceptiveness are those premonitions that cannot be accounted for in terms of telepathy or subtle physical clues. In these cases, by a process of elimination, precognition or presentiment, seem the only remaining possibility." He continues: "But at the very least, the existence of precognition or presentiment implies a blurring of what is happening now and what is about to happen."[36] Dogs, cats, bird, fish and animal life in general, along with human beings, experience precognition. We need to learn from both experiences.

Political Precognition

Dean Radin, in a book that I highly recommend, *The Conscious Universe,* provides several well-known stories dealing with President Lincoln and his assassination. Evidently President Lincoln had experienced events that contributed to his precognitive sense that he would die while in office. In one situation, just after his election in 1860, he had looked into a mirror and saw a double image of himself. He interpreted this intuitively as a matter of fact that he would be elected to a second term but would die before finishing the term. This was substantiated for Lincoln by a disturbing dream he had. Awakened one night by the sound of people grieving aloud, he followed the sound to the East Room of the White House. There he discovered soldiers keeping guard over a corpse dressed in funeral attire. When he questioned them about who had died, they responded that it was the President who had been assassinated.[37]

Radin continues with a lesser known story regarding the precognition experienced by Mrs. Julia Grant, wife of Ulysses S. Grant. Grant, having just accepted the unconditional surrender of General Lee a few days before, was to have been honored at a reception at the capital. The couple was also to have been seated in the same box at Ford's Theater with President and Mrs. Lincoln. Early in the day, Julia Grant had begun to feel an urgent need to leave Washington with her husband and child. Her sense of urgency increased with each passing hour. After sending repeated messages to her husband, who was busy with appointments, he finally agreed to leave, and the family left Washington before evening. It was after arriving in Philadelphia, that they learned of the assassination and that they, too, had been among the intended victims.[38]

Before concluding this section, I have just a note. Such moments of precognition are often so extraordinary that it is tempting to call them coincidences. It certainly is a safe way of handling extraordinary phenomena. However, in doing so, we are denying the possibility of a connection with either the universe or our soul. If we were to consider that there might be something else taking place, we might indeed have an opportunity to expand and enhance our sense of connection with our own spirit or soul.

Near-Death Experiences

How often have you heard about or seen on television someone who has died, been declared officially dead, and then, usually quite miraculously and without explanation, returned to life? And, then, to add to the stunning nature of the event, has talked about what it was like while "on the other side?" These incredible, mystical stories about what happens to individuals at the time of their death have a name. They are referred to as **near-death experiences,** which henceforth will be referred to as **NDEs.**

These events are among the most extraordinary of life experiences. Given that NDEs have been relatively unpublicized, you might think they are uncommon, but think again. According to a poll conducted by George Gallup in 1982, more than eight million Americans have reported NDEs. According to Raymond Moody, M.D., often considered to be the father of near-death research, such experiences occur more frequently than people would think. He believes that he can find at least one person who has had an NDE in any group of thirty.[39]

While a number of researchers had been investigating the NDE, Moody was the first to coin the term and to publish his findings in his first book, *Life After Life,* published in 1975. Keep in mind that, according to Moody, he was not interested in trying to prove that there is life after life. What he did want to do was, first, to bring attention to the phenomenon, and, second, to create a more receptive attitude on the part of the public toward the subject. Moody knew that knowledge of NDEs would make an impact on how individuals go about living their daily lives.[40]

Moody concluded his book with the implication that more research dealing with death and life after life was needed by other professions.[41] As a result of Moody coming forth with his research, other physicians and scientists, including Kübler-Ross,[42] Michael Sabom,[43] Kenneth Ring[44] and Morse[45] have brought their findings to the public. In addition, many authors who have personally experienced an NDE, including Betty Eadie,[46] Dannion Brinkley,[47] Jan Price[48] and Pamela Kircher[49] have written detailed accounts of their frequent breathtaking stories.

Characteristics of an NDE

By now, you may be wondering exactly what an NDE is. If you were having a typical NDE, at the time of your death, perhaps from a heart attack, surgery or accident, you would be likely to experience one or more, though rarely all, of the following:

- A sense of leaving your body, floating up to the ceiling, and looking down on events taking place below as well as surrounding your own body.
- An awareness of those present down below, perhaps paramedics, doctors and others who are trying to revive you, and feeling frustration because they cannot hear you as you try to communicate with them.
- A feeling of suddenly being drawn down a tunnel with a whooshing sound where you experience the presence of deceased loved ones, grandparents, family members and friends, who have a glowing appearance, seem genuinely happy to be with you, and lovingly both comfort and guide you. By this point, you realize that you, too, are glowing.
- A sense of peacefulness and painlessness, especially as you feel yourself being drawn toward the **Light or Being of Light** (often called God, Jesus Christ or Allah) and described by others as unlike anything they have encountered in life, who radiates much warmth and love.
- A review of your life (often conducted by the being of light who gently, but without admonishment, replays a movie of your life in which you not only experience

your own actions, but also how those very actions made others feel, clearly leaving you with lessons learned for future ways of being).

In your meeting with this divine presence, or with a loved one who has died, you are presented with the choice of either staying or returning to physical life, or are simply informed that you must return to finish your life's work, despite your feeling that there is no way you wish to leave this indescribably beautiful, accepting and loving place.

Once returned to your physical body, you experience a transformation of—or change in—your identity, personality, values and your approach to life, such as going from being materialistic to becoming more spiritual and nonmaterialistic.

The Transformative Power of the Light

Let's talk about the Light for a moment. This light, which has been described by NDEers as loving, healing, unforgettable, unconditionally accepting and all-knowing, has been a main focus of attention for Melvin Morse, M.D. Morse, a pediatrician who has devoted a good part of his life to scientifically exploring NDEs, has concluded that the Light is the key element of the NDE experience and that it is the one element that cannot be explained using scientific theories. It is, he believes, located outside our bodies, and once one is exposed to the Light, the effects of the Light remain with the individual for the rest of his or her life.

One of my favorite stories that reinforce the long lasting effect of the Light is that of the Battlefield Angel, described by Morse in *Transformed by the Light*. Morse tells the story of a man who, while wounded in Vietnam, begged God to allow him to die. The man suddenly felt no pain, rose above his body and found himself surrounded by a radiant glowing light and, again, felt no pain. Although the man was neither religious nor spiritual, he found that in the years that followed back on earth, whenever he found himself in pain or very stressed, the Light would appear ever so slightly, always accompanied by peace and calm.[50]

Morse was so impressed with the descriptions of the Light provided by his young patients, and which appear in his first book, *Closer to the Light,* that he felt compelled to further investigate the effects of the Light on his patients' lives as they moved into adulthood. In his second book, *Transformed by the Light,* he writes: "I am convinced, after more than a decade of studying the near-death experience, that this light that comes to us when we die is real. I do not think it is simply a byproduct of human brain activity. Rather, I think it is the very source of all that we consider to be uniquely human, namely the soul."[51]

After many years of my own research dealing with extraordinary and paranormal phenomena, as well as my involvement in studying intuition and various forms of energy, I have come to believe that we are all essentially light or electromagnetic energy, each with our own wavelengths and frequencies. This theory has been put forth by physicists, including Stephen Hawking, who have shown in laboratory settings that everything can be broken down to particles of light or simply forces of light energy. It is this kind of thinking that better enables us to understand those NDEers who describe themselves and everything they see as an incredibly pure, glowing light. Morse quotes one of his own patients: "I could see the light in all my own cells and in the universe. I could see that light was God. . . ."[52]

In order to reassure the medical community of the legitimacy of his work, Morse formed teams of highly respected and conservative thinkers and scientists in the field of medicine for both his Seattle Study and Transformations Study. The results of the work he and his teams of researchers completed led to his belief that the ability to see God is within each of us, and specifically lies within the right temporal lobe.[53] Furthermore, according to Morse, "The real value of my research team's results is that we have established that the near-death experience is a natural and normal event that happens to human beings when they die."[54] This is a powerful conclusion and deserves significant consideration.

When Researchers Are Transformed by the Light

Moody, in *Life After Life*, challenged those researchers who followed him, to pursue the investigation of the NDEs. He believed that in addition to the information that would come forth, the lives of those who chose such an investigation would be forever changed, just as his was.[55] Morse, Kübler-Ross, Ring and others have written of similar NDE experiences that they have also researched.

The results of my investigation into NDEs involve not only more than a decade of research in the area of exceptional, extraordinary and, yes, paranormal experiences, but, more important, the ability to treasure life so much more because of a diminished fear of death and what comes after death. This has been the gift of NDEs for me, personally, and this is what has contributed to my desire to write this book.

Before concluding this section, according to the NDE research results of Morse and others, an NDE is not a true NDE unless there is a transformative effect. You see, Morse and his team definitively determined that only those who experience an authentic NDE are truly transformed by the event. Furthermore, there are a variety of ways in which people may be transformed following an NDE.

For example, some people have experienced a decreased fear of death and dying while others have become less materialistic and more charitable (which may include going into a helping profession). Others have noted an increasing number of paranormal experiences, such as becoming more psychic or adept at healing. Some have reported changes in their electromagnetic energy, often disabling watches and pacemakers from working properly. Many have also reported that following their NDE, they have an increased need to take good care of their body via improved nutrition and exercise. In addition, many in this last group have also reported experiencing an improved sense of emotional, mental, physical and spiritual well-being.[56] (Morse emphasizes that it is the Light, of course, that is responsible for these transformations. This Light, remember, is unlike anything we have ever experienced. It is luminous, alive, warm, incredibly loving and compassionate. Those who experience this, even when it is the light of another individual, are, indeed, forever changed.)

I don't think I shall ever forget the touching story that Dr. Joan Borysenko, psychologist and author, describes in both *Fire in the Soul*[57] and *A Woman's Book of Life*,[58] which deals with the events surrounding the death of her mother. While her mother was dying of emphysema and congestive heart failure and drifting in and out of consciousness, Joan Borysenko and her son Justin sat meditating on opposites sides of her mother's hospital bed. Borysenko describes a vision of hers which took place while meditating in the hospital room in which she had merged with her mother and was both being born and giving birth to her mother's soul. In this extremely powerful meditation Joan Borysenko had the sense of being one with her mother.

Borysenko writes in *Fire in the Soul* that from the perspective of being both mother and child, all the "joys, sorrows, angers and anguishes" of their life together then made absolute and complete sense. She also writes that, as a baby, she was "in wondrous awe of the bright, mysterious and awesome Light at the end of the long, dark birth tunnel." Again, in her words, "I was aware of her consciousness moving down the long, dark tunnel and leaving this world, already rejoicing in the splendor of her return to the Light. She had birthed me into this world, and I felt as though I had birthed her out of it."[59]

As Joan Borysenko opened her eyes, she and her son, Justin, then twenty years old, found that the room "seemed to be suffused with the Light and alive with an indescribable, peaceful power."[60] In describing the experience, she also states, "When I opened my eyes, the entire room seemed made of light, of energy. There were no boundaries between things. My mother's body was an energy form that graded into the air, the floor, the bed, the body of my son whom I saw weeping, a look of awe on his face. I nodded and moved around the bed to sit next to him."[61]

In the few moments during which Justin experienced his grandmother's transition and the Light, he found himself suddenly aware of new revelations of wisdom. Joan Borysenko writes, "He looked deeply into my eyes, and said, 'This is Grandma's last gift. She's holding open the door to eternity so that we can have a glimpse.' He went on to say that I must be very grateful to my mother for the gifts she had given me. . . . He told me that he understood that his grandmother was a wise soul, a very great being and that she had displayed much less wisdom in this life than she actually had. This was part of our combined destiny, he continued, for in order for me to come more fully into my own life purpose I needed something to resist, to push against, so that I could become more fully myself and then share what I had learned with others."[62]

It was just hours after this experience that her mother died. But, as a result of the vision, Joan Borysenko was left with an "expanded" sense of peace and understanding of the life she had shared with her mother. Thanks to the wisdom her son had shared with her, as well as the vision which included the Light, she felt that she could see from a higher perspective the pain and disappointments that were a part of her relationship with her mother and that they had more to do with learning about love and spiritual courage. The need to forgive her mother was no longer an issue. The Light had transformed Borysenko, as it has so many others.[63]

I was, and am, especially moved by Justin's words to his mother, which contributed to her deeper understanding of why she and her mother needed to spend so much of their physical relationship in a state of tension and resistance. Perhaps, had Joan Borysenko had a mom with a different personality, she would not have pushed so hard and might not have been motivated to develop her potential to the extent that she has.

There are reasons we are in the lives of specific family members, friends and colleagues. Neil Donald Walsh, in *Conversations with God*,[64] and Carolyn Myss, in *Sacred Contracts*,[65] address this point. It is while in nonphysical form that we lovingly contract with other nonphysical souls to come in with one another (to be physical beings together) in order to heal an aspect of the soul that is in need of healing. For example, if a soul seeks to learn forgiveness, another soul may lovingly offer to come in at the same time and, in physical form, create a situation that needs to be forgiven. This is similar to what took place in Joan Borysenko's life with her mother.

The key point here is that the wisdom that came to both Justin and his mother came by way of their individually experiencing, and yet sharing, the death of Joan Borysenko's mother. This event took both mother and son to an intensely deeper level of understanding regarding their time together in physical form than either could have possibly envisioned.

Psychic Energy

Psychic energy definitely overlaps several other categories that have been so far discussed, including intuition, presences and enmeshment. For years, I have studied various types of energy. My desire, I believe, has been born out of years of patients sharing their stories of sensing or experiencing the presence of a deceased loved one, as well as more than a decade of researching consciousness and extraordinary or paranormal phenomena. With a hunger to understand energy and how to use it to help others heal emotionally, mentally, spiritually and even physically, I have studied various modalities that include reiki, therapeutic touch, integrative energy therapy, hypnotism, consciousness in healing and intuitive development.

So, how might we define psychic energy, which seems to be expressed in so many ways? It is my belief that what we are talking about here cannot be defined using just one definition. Let us begin with a definition of **psychic.** According to the *American Heritage Dictionary,* psychic is defined as "of or pertaining to the human mind or psyche," and also as "extraordinary, especially extrasensory and nonphysical, mental processes." One might think of psychic energy as energy which may be experienced with the mind.

The Nonlocal & Intuitive Aspects of Psychic Energy

Given this definition of psychic energy, it is in our best interest to then examine the consideration that mind is **nonlocal,** a concept born out of the research of the quantum physicists and the work of Larry Dossey, M.D.,[66] as well as others. By applying the term nonlocal to psychic energy, we are describing mind or consciousness as not being bound to any time, body or place, and therefore available to be experienced and observed by individuals wherever and whenever it may occur. (This has numerous implications, including mind being able to connect with mind at a distance, as in prayer and spiritual healing.) Used in this way, psychic energy has served to help individuals develop their own healing potential or that of others.

Another consideration is that psychic energy may not be energy, per se, but simply a way of knowing. Here, again, we seem to be talking about intuitive wisdom. Three highly respected medical intuitives, Carolyn Myss,[67] Judith Orloff, M.D.[68] and Mona Lisa Schulz, M.D., Ph.D.,[69] have written extensively about the experience of being intuitive regarding the human body. As medical intuitives, they are able to psychically or nonlocally "read" the energy of others. In other words, they are able to connect, consciousness to consciousness, and to "know" what is going on within an individual whether the individual is in their presence or at a distance. Their wish is to inform the public that the ability to "read" another's energy or physical state is something that can be developed with time, patience and guidance. Rosemary Altea,[70] author, medium, intuitive and healer, and Judith Orloff,[71] physician and author, have also written of the power within each of us to develop our intuitive abilities.

Seeing with Our Heart

Rather than something we can "see," psychic energy is more often than not something we "feel." Indeed, my experience is that so much of what takes place psychically is done with the heart—and not the head. This, I believe, is how intuition works. In other words, usually we "see" the energy with our heart and/or our whole being.

For example, many have described moments in which they "felt" the presence of a being, person or animal. They have spoken of how they just knew, though no words were spoken, that their loved one was present. These moments have usually been described as comforting and a "gift," although, for some, they are alarming, confusing and frightening. There are times, however, when energy has been described as a visual experience such as those described by loved ones who have lost spouses, children, parents and friends. That is, after all, what visions are about. These are almost always viewed as special and comforting moments.

It needs to be noted that there are situations in which the term psychic energy is sometimes used, but for which an appropriate definition or explanation cannot be provided. Prayer and distance healing are two examples of this. My own research has led me to conclude that distance healing and prayer are probably not about energy, but about nonlocal mind at work. In such situations, researchers have yet to adequately explain such events. These will be discussed further in a later chapter.

CHAPTER 3

Extraordinary Communication: Key Players

Patience and timing . . . everything comes when it must come . . . A life cannot be rushed, cannot be worked on a schedule, as so many people want it to be. We must accept what comes to us at a given time, and not ask for more. But life is endless, so we never die; we were never really born. We just pass through different phases. There is no end. Humans have many dimensions. But time is not as we see time, but rather, in lessons that we have learned.

THE POET MASTER
FROM *Many Lives, Many Masters*
Brian Weiss, M.D.

The majority of my patients and others whom I have interviewed believe that their extraordinary encounters were moments of communication with spirits of loved ones who had died—or the spirits of those who had died, but who may not have been personally known to them.

Deceased Loved Ones

I offer some statistics here to support those whom I have interviewed who have reported having some form of communication with a deceased loved one. Bill and Judy Guggenheim, who wrote *Hello from Heaven,* have done extensive after-death communication research. They found in a recent poll that 42% of American adults believe they have had contact with someone who has died, and 67% of all widows feel that they also have had communication with loved ones who had died.[72] The authors also noted that their research indicated that approximately 20% of the U.S. population has experienced some kind of communication with a deceased person.[73]

The popularity of authors who are also mediums, such as James Van Praagh,[74] Rosemary Altea,[75] John Edward[76] and Sylvia Browne,[77] is further testament to both the interest and desire of the public to learn and understand such phenomena. My own research in this area leads me to believe that the interest in these celebrities is rooted in attempts to normalize personal experiences that have not been shared with others.

I also believe that large numbers of those who are reading these very words are among those who have had similar experiences. If you are among this particular population, know that I wrote this book with you in mind. My distinct intention was to provide you with both comfort and knowledge that might shed more understanding, insight and wisdom concerning the meaning of such events.

You may be wondering what might contribute to a deceased individual sticking around, sometimes making his or her presence known, sometimes not. The result of my own research allows me to provide some insight here.

Reasons for Staying Close to Home

I have learned that when someone dies, his or her spirit remains close to those physical beings he or she loved while alive, including the children, spouse and family members. The desire to continue the role as caretaker, parent, spouse, etc. appears to continue as long as those with whom they were close remain in need of them. These spirit-beings may become protectors and guides, providing assistance, comfort and support to those in the physical realm when they feel it necessary.

At some point, most loved ones continue on as spirit with their journey when they are reassured of the well-being of their physical family members and/or friends. Their visits decrease in number, though they frequently return to share holidays and anniversaries, as well as always being there for their physical loved ones when emotional or physical assistance is requested or needed.

Locked in by Need and Grief

A problem I have experienced as a therapist is that often my patients choose to hold on to their grief in order to hold on to their loved ones. They fear that by getting emotionally and physically healthier and stronger, their loved ones will move on, leaving them alone. Physical beings need to know that those in the nonphysical realm always hear our calls for help. They can be there instantly no matter where we may be on our own physical journey.

There are some deceased souls who choose to remain, even after a significant period of time, perhaps continuing to feel needed by their physical family and friends or perhaps because they have not yet brought closure to personal unresolved issues and relationships. Those who experience the presence of a deceased loved one often interpret the experience as an expression of love, caring or concern. In addition, the event serves as both a message and a validation that life continues despite the death of the physical body.

I would like to share an observation based on what many have shared with me. Those who have had the experience of meeting their loved one through the help of an individual who serves as a medium have frequently told me a similar story. It is not unusual for a deceased loved one to come to those of us in physical form to let us know that they are doing just fine and that we have grieved enough, and, in their opinion, that we need to move on. I smile each time I am told this.

Evidently, once our loved ones have died, they are privy to the wisdom of the universe which contributes to their recognition that life continues, that the soul continues to live beyond the physical life, and that souls are reunited. Thus, from the perspective of the majority of souls, there is really no need to grieve. Of course, the situation is different for those of us in physical form.

I remind others that when these souls were in physical form, they too grieved the separation due to death from their beloved family members and friends. This is because every cell in the physical body literally feels the impact of being separated from either a loved one or from something about which one has cared very deeply. However, following the transition from physical to nonphysical, the soul knows there is no death and, thus, nothing to grieve. (This most definitely appears to be the more comfortable situation in which to be.)

Creative Means of Communication

Loved ones communicate in many ways, as already discussed. They definitely can and do communicate telepathically. If one considers the possibility that mind is nonlocal, detached from any particular space, time or place, then the idea of telepathic communication makes sense. Telepathic communication is similar to messages being sent from one radio to another by means of radio waves. I encourage individuals to trust their intuitive wisdom, the little voice in one's being, and to remain open to any sense of a presence or to their intuition.

Also, as previously indicated, deceased beings may come to communicate with us in visions during our waking and non-waking hours, including our dreams. These visions, however, may be sensorily experienced. So often stories are shared with me of deceased loved ones who sit down on a bed or sofa, leaving an impression of their presence in the couch, chair or bed. Others tell me that they experience the presence of their loved ones as a soft breeze. In fact, after the loss of a loved one, some have spoken of being gently touched or caressed or of experiencing the sensation of someone running hands through their hair.

Deceased loved ones are remarkably creative! They find unique ways to convey their presence. Some have used a feather; some a specific type of car, van or truck. Others use a specific animal or bird, always one that is meaningful so that there will be little doubt about the source of communication. Some use electrical devices, such as answering machines. There are some who play with lights, causing them to blink and flicker, to get our attention. And there are others who use their energy to move an object or two.

There are also those who choose to communicate with us by merging their energy with ours so that we take on their appearance, mood and spirit. Others speak to us of their presence with the scent of a familiar cologne, perfume or flower. Some even choose to work through us by inspiring us to write what they want us to know. Others gather enough energy to actually appear in physical form to family or other loved ones. I am often amazed at how they manage to make their wishes, concerns, thoughts and feelings known to us.

A Son's Creative Communication with His Family

As I have previously noted, I am presently working with a family that suffered the unanticipated loss of their seventeen-year-old son, Steven. Since his death, all of the family members have experienced their son/brother in unique ways. For example, Carol, Steven's mom, has frequently had the pleasure of being visited by butterflies, even in pouring rainstorms when butterflies are not prone to fly. The butterflies fly close and hover around Carol, who chats with them as easily as though she were conversing with her son.

Since Steven's death, Carol has found solace and comfort sitting and reading on her porch off her kitchen. It is there while reading or looking out at her garden that she has been surprised at hearing Steven's voice and feeling his presence on numerous occasions. Furthermore, there and elsewhere in their home she has smelled the cologne, something that was a combination of musk and vanilla, that Steven loved to wear.

Steven had a great sense of humor and loved to play jokes on his family while in physical form. He evidently still does. While his mom was peeling potatoes for a Sunday dinner, the potato sack suddenly moved, on its own, a few inches to the right, just as though someone had pushed it over. Startled, Carol caught her breath and scolded Steven for scaring her, though she admitted it was good to know that he was close by.

While driving down a local street shortly after Steven's death, Carol barely missed hitting a gentleman walking in the street, something totally atypical for Carol before her son's death. Within a moment of realizing what had almost taken place, Carol suddenly felt the sensation of a hand tapping the side of her seat. Knowing that she had not touched her own seat, Carol believed that Steven was giving her his "wakeup and be alert" call, as well as offering assurance that he was with her and his siblings.

On another occasion, while the two younger children, Matt and Jenny, were attempting to reach for Steven's football on his bed, Jenny's eyes opened wide as she saw the football move backwards, as though someone had pushed it. Jenny, only momentarily scared, immediately realized it was Steven. She grabbed the football and ran downstairs screaming to her mom about what had just taken place. Jenny has told me that even though it was scary for her, it felt good and comforting to know that Steven was there and still up to playing jokes on his little sister.

Tom (Steven's father), Carol and each of the children, including Steven's older sister, Michelle, have all experienced vivid dreams of their son/brother. He has come in a variety of ways in dreams, some of which might be interpreted as psychological in nature, and some of which might very well be considered psychic in nature. This has been one of the most interesting ways in which Steven has communicated with his family—using the language of symbolism to convey some of his most private thoughts and feelings to his parents and his siblings. Some of the material expressed in the dreams represents what I believe Steven would have wanted to share with his family before he died, but which he could not bring himself to do.

Looking for Communicators

Before concluding this topic, the reader needs to be aware that those in the spirit world are often eager to communicate with those who are in the physical world. What I have learned and witnessed is their determination to communicate by means of connecting and working through physical individuals who are extremely sensitive to their energy and who are highly intuitive, called mediums by some. I quite unexpectedly found this to be the case when my own mom died. It was while I sat with my dear friend, Samantha, who is extremely intuitive, that my mom made her presence known to me, along with her concerns for me.

Not having ever experienced this phenomenon before, I was greatly surprised the first time it occurred. However, my initial surprise and discomfort quickly melted away, and I found myself enthusiastically anticipating unannounced visits from my mom whenever I would be with Samantha. In addition to my mom, other family members and even patients whom I have treated and who have died have taken advantage of my time with my friend, and have come to me, offering their concerns, knowledge, insight and wisdom. Furthermore, the work I do as a therapist has been enormously helped by feedback given to me by those nonphysical beings that have chosen to come to me while I am visiting with my good friend who is so gifted intuitively. Needless to say, these experiences have personally confirmed my belief that life continues, despite the death of the physical body.

Indian Guides and Teachers

During the many years in which I interviewed others and did the research for this book, I encountered the works of many physicians, scientists and authors who would describe their personal experiences with their own guides, teachers and masters. While I must admit that I found myself more or less envying those who were blessed with such experiences, I could not fathom what it might be like to have such a guide until I myself was blessed with the meeting of one of my own guides.

Meeting White Feather and Elisabeth Kübler-Ross Forever Change Me

The story of my first meeting with my Native American guide, whom, at the time, I called White Feather (and continue to do so at times, despite knowledge of his real name) will be told in a later chapter. However, the bottom line is that I found myself, quite unexpectedly, seated before my guide several years ago while conducting an emergency session the day after Thanksgiving. He appeared out of nowhere and I had to do a significant amount of determining my own mental well-being at the time. Why? Because my sense was that while I was seeing and feeling the presence of this grand old Native American, I knew that he was not actually present. He was—but he was not, if that makes any sense to you.

Since that was the first time I had experienced the presence of White Feather, I needed reassurance from others that I was not imagining the whole thing. This actually came from several reliable sources in the following weeks and months. In the early spring of 2001, I had the most wonderful opportunity to interview and visit with Elisabeth Kübler-Ross. It was while I was describing my first encounter with White Feather that she corrected me and informed me of my guide's correct name and his writings with which she was familiar. I am so grateful to Elisabeth for the sharing of her own experiences with her guides in her autobiography, *The Wheel of Life*.[78] Had it not been for her courage in sharing her experience, I am not sure I would have risked sharing my own story, and had I not shared my story, I would not have learned the true identity of my guide.

Before the meeting with my own guide, I had been particularly moved by Rosemary Altea's story of her meeting and work with her own guide, Grey Eagle. In *The Eagle and the Rose,* Altea describes her meeting with Grey Eagle as well as the story of how he helped her to develop her intuitive potential and assisted her in her work as a healer.[79] I recommend Altea's story for a closer look at the experience of working with a guide.

Guides and Teachers: What They Do & How They Do It

Let's talk for a moment about the purpose of a guide. I agree with Gary Zukav, who, in *Seat of the Soul,* indicates that he believes that guides and teachers come into our lives to assist our souls in their evolution.[80] According to James Van Praagh in *Heaven and Earth,* every human being has many spirit guides. Furthermore, "the primary function of a spirit guide is to help, protect, assist and inspire you in your spiritual evolution."[81]

In other words, guides and teachers enable us to fulfill our soul's intentions. With loving compassion, kindness and true understanding, they enable us to heal the parts of our soul that need to be healed. And they enable us to learn. Our guides assist us in teaching us what we need to know that will contribute to our peace and feeling contentment, in order to be whole and truly happy.

Van Praagh also describes spirit guides as "highly evolved beings," who are similar to angels in that they continue learning and maturing as they work with us. Furthermore, the guides who come in and out of our lives may have lived on earth as saints, leaders and as spiritual teachers, such as Saint Francis of Assisi, Jesus, Mary and Buddha. These same beings are also considered to be master beings who contributed to the development of spiritual consciousness while in physical form. There are also those guides who have never been physical beings.[82]

Guides come to us in many different ways. As some of you may have guessed, spirit guides may also include deceased family members and friends who guard and protect loved ones whom they have left behind. Guides are also usually dressed in attire that is easily identifiable, such as the robes of a monk or the leather skins of Native American Indians. According to Van Praagh, this is done to gain our trust.[83]

Zukav, in *Seat of the Soul,* makes the following important points: "Your soul knows its guides and Teachers. It drew upon their wisdom and compassion in charting the incarnation that became you, and that part of your soul that is you will be gathered into their waiting arms when the incarnation that is you comes to an end—when you go home." Zukav continues to note that we are guided and assisted in every moment of our lives.[84]

Your Guides and Teachers: What They Need Us to Do

Your guides and teachers are waiting for you to engage them; that is, to ask them for guidance. Whether you ask questions of them from a conscious state, a meditative state or a prayer state, they wait for you to come to them to ask for assistance. They provide answers, solutions, clarity, compassion and alternatives—everything you need. They speak to you via the quiet, still voice you hear speaking to you from within. At times, they are the flash of inspirational thought that appears suddenly and disappears just as suddenly. They depend on you to maintain an open heart and to be ready and listening. But they cannot make the choices for you. In other words, they cannot do the work. You must decide what you will ask and which guidance you will choose to follow. That is your responsibility. This is where you learn to trust your intuitive wisdom.

I begin every day in my office with a prayer of intent to assist those who come to me for help in the healing of their pain. I have a delicious cinnamon scented candle that I burn. There's nothing like the scent of a cinnamon bun or an oatmeal cookie candle! It is while lighting this candle at the beginning of the day that I ask for assistance, guidance and protection in the work that I do with my patients.

Furthermore, I am very much aware that there are times during the day when I am presented with dilemmas that I know I do not, at the time, have answers for, but for which I manage to find solutions or appropriate therapeutic means of handling within the time my patient and I are meeting. In these situations, I once again silently ask for additional guidance and assistance. The result is that I can feel myself being intuitively guided—and it is a thoroughly impressive and awe-inspiring experience for me. The answers always come; the process always amazes me; and I always take time to thank my guides and teachers for being there for me. In fact, I thank them frequently throughout the day.

To connect with one's guides and teachers, I encourage my patients and others to quiet their minds, something that one can learn to do by the simple act of focusing on their breath for three to five minutes, and then to put forth issues needing to be solved. It helps to center, using your breath, and to visualize your heart opening to receive whatever may come. The answers are there, just waiting to be received. But, to do this, we so often need to get out of our own way, to more or less clear the path internally, in order to hear what we need to hear.

I have actually become aware of having more than one guide. In fact, I believe that everyone has at least one guide, if not more. Both Van Praagh and Zukav agree that we have many guides and teachers during our lifetime. I believe that they are, at their deepest level, an extension of our essence. They are also, I believe, simply a part of our true knowing. As to the number of guides that we may have, my sense is that this has to do with what it is that we set out to do—our intentions regarding this lifetime.

Experiencing My Guides and Teachers

My guide, White Feather, whom I later learned is known universally as White Eagle, is recognized for his wisdom and his compassion. While I was initially stunned by his presence, I knew that he had come to reassure me that I was on the "right track" and to guide me as I tread carefully during a critical and difficult session with a patient who had been severely traumatized.

Since first learning of White Feather, I have also learned that I work in the presence of two other guides. These include Chief Rainbow, a sweet, gentle Indian Chief who is a two-hundred-year-old medicine man. He has been helping me develop my intuitive wisdom for more than fourteen years. Also working with me is a surgeon who has indicated that he has chosen to work with me intuitively because of the spiritual, intuitive and alternative therapeutic approach I take in my work, especially since my practice is medically oriented.

Given the research I have done regarding the effectiveness of prayer, I have always encouraged my patients to ask for help and inner guidance when they felt the need. As I have previously described, I do the same thing when I am beginning my session with a patient. I completely concur with Zukav who writes in *Seat of the Soul*, "The ability to draw consciously upon your nonphysical guidance and assistance and to communicate with your nonphysical Teacher is a treasure that cannot be described, a treasure beyond words and value."[85]

The Divine and Other Spiritual Beings

There are so many people who fervently believe that the source of their extraordinary communication is the Divine. The Divine can go by many names. For some, the Divine may be Allah or Buddha. For others, the divine connection may be about Moses, God, Source or Great Spirit. And for still others, the Divine may be viewed as having a personal sense of connection or communication with Jesus or Mary. There are some who believe that they experience the Divine when they believe a particular saint is present, such as St. Francis or St. Germain, or a beloved and renowned figure, such as Padre Pío or Mother Theresa.

What is lovely is that experiencing a connection with the Divine or a spiritual being can occur any time and any place, including during meditations, prayers, quiet moments, a walk in the park, while sitting at your child's baseball or soccer game, during healings or even while having a massage, or they may simply come "out of the blue."

Dr. Melvin Morse, the NDE, the Light and a Meeting with God

Those who are familiar with near-death research will recall the powerful significance of the Light. From my perspective, the experience of the Light is about a connection with the Divine. So many NDEers have described their experience of being in the Light as having the sense of being connected to someone or something that feels incredibly loving, warm and unconditionally accepting. For some, the Light is described as a specific spiritual being, and, for almost all, the Light is said to have a profound impact on their lives.

I particularly love the work of Melvin Morse, author of *Transformed by the Light,* who, as a pediatrician, has carefully studied the effect of the Light on the adult lives of those who have had NDEs as young children. He found that the Light clearly changed the lives of those who had experienced it, and usually in the most positive ways.[86] Morse found that for the majority of those who have had NDEs, the Light may be experienced as a presence like no other: a presence whose essence both represents love and feels like love. One can only imagine how wonderful such an experience must be!

How ironic it was, according to Morse in his newest book, *Where God Lives,* that he, after writing three books that dealt with divine connections (NDEs), had never really experienced a deep sense of connection with the Divine via prayer. While he recognized that it is the right temporal lobe, which he calls the God Spot, that is associated with the characteristics of the near-death experience and other paranormal events, he admitted that he had never really been "turned on" via prayer or any other method. In fact, he even admitted that he had never thought of prayer and religion as being different from one another. He went further in admitting that he honestly did not know what real prayer was. Not being very religious, he had rarely prayed, or prayed in a deeply meaningful and sincere manner, other than when his dad had cancer.

Then, while on a tour in the Midwest, Morse made a promise to a woman who had encouraged him to use prayer to make a real connection with the Creator. She advised Morse to not think of all the problems that have been due to religion, but to "just think about the creator of the universe and about trying to touch that power." She continued, "Just get on your knees and talk to God," and then said, "If you do it right, maybe God will respond."[87]

That evening, in his hotel room, Morse actually got down on his knees by the foot of his bed and prayed. He prayed from his heart, in a way he had never done before. After spending several minutes of lovingly thinking of each of his children and his wife, his blessings, he expressed his gratitude for them and prayed for their well-being, as well as that of his patients. Following this, he put forth his question to God. He asked, "What is the nature of God, and what is the relationship between God and man?" Mentioned within the prayer was his intention to have a response within the next twenty-four hour period. Morse always likes to make things as scientific as possible.

The answer to his prayer came as requested the next day when, after a long journey traveling to Los Angeles and doing radio and television interviews, he returned to his hotel room. That is when he experienced the only real epiphany he has ever experienced. Suddenly, he found himself enveloped in a light so incredible that it filled his entire being with a sense of peace, warmth, love and tranquility.

In the same moment that he again heard the question he had asked the evening before, he was experiencing the answer to the question. In that very moment, he felt a sense of connection to God and to everything in the universe. He writes, "I understood that man and everything else in the universe is a piece of God. As each snowflake contains miniature representations of the entire snowflake, and each strand of human DNA contains the code to create a unique human, we are all tiny pieces of God."[88] Though he felt the rug had been pulled from beneath his feet, he describes the whole experience as so stunning that "I suddenly understood I was a body within a soul, not the other way around."[89] Morse also points out that the result of the experience was his sense of understanding about the meaning of life—and an increased confidence in his own intuitive abilities, all stemming from the stimulation of the right temporal lobe—or the God Spot.

Angels

As I write this, I wonder what can I possibly say about angels that you may not already know. So many patients

I have interviewed have commented that they believe they are watched over, protected by or connected with an angel. In fact, *Time* magazine conducted its own poll regarding the public's belief in angels. The results showed that 69% answered yes to "Do you believe in angels?" and 46% answered yes to "Do you believe you have your own guardian angel?"[90] Indeed, the concept of angels has been a part of religions throughout the world and throughout time—including Buddhism, Hinduism, Christianity and Judaism.

The word angel has its derivation in the Greek word that means messenger. Sophie Burnham, in her classic *A Book of Angels*, provides the *Oxford University Dictionary*'s definition of angel as the following: "A ministering spirit or divine messenger; one of an order of spiritual beings superior to man, in power and intelligence, who are the attendants and messengers of the Deity."[91]

According to Burnham, angels are "remarkable for their warmth and light and all who see them speak in awe of their iridescent and refulgent light, of brilliant colors or else of the unbearable whiteness of their being."[92] She goes on to describe angels as providing needed aid and a sense of well being, bringing messages of hope as well as warnings of danger, positive news, flooding us with laughter and joy, and, of course, leaving us in a state of serenity and calm.[93]

The Power of Angels

Just as I cannot prove the existence of God, neither can I prove that of angels. Yet, those who have been touched by an angel know that their experience is as real as it gets. Being touched by an angel is not about knowing intellectually that your angel is real. It is truly experienced at the heart level where it is felt and known intuitively. Of this, I am sure. What I have come to know regarding angels, both from my research and my many years of interviewing those who have had an encounter or two with an angel, is that the experience fills you with a sense of having a connection with the Divine. It is almost magical and leaves you wondering whether or not you are grounded or floating somewhere other than where you thought you were. Once you have had such an experience, it not only stays with you for the remainder of your life, it also changes you in the most wonderful of ways.

My experience has taught me that angels come in many shapes, forms and sizes. They may be the strangers who suddenly appear out of nowhere to assist you when in need and are suddenly gone, leaving not a trace anywhere. Angels may come to us as the canary that repeatedly crosses our path or the butterfly that lands on our shoulders and stays after a loved one has died. They may also be the thought or voice in your head that offers guidance or warns you of impending danger. I have a perfect example of this to offer you.

I recall a young friend of our family who, after escaping Tower One of the World Trade Center on September 11th, 2001, just before it came crashing down, was considering heading back, thinking that it was safe to do so. He recalled that he was suddenly overwhelmed by an inner guidance that directed him to take a different route and seek the safety of some large buildings. As he came around one of the huge brick and metal office buildings, he could hear the tower falling with pounding force. From his place of safety, he saw huge piles of smoke-filled debris that poured forth down the street he had originally thought to take. Had he gone back the way he had come, he would have been overwhelmed and killed by the onslaught of the mountain of billowing, dark, smoke-colored ashes. It was the sudden inner guidance that saved his life. Was it an angel? Who can say definitively? It certainly felt that way.

Angels: Who and What They Are

Angels, according to Gary Zukav, author of *Seat of the Soul,* belong to the angelic realm. They have never been human. They are not ghosts who, in actuality, are the spirits of those who have died and who, when they appear, appear in the form known to us during their lifetime. Furthermore, Zukav states that angels are extremely evolved beings who continue to evolve. Unlike human beings, angels have no duality. In other words, angels cannot create karma. Thus, they have evolved beyond the need to be tested. They exist in perfection and as perfect beings, they are immortal. Essentially, they are a part of the Light that Melvin Morse speaks of in his research dealing with near-death experiences.[94]

Angels, The Mysterious Messengers, is written in conversational form and is a valuable collection of thoughts, feelings, ideas and opinions dealing with angels. Contributions come from some of the country's most highly respected theologians, authors and physicians. Also included are the thoughts of Dr. Joan Borysenko, Harvard trained biologist and psychologist. According to Borysenko, given the many forms an angel may take, no one knows what an angel is.[95] However, I believe that what she is actually saying is that an angel is whatever you perceive it to be. Its reality is your reality, whether it is the feeling of an overwhelming sense of warmth and love, a presence or a gentle sense of being touched.

In the same book, *Angels, The Mysterious Messengers,* Dr. Raymond Moody and Dr. Melvin Morse are also interviewed individually. Moody emphasizes the difficulty of dealing with questions concerning the existence of angels.[96] However, Morse states that in his extensive work with children who have had an NDE, his research reveals that children see angels about 60 to 70% of the time. Adults, on the other hand, report seeing angels only 10 to 20% of the time.[97] This is very similar to the findings of Kübler-Ross, who is known for her work with the dying, and especially with dying children. Both Moody and Morse believe that the concept of angels and NDEs should be studied, not to prove their existence, but because of their power to transform people, and because these experiences are an important aspect of being a human being. I agree.

On a Walk with the Angels

A classic and favorite story of mine that deals with angels appeared first in *Guidepost* magazine in 1963. It has been completely reprinted in Burnham's *A Book of Angels*, which has greatly impressed me and which I heartily recommend. Though it has been more than a decade since first reading this story, the power of the images evoked by the tale have stayed with me. I hope that you, the reader, enjoy it in your own way.

The story is entitled *The Day We Saw The Angels*,[98] and is authored by Professor S. Ralph Harlow, who was a professor at Smith College at the time the story occurred. It took place in Northampton, Massachusetts, probably in the thirties. With a B.A. from Harvard, an M.A. from Columbia, and a Ph.D. from Hartford Theological Seminary, Professor Harlow establishes not only his credibility, but also the fact that he does not suffer from hallucinations.

According to Professor Harlow, while he and his wife were visiting his wife's parents who lived in New England, they decided to go for a walk. It was an exquisite spring day in May, and they were feeling quite happy and peaceful. While strolling in the fields and woods, they enjoyed both periods of restful silence and moments of shared conversation. Suddenly, they heard voices of strangers approaching—but they heard them from both behind and above them.

Professor Harlow writes that it was difficult to put into words the excitement and exaltation which he and his wife experienced. In his words, "For about ten feet above us, and slightly to our left, was a floating group of glorious, beautiful creatures that glowed with spiritual beauty."[99] He and his wife stopped and simply stared as the heavenly beings floated gracefully and naturally by them. They were, of course, astounded by what they were witnessing.

According to Dr. Harlow, there were six lovely young women, dressed in white garments that seemed to float in the breeze, busily engaged in conversation with one another. In fact, so busy that they did not appear to notice the professor and his wife. Though their words were muffled and were unable to be understood, the couple clearly heard their voices.

Professor Harlow continues: "Their faces were perfectly clear to us, and one woman, slightly older than the rest, was especially beautiful. Her dark hair was pulled back in what today we would call a ponytail, and although I cannot say it was bound at the back of her head, it appeared to be. She was talking to a younger spirit whose back was toward us and who looked up into the face of the woman who was talking."[100]

After the group had passed, Professor Harlow writes that he and his wife had to sit down on a fallen tree beside the path and process what they had just seen and heard. Each needed to hear the other's story to confirm their experience. They knew that what they had seen and heard would be completely unbelievable to most people.

What I feel is especially important here is the professor's admittance that, as incredible as the story seems to be, it was not only real for them, but the event has had a long-lasting impact on their lives. In fact, he writes, "For this experience of almost thirty years ago greatly altered our thinking."[101]

The Angels of World War 1

The Angel of Mons is a story that appears in *Parting Visions* by Melvin Morse and also in *The Book of Angels* by Sophie

Burnham. I love telling the story because it is a true, well doc-
umented event that took place on the battlefield during World
War I. According to Morse, the Allies were suffering from
being badly defeated and, consequently, having heavy casual-
ties. Those soldiers who were taken to the hospital were tell-
ing the staff stories of having seen angels while fighting. The
British soldiers believed that the angel they saw was Saint
George. He was described as riding on a white horse and
having yellow hair and golden armor. The French also saw
angels and believed that they had seen Archangel Michael
mounted on a white horse.

Following the war, the Germans offered their perspective.
According to their cavalry troops, their sense was that the
Allies had thousands of troops who were attacking them. In
truth, the Allies had only two regiments there. The Germans
also stated that their horses suddenly pulled back from pur-
suing the Allies, and chose to turn and flee.[102]

What is so fascinating about this is that there are three
different groups involved—and three different visions, or per-
spectives, of what was taking place. Two of the three visions
specifically involve seeing angels.

The last story I wish to bring you is another favor-
ite of mine. Since first reading it many years ago in *Part-
ing Visions,* it has stayed with me and, I believe, influenced
my work with children who are ill and with their parents.
It has also impacted my work in teaching compassion to
the medical community. The story is especially significant
because, according to Morse, at least 50% of the children in
his research see "guardian angels" as part of their near-death
experience.[103]

Morse writes about Dr. Frank Oski, a highly esteemed
professor of pediatrics under whom he trained at Johns Hop-
kins University, who was touched by the Light. The light he
describes is the same that is so often described in the near-
death experience and in the mystical visions people have

been having for centuries. The story Morse shares in *Parting Visions* is one that Oski had shared with his colleagues and the public by having it published in a renowned pediatric journal. According to Morse, it is in this article that Oski wrote, "I will make no attempt to convince you as to the reality of my story. But I would ask that you keep an open mind on the mysteries of life which occur to you on a daily basis."[104]

Oski's story took place while he was a medical student and caring for a child who, despite all his efforts, was dying. He went to bed one evening feeling helpless regarding his ability to help his young patient—and trying to understand why the child had to die. Not long after falling asleep, a light so bright that it felt as though the sun were shining into his room awakened Oski. As he opened his eyes, a beautiful winged young woman stood before him. Stunned by what he was observing, he heard her hushed voice explaining why children have to die.

Morse quotes Oski: "The angel (I don't know what else to call her) said that life is an endless cycle of improvements and that humans are not perfect yet. She said that most people have this secret revealed to them when they die, but that handicapped children often know this and endure their problems without complaining because they know that their burdens will pass. Some of these children, she said, have even been given the challenge of teaching the rest of us how to love.

"'It stretches our own humanity to love a child who is less than perfect,' said the angel. 'And that is an important lesson for us.'"[105]

Remember that angels are messengers who come when needed to guide and assist us. This particular angel provided Oski with the reassurance he needed to continue on with his goal of healing children, despite the reality of some of his young patients dying. Somehow, when we most need assistance, it often appears in an unusual and extraordinary way.

Spiritual Beings

While the majority of my patients have shared with me stories of visits from loved ones who have died, there have also been, much less frequently, stories of spirits who are not always the friendliest of beings.

According to Gary Zukav in *Seat of the Soul,* other levels of souls do exist. Rather than joining with their higher selves, these souls wish to retain their personalities, and though in nonphysical form, they choose to remain close to earth. Zukav believes that quite possibly their desire to hold onto their personality is about their attempt to hold onto the power they had while in physical form.

The difference between these spirit beings and those deceased loved ones already discussed is that these are negative spirits who are drawn to negative energy, which has the capacity at times to create malevolence. Sometimes considered to be evil spirits, ghosts or possessions, these beings, according to Zukav, choose to remain earthbound and create negative karma.[106]

According to Sophie Burnhan, in *A Book of Angels,* such spirits or ghosts are a part of all cultures and are often described in similar terms. She writes, "Ghosts are attached by their longing and troubled memories to this physical plane; or else, they are lost shadows, unable to reach the other side." They may have a misty, milky appearance, appear as if you can see through them, have no feet, hold onto their old personalities and may be as kind or cruel as they were in physical form. Burnham also states that while there are those who are truly evil and may attempt to possess you, the majority are good and loving that come to comfort us in their own way. I absolutely agree with this statement.[107]

How will you know a spirit is present? Burnham confirms the experiences of my patients when she writes, "When a spirit enters a room, you feel a chill, as if a door's been left ajar, and when it touches you or when its body passes through you, you feel an arctic cold.[108]

In addition to several stories shared with me of personal meetings with evil spirits or energy, author, Betty Eadie, in *Embraced by the Light*,[109] describes her own encounter with a strong evil, demonic form of energy which took place after her near-death experience while in her hospital bed. The story she presents is very similar to that described to me by several members of the Simonton family whose story contributed significantly to the writing of this book.

Masters (Highly Developed Souls)

There is a higher level of intelligence that has the ability to teach and assist us in both healing and making our life experience as meaningful as possible. This level is represented by a group of beings or spirits that I call Masters. My first exposure to the Masters came back in the late eighties when I first read *Many Lives, Many Masters,* a true story by Dr. Brian Weiss. Weiss, who was Chairman of the Department of Psychiatry at the Mount Sinai Medical Center at the time, had had a patient, Catherine, referred to him by several other physicians. Given the multiplicity of problems the patient suffered, Weiss eventually decided to use hypnotic regression with her, never imagining the extent to which he would be able to regress his patient.[110]

Many Lives, Many Masters, a Story of Spiritual Transformation

Not only did Weiss discover that Catherine was experiencing numerous past lives, something with which Weiss, an empirically trained physician and scientist, had no familiarity, but, even more importantly, he learned that Catherine served as a conduit for a higher level of intelligence and wisdom which she wished to communicate toWeiss. *Many Lives, Many Masters* deals with both the transformation of a traditionally trained psychiatrist and the story of the Masters and the wisdom they wished to share with all humanity by way of Brian Weiss.

It was while Weiss was regressing Catherine that she entered a "between lives" quiet trance state, a tranquil place to which one's spirit returns during hypnotic regression. There, Weiss noticed her voice suddenly changed from a soft, low whisper to a loud, husky rasp. He heard her state, "Our task is to learn to become God-like through knowledge. We know so little. You are here to be my teacher. . . . By knowledge we approach God and then we can rest. Then we can come back to teach and help others."[111] These words stunned Weiss, who had absolutely no experience, no knowledge or familiarity with reincarnation and related subjects.

What stunned Weiss even more was the session in which Catherine's voice had become very husky and spiritual, and then stated: "Your father is here, and your son, who is a small child. Your father says you will know him because his name is Avrom, and your daughter is named after him. Also his death was due to his heart."[112] Weiss had never shared any of his private life with Catherine or any of his patients. How could she have known this?

Catherine continued: "Your son's heart was also important, for it was backward, like a chicken's. He made a great sacrifice for you out of his love. His soul is very advanced. . . . His death satisfied his parents' debts. Also he wanted to show you that medicine could only go so far, that its scope is very limited."[113]

Absolutely no one had known of his young son's death or that of his father, let alone his Hebrew name. When asked how she knew such information, she replied, "the Master Spirits tell me. They tell me I have lived eighty-six times in physical state."[114]

Despite the chills he experienced upon hearing her words and despite his initial confusion, Weiss admits that the fact that his loved ones seemed to be talking with him and were providing extremely specific information contributed to his sense that perhaps his loved ones had really never died. This was most comforting for him. He writes: "Beneath my chill, I felt a great love stirring, a strong feeling of oneness and connection with the heavens and the earth. I had missed my father and my son. It was good to hear from them again."[115]

This experience of meeting his father and his baby by way of the Masters forever changed Weiss. As he continued to work with Catherine, and as he frequently became engaged in conversations with the Masters, he noticed that he was undergoing a transformation. Weiss, like Catherine, was becoming more psychic. He was calmer, more peaceful and patient with others; he felt happier and more joyful about everything. What he soon realized was that the fear of dying, of death and of losing others to death was gone.

Weiss learned what I and so many others who have studied the near-death experience and other experiences related to life after life have learned—that once we release the idea that death is the end of life, we become more mindful of our purpose in life. We become more joyful, more aware of what truly matters in life and less obsessed regarding our appearance, being in control and owning material possessions. We recognize the importance of our relationships, and we are able to relax, be less competitive and more loving and compassionate.

The lessons of the Masters so deeply affected me that I believe I was forever changed by the experience of reading this book. Over the years, I have recommended *Many Lives, Many Masters* to those patients who I felt would benefit therapeutically from reading this material. It has significantly contributed to positively changing the course of several of my patients' lives.

The Wisdom of the Masters

Weiss, using teachings of the Masters, has gone on to write several other books that also present the elegant yet simple wisdom of these spiritual beings. One of Weiss's most recent books, *Messages from the Masters*,[116] another favorite of mine, serves to further reinforce the basic points presented in *Many Lives, Many Masters*. The messages presented in his books represent the heart of my work as a psychologist who seeks to assist others in healing their bodies and their pain.

The essential messages of the Masters are that we are immortal, eternal, spiritual beings who live in physical bodies. Thus, we have nothing to fear. Furthermore, we do not die. Death is simply the giving up of our physical bodies. We are also here to learn, to love and to forgive. They teach us that we are here to be compassionate, kind, caring, loving, happy, and joyful beings. The Masters speak to us in various ways, including through dreams, meditations, visions and the little voices we sometimes hear guiding us. They come to assist us on our journey, as well as connect with our soul.

Throughout *Many Lives, Many Masters*, Weiss writes of the appearance of different Masters who share their wisdom through Catherine. For example, one Master speaks of what happens following the shedding of the body. He states:

We don't just stop growing; we continue to grow. When we get to the spiritual plane, we keep growing there, too. We go through different stages of development. When we arrive, we're burned out. We have to go through a renewal stage, a learning stage, and a stage of decision.

We decide when we want to return, where, and for what reasons.

Some choose to not come back. They choose to go on to another stage of development. And they stay in spirit form . . . some for longer than others before they return. It is all growth and learning . . . continuous growth. Our body is just a vehicle for us while we're here. It is our soul and our spirit that last forever.[117]

Recognizing that so many human beings fear death, the Master Spirits offer Weiss the following wisdom through Catherine:

But if people knew that "life is endless; so we never die; we were never really born," then this fear would dissolve. If they knew that they had lived countless times before and would live countless times again, how reassured they would feel. If they knew that guardian "angels" really did exist, how much safer they would feel. If they knew that acts of violence and injustices against people did not go unnoted, but had to be repaid in kind in other lifetimes, how much less anger and desire for vengeance they would harbor.[118]

So much of my work as a psychologist is in enabling others to release their fears. The Masters had this to say to Weiss regarding fears:

You must eradicate the fears from their minds. It is a waste of energy when fear is present. It stifles them from fulfilling what they were sent here to fulfill. . . . Energy . . . everything is energy. So much is wasted.[119]

Regarding the issue of knowledge and what we need to learn, another Master says the following:

But we choose what we need to learn. If we need to come back to work through a relationship, we come back. If we are finished with that, we go on. In spiritual form you can always contact those that are in physical state if you choose to. But only if there is importance there . . . if you have to tell them something that they must know.[120]

When Weiss asked the Masters why it was necessary for us to have to be physical to continue learning, they replied:

There are different levels of learning, and we must learn some of them in the flesh. We must feel the pain. When you're a spirit you feel no pain. It is a period of renewal. Your soul is being renewed. When you're in physical state in the flesh, you can feel pain; you can hurt. In spiritual form you do not feel. There is only happiness, a sense of well-being. But it's a renewal period for . . . us. The interaction between people in the spiritual form is different. When you are in physical state . . . you can experience relationships.[121]

Weiss writes in *Many Lives, Many Masters,* that he too had wondered about the hierarchy of spirits. It is his thinking that the divisions as to who becomes a guardian angel, guide or Master is probably a function of gaining certain knowledge and wisdom. His belief parallels that of the great mystics and theologians in that he believes that the ultimate goal of the soul is to achieve a sense of merging or uniting with the Divine and of becoming God-like.[122]

In addition to lessons dealing with love, the Master Spirits emphasize the importance of balance and harmony and offered, along with the message, the ominous prediction that unless all of mankind can establish the needed balance, it will destroy itself. Look to Nature, the Masters advise, because Nature is about energy, harmony, balance and restoration. Man, they tell us, is about destruction only.[123] It is because of these messages that Weiss has so fervently dedicated himself to his writings and to sharing with the public the messages dealing with love, compassion, harmony, charity, faith and forgiveness.

Moving Toward an Intuitive Transformation

Through Weiss, the Masters speak to us about the importance of trusting our intuition. They repeatedly refer to the importance of being in a relaxed state, such as in a hypnotic or meditative state of being, in order to allow intuitive wisdom to be noticed or received. At one point, the Masters state to Weiss: "What we tell you is for now. You must now learn through your own intuition."[124]

As I have stated earlier, I believe strongly in the importance of developing one's own intuitive wisdom. I encourage you, just as I do my patients, to do this through meditation and/or formal classes. It is entirely doable and more rewarding than words can possibly express. One wonderful gift is the sense of increased awareness of what is occurring both physically and nonphysically. The greatest gift of all is the recognition that we are, as the Masters tell us, all truly one and connected. You see this when you begin to sense what one is thinking or who may be present. It is a recognition that mind and consciousness exist, regardless of person, time or place. It is not as difficult to tap into that consciousness. Furthermore, with such awareness gained through intuition, we come to realize that we need to love one another, for we are all brothers and sisters.

As I have previously written, Weiss's work has tremendously influenced my own work as a psychologist. With the help of the Masters, Weiss was transformed as he expanded his own spiritual knowledge, identity and consciousness and found that this enabled him to heal patients more quickly and effectively. I have experienced a similar transformation personally and professionally—and one which has contributed to the well-being of my patients.

I, like Weiss, very much wish to see therapists integrating the possibility of life after life or death into their therapeutic work. Doing this helps individuals open themselves up to the possibilities of being immortal and eternal, and deeply affects their perspective regarding their life and their purpose for being in physical form. Denying such experiences or stories denies one's truth and hinders awareness, growth and healing. Please know that your experiences are real from your perspective and deserve both recognition and validation.

Connecting with the Wisdom of the Masters

During the past decade, I have had the privilege of studying with a teacher, Yanni Maniates,[125] who has taught me the gift of engaging the Masters on a first-hand basis. This takes place through intuitive development and meditation. An even greater gift that he has given me is the recognition that I, too, am a Master—and that we are all capable of being Masters, if we so desire. We are all truly united and draw from the same great consciousness. It is through Love that we can connect with one another and, at the same time, heal both others and ourselves.

Those we call Masters, be they Buddha, Christ, Moses, Mohammed, Mary, Mother Theresa or Padre Pío, are all of the same energetic constellation. They are of the Divine, just as you and I are. By tapping into the Collective Consciousness or Universal Mind, it is possible to merge with such sacred, divine or holy energy. When we do this, merge with the Divine, we are expanding our consciousness, something that fills our being with a sense of love for all there is. It is here, in this state of connectedness, that we may recognize our own Mastery, as well as that of others.

We are all spiritual beings, having a spiritual experience, while in physical bodies. What this means is that we continue *to be* through eternity, always changing and expanding. When we accept this, we realize that there are no limitations, other than those that we impose upon ourselves. Mastery is within our power—if we wish it to be.

CHAPTER 4

More About the Extraordinary

If there is an aspect of the mind that is indeed nonlocal, then this entity comes to resemble the soul—something that is timeless, spaceless and immortal. Recovering the nonlocal nature of the mind, then, is essentially a recovery of the soul.

LARRY DOSSEY, M.D.

Prayer is moving into a personal relationship with Divine Intelligence . . . It is impossible to have a prayer without power. It is impossible to have a thought that is a secret for all energy is heard. When you pray, you draw to you and invoke grace. Grace is uncontaminated conscious Light. It is Divinity. Prayer brings grace and grace calms you. That is the cycle. Grace is the tranquilizer of the soul.

GARY ZUKAV, *The Seat of the Soul*[126]

There are many questions to ask about the extraordinary: Where and when does the extraordinary take place? What do extraordinary events have in common with those that take place in the laboratory of the quantum physicists? What purpose do such events serve?

Dr. Lawrence LeShan, psychologist and author, in *The Medium, the Mystic and the Physicist,* takes a serious look at the question, What is man? He concludes that, in addition to the many preconceived ideas regarding our separateness, our being flesh and bone and our nature, there are facts that contribute to answering this question that simply do not add up. Such facts fall into the category of *psi,* the study of the paranormal, or extrasensory perception (ESP), which includes clairvoyance, precognition and telepathy.[127]

Psi and the Clairvoyant Reality

Psi is actually a collective word that sums up our psychic abilities. It implies a sense of connection with everything and everyone. According to Russell Targ and Jane Katra in *Miracles of Mind,* "These abilities known collectively as *psi,* from the Greek word for soul, reveal numerous kinds of connections—mind to mind, mind to body, mind to the world and what some would call one-mindedness with God."[128] In fact, those in the field of quantum physics, including Einstein, Bohm and Margenau, have long believed that separation is only an illusion.

Those of you who use some aspects of psi, or extrasensory perception, have found, or will find, that it allows you to both make use of and to enjoy being a part of all consciousness. Targ and Katra demonstrate this exquisite value of using ESP, or psi as they share with the reader the countless experiments conducted by the United States government involving Russia during the Cold War, as well as the role it plays in spiritual healing.[129] That's right—spiritual healing. It is a powerful application of psi. Jane Katra describes the many facets of what is considered to be spiritual healing in *Miracles of Mind,* which is a fascinating collection of research written in a down-to-earth manner and is a "must read" for anyone seriously interested in learning both what psi is and how to put it to use.

Parapsychology or psychical research, according to LeShan, in the most profound sense, is the scientific study of the basic nature of man.[130] What LeShan is saying is that we need to recognize that a new concept of man is required, one that recognizes and honors the many ways in which he perceives and experiences the world. Furthermore, as we study those facts and events that are not supposed to take place, but do, we are formulating this broader, more realistic, understanding of man. This is a good thing. It allows us to move into and realize our potential.

LeShan's Four Aspects of the Clairvoyant Reality

What I especially appreciate in reading LeShan's work is his honesty. Like so many other men of science, LeShan, trained as an experimental psychologist, writes with candor of beginning a fifteen-year research project on psychosomatic medicine. He had strongly believed that he would find little validity in studying ESP.[131] However, having approached his research with a true scientific approach, LeShan surprised himself by concluding that **two realities truly exist for man:** the Sensory (ordinary) Reality, and the Clairvoyant Reality that occurs in the moment one is experiencing ESP—or receiving paranormal information.

What I call *The Extraordinary* is, I believe, an expression of the Clairvoyant or Mystical Reality. Keeping this in mind, I offer you the four aspects of the Clairvoyant Reality because I believe this will help you, the reader, to interpret and integrate the many extraordinary experiences that are presented in this book.

The first aspect of the Clairvoyant Reality is that what matters most about a thing or person is its relationship to everything else, rather than any particular individual aspects or qualities. This may explain why it is that mediums tend to share with us their sense of others with whom we have had or do have relationships. Also, what is emphasized is the unity or sense of connection of everyone to everyone else. What is most significant here is that the individual is seen as part of something greater than himself or herself.[132]

The second aspect is that time is an illusion, meaning that everything, including the past, present and future, simply *is*. Everything exists at the same time, and there are no delineations of time. LeShan quotes Evelyn Garrett, renowned clairvoyant, regarding time: "On clairvoyant levels there exists simultaneity of time, and the clairvoyant message may concern future events and future relationships which today seem impossible or meaningless to the person to whom they are revealed."[133] It is accepting that *all events are occurring at the same time* that makes precognition explainable.

The third aspect follows from the second. Since there is no separation in time, and everything simply is, the Clairvoyant Reality sees neither good nor evil. This does not mean that while in the Sensory Reality, good and evil do not exist. What it does mean is that while in the Clairvoyant Reality, you simply are aware and take notice of what occurs, without judgment or criticism.[134]

The last aspect of the Clairvoyant Reality is that information is best gained not by the use of our sensory organs, but rather through a sense of unity with everything and everyone else. In other words, if you were to be experiencing a Clairvoyant Reality, you would have a sense of being one with all there is, which makes it logical and possible for information to simply flow and circulate from one to another. This aspect helps to explain the experiences of both telepathy and clair-voyance.[135]

LeShan formulated these conclusions from conducting his own research, which included meetings with numerous cele-brated and highly respected mediums, mystics and physicists. What surprised him even more, and probably delighted him as well, was that the physicists also shared the characteristics of the Clairvoyant Reality. LeShan had expected that the four basic characteristics would be applicable for the mediums and the mystics but doubted this would be the case for the physi-cists. In other words, he discovered that there was complete agreement among the three groups regarding how the world is constructed. From my perspective, this is an extremely impor-tant finding.

As I present these to you, it is my hope that you will take a few moments to step back into your own life history and recall moments when you knew you were experiencing reality from the clairvoyant's perspective. Know that both realities are necessary for you and all of us to live fully and completely. In fact, LeShan, in 1966, wrote "The deepest goal is to integrate the two in our lives, so that each viewpoint is heightened and sharpened by the knowledge of the other."[136] One of my favor-ite quotes that substantiate this is by Eileen Garrett who states: "I asked these spirit figures if I was seeing them or if I was seeing what was in my own brain. They answered, 'both.'"[137]

The thinking of Gary Zukav, author of *Seat of the Soul*, parallels that of LeShan. Zukav writes of mankind's need to perceive the world from the multisensory personality, rather than the five sensory personality. Like LeShan, who wrote approximately twenty-five years before, Zukav wrote of man-kind's need to develop its intuitive wisdom, something Zukav believed would greatly contribute to the development of man's potential.[138]

Meditation, Intercessory Prayer
and Distant Healing

For many years I had heard about an experience called medi-
tation and thought it to be some type of elusive spiritual
experience. Though I was fully aware of the value of medita-
tion, I also knew the demands of my lifestyle. I doubted that
I had sufficient time and energy to even attempt to pursue the
development of a meditative mindset. As always, life is full of
delightful twists and turns and certainly brings to us its own
sense of humor. Little did I know that the practice of medita-
tion would become the grounding of so much of my life, and
that it would be the basis of not only a healthy lifestyle (mine
and that of my patients), but also of much of the healing work
that I do.

The Relaxation Response—
the Little Pill That Works

Not long after beginning my practice, I began to teach a won-
derful technique called the *relaxation response,* which was
developed by Dr. Herbert Benson, a cardiologist associated
with Harvard University. In his desire to help his patients
better manage their own stress and thereby reduce associated
cardiac problems, Benson began his search for an intervention
that appeared to be at the heart of those who practiced such
modalities as meditation, yoga and biofeedback. The core of
this technique is the breath.[139]

Having first learned the technique while taking a biofeed-
back class during my doctoral studies, I found the use of breath
to be invaluable in reducing my own level of pain as well as
calming and relaxing me in times of great stress and anxiety. I
knew I was on to something valuable. Considering that I began

my practice of psychology specializing in stress reduction and pain management, the relaxation response became, and still is, an important tool in restoring a sense of well-being.

Essentially, the technique involves learning to breathe correctly, which leads to a particular response of the body called the relaxation response. As one learns to breathe appropriately, a number of physiological changes occur that contribute to a sense of calm, peace and well-being. These changes, which are due to a decreased need for oxygen and a decrease in carbon dioxide production, include a decrease in heart rate, breath rate, blood pressure and metabolism.

But something else was becoming quite apparent. Those, including myself, who chose to practice the relaxation response for fifteen to twenty minutes once or twice a day, were realizing a meditative state of being. The process of learning to place the focus of attention on your breath is actually a very successful means of quieting the mind. In the quieting of the mind, there is the sense of "going inside," and of centering or grounding. This is all part of the meditative state. The more you practice the breath, the easier it becomes to invoke the relaxation response. It is essentially a means of training your mind and body to quickly go into a lovely place of well-being and peace.

Furthermore, in learning the relaxation response, as well as in meditation, you raise the level at which your energy vibrates. This facilitates a sense of connection with God, Universal Consciousness, Source, Great Spirit or whatever divine power or beings with which you are comfortable. It is this raising of your energetic vibrations, achieved by focusing your breath, or meditating, that contributes to the development of your intuitive wisdom as well as your increased sense of peace, tranquility and well-being.

I have come to realize that I do not care for this word *meditation* because it is both so much simpler and yet so much more than it suggests. It is simpler because I think there is nothing much simpler and more pleasant than choosing to focus on and stay with your breath. It really is so easy to do, though I admit the trick is developing the ability to stay with and return to your breath when your mind wanders, which it certainly will do. There is more because the gift of staying focused on your breath is not only life-preserving, but extremely profound.

Having mastered the relaxation technique and used it as the basis of developing my meditative skills, I have gone on to study meditation with superb teachers and have used my skills to develop my own intuition, which has been incredibly gratifying. I recommend using breath and meditation to develop intuitive skills to my patients and to you. Simply by learning to shift your focus to your breath, you can develop those parts of your being, including your potential, that you only knew existed in the world of possibilities.

Furthermore, I highly recommend the audiotapes called *Breathing*, by physician Andrew Weil, to expedite learning breath work.[140] Weil is a gentle, clear, patient and excellent teacher. I cannot think of a more enjoyable way to learn the basics of breath.

As you stay with the breath, you have a sense of a quieting of your very being, of peace and tranquility, and even of beginning to connect with your intuition, otherwise known as the wisdom of your soul or consciousness. In the development of your intuition or connection with consciousness, via meditation (the breath), you are actually engaged in activities of nonlocal mind. This is where my research dealing with prayer comes into play.

Prayer in the Laboratory—the Spindrift Studies

While busy studying and teaching the relaxation response and developing the beginnings of a meditative state, I found myself actively involved in researching consciousness, including intercessory prayer and distant healing. I have spent years reading and studying the writings of physician Larry Dossey; the quantum physicists, including Albert Einstein, David Bohm, Henry Margenau and others; psychologists Carl Jung and Lawrence LeShan; physicists Dean Radin and Russell Targ; biologist Rupert Sheldrake; healers Jane Katra and Doris Kunz;[141] and so many others. The result of this research has led me to understand that *intercessory prayer and distant healing* work. This is, I believe, because mind is nonlocal. Mind is, as indicated earlier, transpersonal, transpatial and transtemporal.

The world of modern day science is filled with beautifully conducted studies that have been able to be successfully replicated regarding psi and the effects of prayer. Scientists cannot afford to disregard the results of such studies.

It has been many years since my first reading of the impressive early studies that proved prayer to be a significant intervention, but the feeling of joy and excitement regarding the conclusions of these studies has stayed with me. I would like to share just a few of these studies with you because they are truly special.

The first experiments that come to mind are those that were conducted by the Spindrift Organization in Salem, Oregon, beginning in 1975. Scientists wished to establish whether or not spiritual healing is real, whether or not prayer works, and if the effects of prayer can be measured and reproduced.[142] The organization was one of the first, if not the very first, to conduct such studies in a laboratory setting.

According to physician Larry Dossey in *Recovering the Soul,* "A central assumption made by the Spindrift researchers is that all humans have 'divine attributes, a qualitative oneness with God'"[143] This assumption is significant because it speaks to the nonlocal nature of mind that is characteristic of every human being and, therefore, something that makes possible the ability to use mind to influence the well-being of another individual at a distance. That is where the use of prayer to heal those not present comes into play.

What these individuals did was actually rather basic and fundamental. They took a batch of rye seeds, placed them in a container of vermiculite, and divided them into two equal groups by placing a string down the middle of the container. This created Group A, the control group and Group B, the treated or prayed-for group. After treating the experimental group (which involved praying for the seeds), the rye shoots were counted. The findings were that the prayed-for group yielded more sprouts than the nonprayed-for group. After repeating this experiment many times, it was determined that "the effect of thought on living organisms outside the human body was significant, quantifiable and reproducible; and that the effects of human consciousness are not confined to the brain and body.[144] These findings were impressive. But, the scientists wanted to know more.

The researchers, like so many of us, were eager to see what effect, if any, prayer would have on seeds that were unhealthy, since prayer is so often used for unhealthy individuals. To do this, they intentionally stressed a batch of rye seeds by adding salt water to the container. The results were powerful because they demonstrated that prayer is even more effective for organisms that are stressed. The numbers of the prayed for shoots were greater than those of the control group, the shoots not prayed for.[145]

As if these findings were not significant enough, the Spindrift Organization then fine-tuned their examination of prayer effectiveness. They sought to determine which is more effective: direct prayer, which is similar to telling the Universe what to do and asking for something specific (such as a cure for a loved one's cancer or a heart condition); or nondirected prayer, which is open-ended, nonspecific and trusts the Universe or God to do what is best ("best" expressed by the sentiment, *Let thy will be done*).

To determine which type of prayer is more effective, the Spindrift researchers grew a mold on top of a rice agar plate similar to the type used by microbiologists. After stressing the mold by dipping it in alcohol to damage it and slow its growth, but not enough to kill it, a string was put down the middle to divide the sample into the experimental group, for which there were prayers and treatment, and the control group, for which there were no prayers. The results were significant. When directed prayer was used for the experimental group, there was no change. It was only after the replacement of directed prayer with nondirected prayer, in which no specific goal was stated, that side B began to grow and multiply.

The bottom line here regarding prayer is that the findings of the Spindrift organization show that **prayer works.** Furthermore, while the researchers determined that *both methods of prayer work,* the nondirective technique yielded results that were twice as effective as those of the direct technique.[146]

Prayer and Healing for Coronary Care Patients

Another experiment worthy of special attention here is a well-known study conducted in 1988 by cardiologist Randolph Byrd. This study demonstrated the power of nonlocal healing in the form of intercessory prayer, or prayer at a distance. Byrd, who was a devout Christian, had hoped to establish the therapeutic value of prayer by performing a rigidly-run, double-blind scientific study of coronary patients at San Francisco General Hospital. Over a ten-month period, Byrd had 393 patients divided into two groups. The names, diagnoses and conditions of one group consisting of 193 randomly selected coronary care patients, were sent to individuals of varying religious affiliations who prayed for them. The designated treatment for the remaining group of coronary care did not include prayers.

According to physicist Dean Radin in *The Conscious Universe,* the original findings of this study were impressive.

"The prayed-for patients were five times less likely to require antibiotics and three times less likely to develop pulmonary edema. None of the prayed-for group required endotracheal intubation, and fewer patients in the prayed-for group died."[147]

Even with consideration given to criticisms of the study, the study speaks to the implications of mind and its ability to communicate nonlocally with other minds at a distance. The conservatively-minded and notable Dr. William Nolan, who had been known for being critical of faith healing, was impressed enough by this study that he made the following statement: "It sounds like this study will stand up to scrutiny . . . maybe we doctors ought to be writing on our order sheets, 'Pray three times a day.' If it works, it works."[148]

The results of Byrd's experiment were so impressive that after reading the account of the study, physician Larry Dossey embarked on his own research of the therapeutic effects of distant healing and intercessory prayer. This eventually led to the publication *Healing Words: The Power of Medicine and the Practice of Medicine*[149] and also *Prayer is Good Medicine*.[150] In addition, he, like myself, feels that he would be doing a disservice to his patients if he did not pray for them. He writes in *Prayer is Good Medicine,* "I soon came to regard this evidence as one of the best-kept secrets in modern medicine, and I began actively to pray for my patients."[151]

Putting Prayer in Your Back Pocket

If you are wondering how might you use this material, you may begin by simply recognizing that when in a difficult situation, *prayer is effective.* Some people think one has to engage in lengthy and involved prayers to truly pray. But this is absolutely not the case. Prayer may be nothing more than a simple acknowledgement that you need and wish to ask for help.

Help, after all, is the briefest, most effective request for assistance when nothing else seems to be working.

For some of you, prayer may be the state of being fully present, such as the physician who is engaged in hours of intense surgery, or as one who is involved in a skating, swimming, musical, gardening, bread-baking or walking meditative experience. And, of course, prayer may be that chat you have with the Divine while carpooling, cooking dinner, showering, walking on the treadmill or in church or synagogue. There is no one way or one place to pray. It is, like breath, a beautiful gift you can put in your back pocket and have available any time you need it! To quote Amy Doherty, a dear friend and reader of this manuscript, who scribbled on a post-note regarding this very paragraph, "Love this . . . Prayer is portable!"

As a result of my own investigation into prayer, I began praying for my patients many years ago, and I continue to do this on a daily basis. I also enlist the assistance of prayer circles for some of my most seriously ill patients. As one of my recommended therapeutic interventions, I encourage my patients to use prayer.

Nonlocal Healing in the Laboratory— the Grad Studies

Before moving on, I wish to offer you a few points regarding recent research dealing with intercessory prayer, healing and miracles, or to use a broader term, consciousness. The interest in this area continues to grow. For those of you who are interested in learning more of leading-edge research concerning consciousness, I refer you to the recently published work of Larry Dossey, Dean Radin and Larry LeShan,[152] as well as the publications and conferences of the Institute of Noetic Sciences.[153]

I also highly recommend that you take time to read of the research of psychologist Bernie Grad of Montreal's McGill

University who has, along with LeShan, been honored by Harvard University for his work in studying nonlocal healing intention, i.e., the effect of mind on mind and mind on matter. In describing the experiments of Grad, which are of "Nobel quality," Dossey states: "They are ingenious and profound and have set a standard for all the experiments in nonlocal healing that have followed."[154]

For example, Grad was one of the very first in his field to test whether or not our mood can affect others in our environment. In other words, if one were depressed, would the water he might use to water a plant negatively affect the plant—in contrast to water held by someone in a very positive emotional state? In a controlled experiment, three subjects, including two patients who were clinically depressed and an upbeat, positive individual with a green thumb, were tested. Each subject held a sealed bottle in his or her hands for one half hour that was then used to water barley seeds.

The results were interesting. The depressed female happened to be in a positive mood and had held the bottle as though she were cradling a child. Consequently, her seeds actually grew more quickly than those of the other two subjects. Otherwise, the results were as expected: the seeds watered by the man with the green thumb grew the fastest, and the seeds watered by the extremely depressed gentleman grew the slowest. The findings suggest that our emotions have both positive and negative influence and that the objects we hold may pick up our emotions and therefore mediate these influences.[155]

The results of this experiment led some, including Dossey and myself, to wonder whether the stethoscopes, syringes, Band-Aids and other physical objects that healthcare workers use on their patients might be affected by the mood of the healthcare worker. And if this is the case, does this then affect the patient on whom the object is used? According to Grad's work, which indicates that secondary objects mediate healing intentions, objects used (IV solution, stethoscope, etc.) may indeed affect the response of the patient.[156]

The implication is that if a nurse or doctor who is emotionally very negative or distraught, due perhaps to personal problems or to just having a "bad" day, uses the stethoscope he or she has in a pocket which is used to help establish a blood pressure reading, he or she may somehow mediate or transmit the negativity on some level to the patient. In energetic terms, Grad's findings make sense and should be honored by those in the healing profession. Remember those "Smile" buttons that we used to see? Perhaps gentle reminders to smile and be happy might not be such a bad idea throughout our healing institutions.

For those who wish to expedite healing in a home setting, these findings are especially helpful. Consider wrapping a loved one in a robe or favorite afghan or quilt lovingly made by you or a dear relative or friend. Holding a treasured stuffed animal that has been close to a loved one may also be helpful.

Grad was also the first to examine nonlocal healing intention on the ability to heal wounds. He conducted experiments using mice which had been anesthetized, and in which surgical incisions had been made in order to remove a small piece of skin. The mice were divided into three groups. In one of the three groups a healer, using his or her healing mental ability and intentions, would hold the cage of the wounded mice for fifteen minutes twice a day for two weeks. The treatment of the second group was simply placement in a cage that was heated to the temperature of that of the healer held group. The third group, the control group, was moved about, but received neither heat nor healing intentions. The results indicated that the mice in the treated group, the group which was held by the healer, healed significantly faster than the control groups.

Once again, these are impressive findings. What is special about Grad's work, and the reason that Harvard has honored him, is that he was the first to show us in the laboratory that our thoughts and our intentions are powerful enough to influence other living things, be they mice or seeds. According to Dossey, until Grad began his research, the tendency was to explain away the effects of distant healing by the placebo effect (the power of suggestion or positive thought).

The extraordinary research of Bernie Grad corroborates the work of the quantum physicists. In fact, the belief held by Einstein that all life is connected, and that we therefore need to be compassionate for all living beings, is supported by Grad, who has stated: "(These) phenomena . . . throw new light on the basic unity of man, animal and plant . . . "[157]

Distant Healing with Aids Patients

In 1999, Elisabeth Targ, then Director of the Complementary Medicine Research Institute at California Pacific Medical Center (CPMC) and assistant clinical professor in the Department of Psychiatry at the University of California, San Francisco, published an important article on distant healing in IONS (Institute of Noetic Sciences) Review (Number 49). In the article, Targ, the principal investigator of the studies of distant healing of AIDS patients, states: "The term 'Distant healing'— and the more precise but cumbersome 'distant mental influence on biologic systems' (now adopted by the National Institute of Health)—is an attempt to find a way to objectively describe the outcome of what others call psychic healing, energy healing, or prayer."[158] She then notes that of the more than 150 published formal studies of distant healing in the past forty years, **more than two-thirds show that significant positive effects are possible.** This, in my opinion, is impressive and serves to further validate the power of prayer.[159]

I cite this article for several reasons. Targ writes of important findings of one of the members of her research team at CPMC, Fred Sicher, whose research results were published in the *Western Journal of Medicine.* These results represent more than five years of work at CPMC. According to Sicher, many of the healers whom he had interviewed believed that **their best work occurred with those patients whose needs were the greatest.** In Targ's words: "The healers suggested that if we want to see a significant effect on someone's health, there has to be a significant motivation—the patient should be in extremis."[160]

Targ continues with a point that I believe is extremely valuable regarding distant healing, and which validates what I have determined and known for many years. She states: "Sicher also found that, unlike in many healing studies, distant healing is not usually performed as a one-time effort. Most of his interviewees stated that they tend to work with patients over a period of time, often many weeks." It has been my experience in praying for my patients and my loved ones that the best gift for them is the offering of **repeated and daily prayers by as many as possible.** Sicher also proposed a distant healing study of a population dealing with an incurable disease, such as AIDS, and one which would involve many healers who would treat patients for at least two months.[161]

The article in IONS reports in detail the findings of the study proposed by Sicher, which was designed for the specific purpose of determining "whether or not there is an effect of healing intentions over distance."[162]

According to Targ, there were actually two completed studies: the pilot study, with 20 patients, and the confirmatory study with 40 patients. Neither the patients nor the researchers were aware of who was in the treatment group and the two groups had been balanced in regards to their disease status. The results were stunning. Findings produced by the pilot study revealed a 40% mortality rate in the control group and absolutely **no** deaths in the treatment group.[163] This took my breath away.

In this study, each patient in the treatment group, by the end of the study, had received healing intentions, or "healing effort," from ten different healers (one healer at a time, one hour each day, six days a week, over a ten-week period). Using a variety of healing techniques, each healer viewed a photograph of a treatment patient, knowing only his or her first name, the CD4 count and a line or two regarding the nature of the illness, while holding the intention for the patient's health and well-being for one hour a day.[164]

The results were remarkable. Targ reports that after six months, "patients in the treatment group had acquired significantly fewer new AIDS-defining diseases than people in the control group, their overall illness severity scores were significantly lower, they had had significantly fewer hospitalizations and those hospitalizations were significantly shorter."[165] In addition, those patients in the treatment group experienced more recoveries from AIDS-defining illnesses and demonstrated significant improvement psychologically.[166]

This study is powerful in its own right because it provides you with an understanding of what you can offer those who are in need of healing intentions. We are all capable of praying and of asking for blessings for the well-being of those who are ill or dying. As I have previously emphasized, prayer works. It may not work every time, but it has been shown to be significantly effective and, therefore, deserves consideration. Although your prayers may not stop a loved one from dying, if there is even the slightest indication that they contribute to an alleviation of pain, isn't it worth making the effort? I believe it is.

Harvard and Benson—the Respectability of Prayer

Prayer research has earned its place of respectability. This is indicated by the fact that Harvard University in 1997 sponsored a conference called "Intercessory Prayer and Distant Healing Intention: Clinical and Laboratory Research." It brought together researchers from the various parts of the United States for the purpose of sharing research conclusions regarding prayer or distant intentionality. Essentially, the material being presented dealt with studies concerning consciousness which functions apart from one's body and mind.[167]

At the present time, Dr. Herbert Benson, long affiliated with Harvard Medical School and Boston's New England Deaconess Hospital, is conducting research that deals with the nonlocal effects of meditation and prayer on the body, especially when the body is relaxed. Benson has undertaken a study to examine the effects of nonlocal prayer, or distant healing, on patients.

Over twelve hundred patients undergoing coronary artery bypass surgery in three Boston hospitals are included in the study. One-third of the group will receive prayers from various religious groups without knowing they are being prayed for. One-third of the group will be told they are receiving prayers, and one-third of the group will receive no prayers. Benson hopes to determine from the first two groups whether or not prayer affects healing, and if being informed about this has an influence on the outcome. The importance of this study is that more scientists at prestigious research institutions are taking seriously the study of consciousness—or nonlocal mind—and examining it in a scientific and respectable manner.[168]

One of the results of my research over the past decade is that I have personally developed my own practice of both meditation and prayer. What this has frequently led me to consider is that prayer and meditation appear to have a similar impact on the body physiologically. While the intentions may differ, the end result has been the same. That is, I find that both prayer and meditation lead to a state of calm, serenity and peace. The reason for this is that in each practice, what one seeks to achieve is a connection, a unity and a merging with a sense of something greater that may be called Buddha, God, Great Spirit, the Universe or Source.

Benson's research that led to the discovery of the Relaxation Response serves to further explain this, given that breath work leads to a reduction of heart beats, breath rate, blood pressure, oxygen consumption and carbon dioxide production. When praying or meditating, the ability to merge with something greater is enhanced by the body slowing down its normal life-serving functions. Dossey, in *Prayer is Good Medicine,* validates my own findings. He states: "Both prayer and meditation come from the heart, and there are more similarities than differences between them."[169]

I wish to take a moment here to note the following: In my journey to make sense of the extraordinary events that so many have shared with me, I have found that the research regarding consciousness has opened up doors, if you will, physically, mentally, emotionally and spiritually, for all those who choose to allow it into their lives. Both transformation and understanding take place as we move toward a greater interest in mind and consciousness. We grow in so many ways as a result of this process. It is because of this recognition of its power to transform us that I have offered you a sampling of the research that validates the meaningfulness of both the extraordinary experiences you may have had up to this point, and the stories that are presented in this book.

Saved By a Prayer

One of my favorite stories dealing with the value of prayer and its effect on healing comes from the work of Elisabeth Kübler-Ross, though I am unsure in which book or lecture it actually appears. The story touched me deeply and is one I have recalled over the span of many decades. According to Kübler-Ross, a young woman was driving on a major highway in the northeastern part of the United States when she suddenly was forced to come to a complete stop. Traffic had stopped due to an accident that had occurred perhaps a half a mile away. Time passed as she sat patiently in her car, waiting for the traffic to begin moving.

Upon hearing the sirens of an approaching ambulance, she became concerned about the well-being of those who might have been injured. She began to pray for the individual or individuals who were in the accident, although she had no idea of just how serious the injuries might be. Not knowing exactly what had taken place, she could only pray that God would bless whoever was hurt.

As it turned out, there was a gentleman in one of the cars who came very close to dying. Being so close to death, he had what one might call a near-death experience. Following the accident, the man left his body, floated above the scene of the accident and proceeded to wander back through the rows of cars. As he passed by the woman's car, he became aware of the prayers she was offering on his behalf. Deeply moved by her prayers for him, an individual she did not know, he made a note of her license plate number just before returning to his body. He was then rushed by ambulance to the nearest hospital where he remained for some time. Despite his near-death experience, the gentleman made a full recovery.

What is so remarkable is the fact that upon leaving the hospital, the man contacted the local police to gain their assistance in locating the woman's name and address. We can only imagine how surprised this woman must have been when the gentleman for whom she had prayed showed up at her door with a bouquet of roses to thank her for her blessings.

I especially love this story because it validates several things: first, that our prayers are heard; second, that we are truly nonlocal beings who can and do function apart from our bodies across space and time; and last, that we can have an impact, via our intentions, on the well-being of others. Perhaps what is most beautiful about this tale is that it speaks to our immortality and the nature of our soul.

A Listening Ear

I would like to share several stories that come from a patient of mine, Pat,* a very "normal" and "together" individual, who has found prayer to be the means by which she believes that she and her family have survived numerous difficult situations. During my interview with her, she told me that for several years her prayers, either for herself or for others, had been answered so specifically and quickly that she had come to consider prayer her own "hotline" to God.

The first incident that Pat described dealt with her daughter, Cathy,* who was three years old at the time. Doctors had diagnosed Cathy with a bleeding disorder, but felt that they had to consider the possibility of leukemia. While in the hospital for tests, doctors learned that Cathy's platelets were extremely low, just 40,000, when the count should have been 150,000 to 400,000. Though Cathy went home on a Friday afternoon, the family was told that if her platelets continued to drop, she would have to go into the hospital for transfusions.

Believing in the power of prayer, Pat asked everyone to pray. The word went out to the community. Prayer circles were formed and prayer groups were notified. Family, friends, neighbors, colleagues and strangers prayed for Cathy throughout the weekend.

In addition to their strong belief in the value of prayer, Pat and her husband believed in the value of touch and hands-on healing. They made a point of hugging, holding and touching Cathy every time they walked by her. Their intentions were those of a traditional healer. That is, each time they touched her, they experienced a sense of God coming through their hands and helping to heal their daughter.

In fact, Pat smiled as she recalled her husband hugging Cathy and saying, "Grow, grow, grow!"—as if he were speaking directly to her platelets. What he was doing was visualizing or imaging them growing, something I frequently teach my cancer patients to do. This situation is an example of intercessory prayer, or nonlocal mind, at work.

As you have probably already guessed, when Pat, her husband and Cathy returned to the hospital to redo the blood work on the following Monday, the results had improved significantly. Cathy's count was 76,000—an increase of 36,000 platelets in just two days. The doctors were incredulous, and Pat and her husband were both grateful and pleased, but not surprised.

The doctors were extremely encouraged by this and conveyed their sense of optimism and hope to the family. According to Pat, the physicians believed that once the platelets started to increase, it was unlikely that the numbers would again drop. This was a turning point for the family. Consequently, the intensity of the praying waned, and as it decreased, so did the platelet growth. The increase in platelets fell to about 1,000 per week. However, Pat and her husband continued to express their gratitude and, of course, continued to pray for Cathy.

On another occasion, Pat confided to me that she awakened one morning feeling totally overwhelmed regarding a problem that was interfering with her relationship with her husband. She was extremely distraught and troubled, and felt that if she did not receive some type of assistance that very day, she might not be able to handle her parenting responsibilities.

According to Pat, she wanted to call my office for an appointment. However, she simply could not bear the thought of having to wait several days or more if nothing were available. Having had success with prayer, Pat decided to ask for help. Just before she picked up the phone at her kitchen desk, she sat down and began to pray, asking for immediate assistance in securing an appointment. After leaving a message with my answering service, she said that she prayed once more.

Some might call it luck, and others might call it a coincidence. Nevertheless, within the same hour of Pat's call to my office, my secretary called Pat to tell her that a cancellation for 2:00 P.M. later that same day had just been received. Despite the hassle of needing to get sitters and reschedule other appointments, Pat was thrilled about the sequence of events. She said, "yes" to my secretary and "thank you" to God for listening. From Pat's vantage point, there was nothing coincidental about this. It was, as she had experienced so many times before, an answer to her prayers.

Several years before my interview with Pat, she had been struggling and trying to cope with an enormous problem that was placing far too many limitations on her life and making it difficult for her to function normally. She was desperate. Once again, she decided to ask for help through prayer. And so she prayed, she cried and she prayed again.

She recalls that on a beautiful, warm, fall day, she sat on her favorite blue and white family room couch, peering out into her garden, sobbing, praying and asking for help. She told God, "You have to get me out of this, Lord. I don't know what more I can do. Please, just show me how I can help myself!" Worn out from several hours of tears, she regrouped, got up and went out to run errands.

That very day when she returned home, just before the children arrived home from school, she went to the mailbox, and there she found the answer to her prayers. Along with the many magazines and letters, there was a bright pink flyer. It described a local support group that was facilitated by an individual who had succeeded in winning his own struggle with the very same problem with which she was dealing. Now he was devoting his life to helping others heal.

Pat still recalls exactly what the flyer looked like and what it said. "I can see it so vividly," she says. "I can see the printing and the color of the paper." She was so excited that she ran to the phone to make an appointment for an interview.

Just after arriving for the interview, Pat was asked who had referred her to the group. Specifically, she was asked, "How did you hear about us?" When she responded that she had received their flyer in the mail, the interviewer stopped what he was doing and said, "We don't mail out flyers nor have we ever done such a thing." Even when she went on to describe the flyer in detail, he said, "I don't know what you are talking about." At that point he suggested that she bring in the flyer.

Now here's the odd thing. Pat described herself as a saver and one who never throws anything away. However, when she went home to find the flyer, it had absolutely disappeared. To this day, it has never been found!

As for Pat, the group had a powerful impact on her life. Her life changed immeasurably due to her experience in the group, and she told me that she felt it was the beginning of her new life.

I love this story because not only does it illustrate the value of prayer, but it also provides us with a sense of being watched over, perhaps by loved ones, or angels or guides or some other expression of the Divine.

Thanks and Guidance From the Other Side

Yes, our prayers are heard. This has been validated for me personally several times in my lifetime. I offer you one personal story that makes me smile every time I think of it. In September 1998, just before the Jewish holidays, I was blessed with an extraordinary visit from my father-in-law, who had died on September 17th 1997. As I have noted previously, deceased loved ones like to make their presence known to living family members during special times, such as anniversaries and holidays.

On the evening of the 16th of September, just after finishing dinner, my husband, son and I gathered in our kitchen and lit a yartzheit candle, a Jewish tradition in which we remember a loved one on the eve of the anniversary of his or her death by lighting a special candle that burns for twenty-four hours and by saying a prayer in his or her memory. My family and I hold hands while doing this and often finish by giving one another a hug and a kiss. As my husband and my son walked away, I recall telling my father-in-law, "We love you, Dad." I then returned to the kitchen sink and continued washing the dinner dishes.

The following day, I had my usual visit with my good friend, Samantha, whose intuitive sensitivity allows her to serve as a medium and whose story appears in other parts of this book. Just after sitting down with her, she immediately told me she sensed a male presence of someone with a large build and whose name began with Er or Her. . . . Since this was the anniversary of the death of my father-in-law, Herb, I instantly recognized that this was Dad.

Samantha went on to ask me if our son's arm was hurting, and then told me that Dad was worried about our son David's right shoulder. This made perfect sense to me because David had been having significant problems with his right shoulder for quite some time as a result of his intensive experience as a collegiate baseball player. He was actually preparing for his shoulder surgery the following day. Honestly, I felt good knowing that Dad was keeping a loving eye on David.

The reason I bring this story to you is because of what followed. Samantha then asked me if I or we had been praying recently. When I explained that we had, indeed, said yartzheit for Dad the evening before, my father-in-law then announced that he had been right there with us while we were praying and that he wanted us to know how much it meant to him that we were praying in honor of his memory. He thanked us, through Samantha, for our prayers.

I have never forgotten the moment I heard this message from Dad. Each time we had previously prayed for my mom, my father-in-law and my mother-in-law, I had experienced the sense of their presence. However, I had never received anything to substantiate this. Dad's visit, however, was the validation for which I had long waited, a validation that our prayers are not only heard, but that they are valued and appreciated.

My mom's visit, which came just about a year later, again through Samantha, also served as a validation that our prayers are heard. However, the purpose of this particular visit was to impart guidance and wisdom. You see, she had been listening, perhaps for several months, to my concerns, worries and prayers for my children. Her message was essentially to remind me that they needed to be responsible for their own journey during this lifetime. She was letting me know that they were capable of taking care of themselves and that I did not have to devote so much time and energy to worrying about them.

I knew that my mom spoke the truth. In fact, her wisdom is what I frequently share with my own patients. Yet, I also thought, *It must be easier to be so wise when we are nonphysical beings who no longer have to deal with the many trials and tribulations of a physical experience. After all,* I thought to myself, *I wonder if mom could have successfully pulled off not worrying or praying for my brothers and me and our families while she was alive.*

Having shared these thoughts with you, I can tell you that I took my mom's words of advice to heart. I continued to pray for my children, but from a level of anticipated joy while in the moment, rather than from worry and anxiety about the past or future. I write of this experience because it was a precious gift that can benefit all of us, if we so choose. Pray for your loved ones. But, remember to pray for them *in the moment* and always from a place in your heart that is filled with warmth, love and joyful excitement about their well-being.

Through my own research and the invaluable information offered to me by a patient of mine who, though Jewish, studies Buddhism, I have learned of the value of prayer regarding the journey of the soul. Furthermore, many have shared stories with me that support the importance of praying for those who have died. Perhaps you may remember this the next time you say a prayer for your deceased love one. Your prayers not only deeply touch them, but also play a role in caring for their soul.

Prayers and miracles go hand in hand; there will be more about prayers in the next section.

Miracles—Large and Small

Essentially, everything that has been so far described can be classified as either a miracle or as miraculous—or not, depending on your vantage point. For those of you who view reality from the perspective of only your five senses, the events so far mentioned do appear to be extraordinary as well as miraculous—and I believe that you will find that to be true for so for many of the stories that follow.

Helen Schucman, a collaborator on the recording of material for *A Course in Miracles,* a highly respected group of spiritual teachings, notes that the *Course* distinguishes between what is real and what is unreal: between knowledge, which is truth, and perception. "Truth is unalterable, eternal and unambiguous. It can be unrecognized, but it cannot be changed. . . . It is beyond learning because it is beyond time and process. It has no beginning and no end. It merely is."[170] Perception is a different story. Given that it is based on interpretation, it reflects what is going on with us; it is a projection of our emotions, ideas and thoughts.[171]

We essentially bring to the world our sense of interpretation. *A Course in Miracles* sums up the ability of human beings to make something either taste sweet and delicious, such as an event being miraculous, or bitter and revolting, such as differences in viewpoints. It states: "Projection makes perception." The authors write in the Preface, "We look inside first, decide the kind of world we want to see and then project that world outside, making it the truth *as we see it.*"[172] The issue, I believe, is one of choice.

It's All a Matter of Perspective—and Choice

For a number of years now, Yitta Halberstam and Judith Leventhal have been writing a series of books called *Small Miracles,* which I highly recommend. In *Small Miracles for the Jewish Heart,* they quote the Talmud: "We do not see things as *they* are; we see things as *we* are."[173] These words accurately reinforce the previously-noted thoughts from *A Course in Miracles.* Whatever your perspective, your thoughts, your feelings, your life experience, whatever you bring to the moment, that is what you shall bring to your interpretation of what comes before you on your path.

I share with you a story these authors present that addresses a phenomenon with which I am familiar as a psychologist because it has been studied in the scientific laboratory. They write of scientists who traveled to Micronesia, which at the time was a remote island whose inhabitants were extremely primitive and had no real conception of modern realities. These natives, when exposed to the electronic devices of the scientists, ascribed magical powers to their ability to function. According to the scientists, when several ships appeared on the horizon, they eagerly pointed them out to the natives. Though the ships were clearly visible to the scientists—and very much a reality—the natives were unable to see them, nor comprehend the possibility of their existence. The explanation is actually rather simple. In the author's words, "They were outside the milieu of their experience and thus beyond their perception."[174]

This is an excellent example of how we choose what we allow into our experience. The ships were real, at least from the perspective of the scientists, but because the natives were neither comfortable nor familiar with the event, they chose not to allow it into their experience. Experiments with rats in the laboratory have confirmed that we perceive what we are conditioned to receive. When this occurs at an early period of development, while the brain and mental functions are being developed, it is difficult to see the very thing that may later appear right before us. This is the key: that which appears later is real. We simply choose not to allow it in.

As a psychologist who has sat with patients who have shared countless wondrous stories of small and large miraculous events in their lives, I have come to recognize that the ability to experience miracles is often dependent on whether or not you choose to allow for the possibility of miracles in your life. Choice, remember, is the key.

The section that follows this will deal with coincidental synchronicities—and every one of the stories I share with you, the reader, can be considered a miracle, if you so choose. The meaning of such experiences is what will influence your perspective regarding life and your sense of purpose.

While at a retreat recently, I had the pleasure of being paired off with the husband of a friend of mine, who shared some of his own personal wisdom regarding his life experience. He said that he felt his life had been blessed with many miracles. This amused me because I knew that I was just about to write this very section that deals with miracles. Throughout his life, whenever he needed something (such as a new job, increased income, or a new home)—lo and behold! Whatever it was it would appear and his needs and those of his family were met. It was as though his life was being carefully orchestrated, movement by movement. There was a miraculous quality to this, according to my new friend. He seemed to feel that it all flowed to him with the greatest of ease and certainly no resistance.

When I asked him how he would define miracle, he answered: "Well, miracles are those events over which you have no control, which, when they occur, serve your purpose." This clearly made sense to me. I interpret those events that "serve your purpose" as being *meaningful* occurrences. Some might call such events *coincidental synchronicities*—and others might call them miracles. My new friend clearly seemed to feel the miraculous quality about such experiences.

Since beginning my research into extraordinary and paranormal phenomena, I have been witness to numerous kinds of miraculous stories. There are the frequent stories dealing with those who barely survive horrific car, plane or train accidents; those whose homes and valued possessions come through the most frightening weather conditions; those who are separated by life circumstances and decades later find themselves reconnecting with one another; and those who survive life-threatening illnesses against all odds and predictions. However, there are other kinds of miracles that include our ability to affect events across time.

The Miracle of All Time Being Available in Present Time

As previously stated, *Miracles of Mind*, by Targ and Katra, is an impressive exploration of nonlocal consciousness and spiritual healing. The authors have looked at various phenomena that easily fall into the category of miracles and have described research findings that explain such events. The work of Targ and Katra assists readers to better understand how the capabilities of mind can help to explain the Principles of Miracles as presented in *A Course in Miracles*. For example, they present substantial research that deals with man's difficulty in measuring time.[175]

Regarding the relationship of miracles and time, one of the Principles of Miracles, #13, states: "Miracles are both beginnings and endings, and so they alter the temporal order. They are always affirmations of rebirth, which seem to go back but really go forward. They undo the past in the present, and thus release the future."[176] Miracles, then, are those moments when time either stands still or seems to be in a state of reversal. Let us not forget the concept of nonlocality, which suggests that the mind is transpersonal, transpatial and, of utmost importance here, transtemporal—which allows for miraculous events that appear to transcend time.

Another Principle, #47, implies that time is really unnecessary. It states: "The miracle is a learning device that lessens the need for time. It establishes an out-of-pattern time interval not under the usual laws of time. In this sense it is timeless."[177] Remember, please, that the quantum physicists have long emphasized that from their vantage point, time does not exist. That is, all time is the present time. Their thinking seems to parallel that of the Principles of Miracles.

In the chapter called "*Precognition: Time and Time Again*"[178] Targ and Katra go beyond the remote viewing evidence and references to healings presented in earlier chapters which indicate that mind can instantly connect with mind (remember the concept of nonlocal mind?), be it at a distance or in a future time. Just think about that for a moment, and consider the miraculousness of mind connecting with mind, regardless of time, place or space. That is significant in itself. What these authors attempt to help us understand, by presenting the fascinating theories and research of physicists such as Einstein, Bohm and others, is how precognitive dreams, very common psi occurrences, are able to convey to us with great clarity the events of the following day or near future.

In presenting the summary of a large body of research dealing with precognition experiments, they concluded the following: "This body of data offers very strong evidence for confirming the existence of foreknowledge of the future that cannot be ascribed to somebody's lucky day. There is no doubt that we have contact with the future in a way that shows unequivocally that we misunderstand our relationship to the dimension of time."[179] Using the collected data regarding psi, the authors "believe that an experienced viewer can answer any answerable question about events in the past, present, or future."[180]

What is even more impressive is the fact that Targ and Katra dare to address those questions you have but are afraid to ask. For example, while we cannot undo past events that have actually happened, can we, by sending information in the present, affect the past? The answer appears to be yes. To answer this question, a vast body of research is examined, as well as the work of quantum physicists such as David Bohm and Norma Friedman, who view consciousness or nonlocal mind as having "many of the omnipresent and omniscient properties that people customarily associate with God."[181] Translation: like God, our consciousness is not strapped by limitations of time, place or space and therefore may allow us to move across time barriers in order to fulfill a particular desire.

With regard to healing, the authors ask the question: "Can we send healing thoughts into someone's past, to help them be less sick than they presently are?" They also indicate that there is a body of research that is suggestive of such healing, provided the condition of the patient's illness is not actually known.[182] Talk about miracles!

The Miracles of Spontaneous Remissions or Remarkable Recoveries

We cannot leave the subject of miracles without examining the many medical miracles so often called spontaneous remissions. It has been suggested by Caryle Hirshberg and Marc Barasch, authors of *Remarkable Recovery,*[183] that spontaneous remissions would be better served if they were called *remarkable recoveries*. Why? Well, for several reasons. For one thing, if called remarkable recoveries, doctors would be more willing to discuss them. An explanation is in order here.

In the Foreword to *Remarkable Recovery,* Larry Dossey, M.D., describes the difficulty many physicians have in dealing with spontaneous remissions. He writes of the "cancer mentality" that many doctors have, as does much of the public, which contributes to the projection of their negative expectations onto patients. This occurs despite the research conducted by insurance companies that indicates that coronary disease has a much worse prognosis than does cancer.[184]

Dossey also writes of the fact that physicians bring their psychological perspectives to the treatment of their patients. Indeed, he addresses the psychology of each physician and that he sees it affecting her or his attitude regarding the possibility of a remarkable recovery of a patient. The problem is that doctors do not know what to do with such events, often dismissing them as anecdotal stories, rather than interesting case histories that might in some way be related to something scientific.[185] This is due in part to the fact that physicians like being in control, and they therefore tend to discount those events that appear to be flukes or which happen by chance and over which they have no sense of control.

Along the same line, Dossey notes that another aspect of the problem is that spontaneous remissions are assumed to be due primarily to chance. In Dossey's words, "If we physicians were more fully informed about the nature of remarkable recoveries, including the fact that these events are almost certainly more frequent than we've been taught, perhaps we could create a larger place for what authors Hirshberg and Barasch call 'ethical hope.' Ethical hope is different from false hope. It rests on possibilities, not fantasy."[186]

The question that you probably have is whether these remarkable recoveries or spontaneous remissions are actually miracles. The answer, I believe, is totally dependent on your own perspective, whether or not there is a body of formidable research that demonstrates the various elements that appear to be part of the explanation. The authors of *Remarkable Recovery* provide several different considerations of what a miracle might possibly mean. These range from miraculous recoveries that follow no treatment or inadequate treatment; those that include a delayed progression, which is living with the disease for a relatively long time; those that have a long period of survival, which is living well beyond predictions after completing treatment; those who survive after combining both conventional and nonconventional treatments; and those who are considered miracles because of their spiritual components.[187] Perhaps one or all will fit the criteria for you.

Elements Needed for the Creation of Miracles

What they and other authors, including Paul Raud, author of *Making Miracles,* provide us with are detailed and thorough examinations of patients who have had what appear to be miraculous recoveries from life-threatening illnesses. What becomes clear is that *there are similarities,* and this is the authors' point. With a willingness to look beneath the surface of what appears to be a miracle of sorts, researchers are discovering elements that are common to many of these miraculous events.

For example, Hirshberg and Barasch have addressed the idea that miracles are due in part to the *Healing System* of the body and that there are a number of influences, some psychological and some spiritual, that contribute to the ability of the body to heal. These may include the following: changing long held thoughts, beliefs, attitudes and feelings; rediscovering spirituality, as well as one's faith, religion and prayer; engaging in a release of age-old emotions of anger, pain and rage; finding and engaging in one's passion; being playful and happy; engaging in forgiveness as well as the idea of "Let go and let God;" practicing various modalities that employ the mind and consciousness, such as visualization, imagery and fantasizing; and bringing humor, laughter and joy into one's life. Those patients in Raud's *Making Miracles* share many, if not almost all, of these experiences.[188]

The key to creating healing miracles, I believe, is becoming excited, passionate and joyful, no longer focusing on the diagnosis, but rather what you want out of life. It is about love, love for yourself and for everything that is important to you. It is also about letting go, letting go of the emotional and mental baggage you have been carrying with you for a lifetime. I believe the key to miracles is related to energetic change: to a sense of one's energy shifting from a low, negative experience to one that is lighter, more positive and definitely more uplifting.

For a more intimate look at what goes into the making of miracles, I highly recommend Dr. Paul Pearsall's *Miracle in Maui*.[189] Pearsall, a renowned clinical psychologist, has incorporated into the story of his most inspirational recovery from Stage 4 bone cancer his own insights regarding the process of making miracles. Pearsall blends a description of his spiritual experience while in Maui with his understanding of the basic scientific principles and laws of the universe, as well as with the research findings of Dr. Larry Dossey and the quantum physicists. This combination reinforces the very principles stated in *A Course in Miracles*. Whether the message relates to miracles being a manifestation of expressions of love or that miracles happen because of the oneness of all there is, Pearsall's story aligns with the basic tenets of not only *A Course in Miracles*, but also the work of Targ and Katra and Larry Dossey. Those who either engage in miracle making or who study miracles are all pretty much in agreement about what contributes to the making of miracles.

Era III—a Medicine of Miracles

Miracles are becoming acknowledged elements in the medicine of the twenty-first century. We see this especially when looking at medicine from Larry Dossey's perspective. In fact, in his book, *Reinventing Medicine,* Dossey breaks medicine into three eras of medicine. Era III includes Era I medicine of modern technology (including medications, radiation, surgery, even acupuncture and herbs), but not mind, and Era II mind-body medicine, which recognizes a connection between the mind and organs of the body. However, Era III goes one step further and recognizes that mind, which is a part of consciousness, is nonlocal. It has no boundaries and no limitations of time.

Era III recognizes that mind is not localized to one's body. What this means is that Era III allows for mind to affect healing within one's own body as well as within the body of others, be they near or far. Furthermore, the implication of this for Era III medicine is that it now includes, along with the therapeutic interventions of Eras I and II, the recognition and importance of miracles, intuitive wisdom, intercessory prayer and distance healing.[190]

Dossey's present-day doctors and hospitals value and invite those who are trained in complementary medicine, much of which recognizes the importance of not only nonlocal mind, but understands the relationship of universal energy and the body's capacity to heal itself. This is a medicine that values one's spirit and one's soul, and it is from this that miracles are born.

Love, the Essence of Miracles and Healing

Before concluding this section (I could go on and on about the nature of miracles), it is important to focus on the role that Love plays in all miracles and in all healings. *A Course in Miracles* clearly conveys the message that Love is the essence of miracles. The very first principle of *A Course in Miracles* states: "There is no order of difficulty in miracles. One is not 'harder' or 'bigger' than another. They are all the same. All expressions of love are maximal."[191] Miracles are expressions of our feelings of compassion and love—and the very best of all there is. What we need to keep in mind is that no one miracle, be it physical or nonphysical, is considered to be greater, smaller or more or less important than another. This speaks to the equality of all life and of our need for loving compassion for one another.

Principle #3 states: "Miracles occur naturally as expressions of love. The real miracle is the love that inspires them. In this sense, everything that comes from love is a miracle."[192] Often, I find that events that seem almost miraculous follow my sense of my heart filling up with loving feelings. Principle #35[193] emphasizes this, but takes it one step further. It states: "Miracles are expressions of love, but they may not always have observable effects." Think for a moment about those special and wonderful events that have caught you by surprise or which may not even seem to be significant, except that they seem to be answers to your prayers.

Speaking of prayers, Principle #11 states: "Prayer is the medium of miracles. It is a means of communication of the created with the Creator. ***Through prayer love is received and through miracles love is expressed.***"[194] These words move me even as I write this, because they so exquisitely express the meaning of both prayer and miracles. This thought, which combines both the power of prayer and love, is not only very meaningful, but represents truth, and therein lies its power.

Love, prayer and miracles do go hand in hand. Every great Master who has come forth to teach humanity has spoken of love. Those sites where miracles have occurred, such as Medjugorje and Lourdes, have taken on sacred meaning not only because there has been a miracle, but because individuals come with love in their hearts, seeking to have a connection with something or someone that represents the Divine.

Those who practice the art of spiritual healing know that it is through love that healing and miracles take place. More specifically, spiritual healing includes the process of filling with love and the sense of merging with the consciousness of the individual in need of healing. Jane Katra, a spiritual healer for more than twenty years, in *Miracles of Mind,* describes this in the following manner: "I think of this state as being one in which my brain waves are in some way synchronized with those of the patient. The healing interaction in which the patient and I participate feels like some sort of merged consciousness."[195] Further on, Katra describes spiritual healing as "an experience of one universal mind unifying with itself, which is the main aspect of love."[196]

The two key aspects of spiritual healing are love, recognized as being unconditional and compassionate, and surrender, the surrendering of the ego consciousness to the greater consciousness or the Oneness that connects us all. This is mind connecting with mind. There is nothing logical nor rational about such healing. There is only being in a state of connectedness with all there is, or with Source, and the person in need of healing. It is in such a state that "miracles" happen.

Larry Dossey's Era III medicine marries traditional Western medicine with the wisdom of Eastern medicine. Combining the methodology of the East with the research of the quantum physicists and contemporary technological advances, Era III includes energy, psychic and spiritual healing, as well as any other experience that is a function of nonlocal mind. This is what best serves one's ability to heal. When a healer such as Katra heals someone, it appears extraordinary or miraculous because we have not been accustomed to, or trained to expect, our mind being able to operate in this capacity, nor have we been trained to recognize the role that compassionate, unconditional love plays in the process of healing. However, the recognition of nonlocal mind and the power of love can, if you so choose, contribute to you learning to develop a similar healing capacity.

In *Reinventing Medicine,* Dossey calls his Era III medicine "Eternity Medicine," and those who practice this medicine are Eternists. Why? Quite simply because the very nature of this type of medicine, or healing, implies that we are immortal and eternal. After all, isn't that what nonlocal mind is about? We are talking about a medicine that brings hope and comfort to patients because they recognize mind is timeless and without boundaries. **Miracles happen frequently in Era III medicine** because, once we accept the mind as nonlocal, we recognize that life continues, perhaps in a different format, but it does continue and it is eternal. We are better able to use our full potential—and that includes our ability *to transform* by merging with consciousness. In Dossey's words, "Era III has the capacity not only to heal our bodies but also to transfigure our sense of our origin, nature, and destiny. **The key to this transformation is our awareness of the nonlocal nature of our own mind that it is infinite, indestructible, and immortal."**[197]

In *Miracles of Mind,* Katra writes of her personal journey in becoming a spiritual healer. Her Ph.D. in health education, combined with her knowledge and expertise in nutrition and mind-body health, have contributed to her abilities to be both an immune system coach and a spiritual healer. This is the "down-to-earth" story of a woman who, after having a miraculous recovery of her own from a close to death experience, has devoted her life to learning as much as she can regarding various healing modalities and then to sharing the knowledge with others in her practice, teaching and writing. The book beautifully presents both her and Targ's perspective on how she assisted him, as a spiritual healer and an immune system coach, to miraculously recover from Stage IV cancer.[198] *Miracles of Mind* is important and a book that I strongly recommend to you.

Spiritual Healing—a Personal Perspective

I must admit that this area, dealing with spiritual healing, love and miracles, is very comfortable and familiar to me. Coming from a medical family, I have always had a strong need to assist others in the healing process. As a psychologist, my personal evolution has contributed to being able to treat pain patients, those dealing with cancer and other life-threatening illnesses, and those who are bereaved and/or traumatized in some way. My work is about helping those who are in physical, mental, emotional and spiritual pain. I believe that, essentially, I am here to help those who seek me out to regain a sense of their own power, or well-being, and, in doing so, to enable them to take back their lives. Clearly, a transformation of sorts takes place in my work with my patients.

Without question, I see myself, like Dossey, as an Eternist in my approach to helping others heal. And, without question, I see myself as similar to Katra, as a spiritual healer.

Several years ago, not long after making the decision to study intuitive development and probably after conducting some research dealing with various kinds of healing, I felt strongly drawn to the idea that part of my life's purpose included healing both spiritually and physically. I had studied various types of energy healing work, including reiki, therapeutic touch and

Integrated Energy Therapy (IET),[199] and had begun to employ some of the spiritual healing I had learned on my own. Yet, I was feeling a strong pull to seek out teachers who could assist me with this—and because I am a psychologist, I was seeking a respectability that accompanied such training.

I decided to make my desire for an excellent teacher known to the universe through prayer. Not long after this, I was delighted, but not surprised, to receive a letter from Dr. Joyce Goodrich, psychotherapist and Coordinator of the Consciousness Research and Training Project, who teaches the LeShan approach to healing.[200] This was especially meaningful for me because I have thought of Larry LeShan, who has been honored by Harvard for his research dealing with consciousness and distant healing, as my mentor in my work with cancer patients since the late eighties. Consequently, I began my training with Joyce in the fall of 2001 and plan to continue with these studies. Furthermore, I have met with success and would like to share one wonderful, miraculous story with you.

Amber's Miracle

In late October of 2000, our family learned that Amber, our then fifteen-year-old golden retriever had a nonoperable form of mucocutaneous lymphosarcoma. Blood work and two biopsies confirmed the diagnosis. The cancer came in the form of an ugly tumor located on the lower lip of the right side of her mouth. The prognosis was "guarded." Furthermore, the pathology lab report from the University of Pennsylvania stated, "The regional lymph nodes, liver, and spleen are the most likely sites of metastasis." The situation did not look promising.

Working with a gifted veterinarian and friend, Louise Morin,[201] who uses both traditional and alternative approaches to veterinary medicine, we began to make significant changes that would enhance Amber's immune system. We changed her diet to one designed for dogs with cancer, added Tahitian Noni juice[202] to bolster her immune system, along with many nutrients and vitamins, and began acupuncture and aquapuncture every two weeks. I also began to apply to Amber some of the spiritual, psychic and energy healing interventions that I had been studying.

Over the next year, the growth seemed to go through periods in which it appeared to improve or worsen. There was, however, no indication that it had metastasized and, except for the growth, Amber appeared to be thriving. On October 10th, 2001, Louise and I decided to start Amber on a product called Transfer Factor,[203] an immune system supplement for humans and animals, which Louise had been taking for some time and which she felt, given the research findings, might be able to help Amber.

Within two weeks of beginning Transfer Factor, in early November, I drove to Boston for a four-day seminar/retreat in which I studied the LeShan healing method taught by Dr. Joyce Goodrich. During our four days of intense training in Type I healing meditations, there were times when we directed our healing intentions to those for whom the need was greatest. Amber, of course, was a receiver of my healing intentions. During each of my healing meditation experiences, I would feel great love and compassion for Amber and experience a sense of merging with her, as I had so often done before this weekend. I had no way of knowing, at the time, whether or not the work I had done had helped those who had been the recipients of my healing intentions. However, I do recall that I left Boston feeling richly blessed, with an increased awareness of my ability to assist others in the healing process.

I returned home late on a Monday evening, exhausted from the long ride, and went to bed soon after arriving home. I clearly recall the next morning when I turned to Amber, who was standing in the upstairs hall, between my bathroom and the bedroom. I remember talking lovingly to her, telling her how much I loved her, while lowering her right lip on the side of her mouth, which would normally expose both her teeth and the tumor. I couldn't see the tumor and, thinking I had been mistaken regarding which side of the mouth the tumor was located, I went to the other side of her mouth and lowered her left lip. Seeing only a normal pink gum, I thought I must have missed it on the original side, so I went back to the first side, the right side, lowered the lip, and again saw only normal-looking pink gum tissue. I was stunned! *Oh my God,* I thought, *it is gone. It's really gone!*

I still recall going in to see Louise a few days later. Even she, a vet who has met with great success in the use of alternative treatment with her patients, could not believe what she was seeing. We all knew what the test results had shown. We had all known the tumor to be there just before my trip to Boston, several days before. Yet, it was no longer there. How incredible this was for all of us! Even now, I smile as I recall the many times I have taken Amber in for her acupuncture and aquapuncture treatments and have observed Louise as she lifts Amber's mouth, looks with amazement, shakes her head in disbelief and, with a huge smile, says, "Well, there's still nothing there, Amber."

So, what happened? You may be wondering. No one can say for sure. The only things we know for certain are that there was a nonoperable cancer tumor in her mouth before I left for Boston, that she had been on Transfer Factor for almost two weeks at that point and that I had done healing meditation work directed at Amber. Yes, there was a miracle that occurred here. Yes, I have continued the same medications and supplements and, yes, I still include Amber in my spiritual healing meditation work. From my perspective, this is an excellent example of what can occur, in terms of healing, when we recognize the power of nonlocal mind.

Creating Miracles with Prayers of Love and Gratitude

Perhaps the relationship of love and prayer can best be understood by recognizing how much love is felt and expressed each and every time you have expressed your gratitude for a loved one being a part of your life. Prayers, after all, are not only about petitioning. They are also offered as a means of expressing gratitude for our blessings, and gratitude for our blessings is about expressing and receiving loving feelings. When experiencing feelings of gratitude, the heart opens and fills with warmth and love.

Honestly, I cannot think of a better way to instantly connect with the Divine than by saying or thinking *Thank You, God, for my blessings,* or *Thank you, God, for this beautiful day.* The very act of thinking or verbalizing such gratitude carries a vibration of well-being and joy. Simply thinking or saying the words *Thank you, God,* has the power to shift your vibrational energetic patterns and, in so doing, contributes to what may be experienced by some as a miraculous shift in how you are feeling. It is that simple! And it includes feelings of compassion, gratitude and love.

Knowing how therapeutically valuable all of this is, I recommend to my patients that they snatch a moment wherever they can and offer prayers of thanks for their blessings. For example, as soon as I pull out of my driveway and head down my street on my way to my office or town, I make it a point to look around me and to give thanks for the magnificence of the sky; the lovely shrubs, plants and landscapes; the changing foliage; the children playing on our township's baseball, soccer and football fields; the kindergarteners playing kickball on the elementary school's playing field and having so much fun. When I leave the food market, I find myself offering brief prayers that include words of enormous heartfelt gratitude as I breathe in the crisp, delicious air. Always, while giving thanks, I am aware that every cell in my body is experiencing the same feelings of exhilaration, excitement and thanks.

Having spent many years studying and researching the power of prayer, I have made prayer an integral part of my life. I do this because of how wonderful I feel while in the process of praying as well as following my prayers. Quite simply, I feel as though my heart opens and fills with sensations of warmth, love and peace. Following the experience, I have an enhanced sense of well-being and a feeling of connection with Source or God, or whatever you might wish to call the Divine, that is extremely comforting. I find that things go far more smoothly and well after my moments of prayer. I say "moments" because I also incorporate prayer into those mini-moments when I am driving or sitting in a doctor's office or wherever.

I therefore recommend to many of my patients that they begin their day by engaging in a daily practice of prayer or a prayer/meditation ritual. Those of you who do this may find that you experience heightened feelings of peace, joy, well-being, contentment, greater self-love and more compassionate and loving feelings for others. What is even more wonderful is that what eventually follows or accompanies moments of prayer are events that may feel like answers to prayers. This is where life feels particularly amazing.

My advice to patients is that with their hearts filled with love, they speak to the Divine, or God, and ask for help or, more specifically, for what it is that they need. It helps to picture this clearly in their mind, to do this often and to allow every cell in their body to experience both joy and excitement as they anticipate their prayers being answered.

Coincidental Synchronicity (There Are No Coincidences)

Think for a moment of the extraordinary "coincidences" in your life, in which things happened that both surprised and moved you because they were so meaningful, but which appeared to have had no causal relationship. Yet somehow, you knew that something more was going on than pure coincidence. Perhaps the events that occurred in the external world touched your heartstrings, enabling you to experience a sense of connection with something greater than yourself and/or which contributed to your feeling safe and content in the universe.

The Coincidental Synchronicity of Carl Jung

Carl Jung, a renowned Swiss psychiatrist, wrote of *coincidental synchronicity,* a concept that seemed to flow naturally from his theory that we all have access to a *collective unconscious,* which is similar to a wealth of pooled knowledge. Coincidental synchronicities assure us of our commonality; that is, our connective links with one another. According to Judith Orloff in her book, *Second Sight,* Jung defines coincidental synchronicity as "a meaningful coincidence of the past outer and inner events that are not causally related."[204] Joining the ranks of the great teachers of the past 3000 years and those of the quantum physicists, Jung adhered to the belief, as I do, that all life is connected and that we are all tapping into a collective unconscious.

The classic Jung story that supports his belief regarding synchronicity is another favorite of mine. It deals with a patient of his whose excessive tendencies to being rational and cognitive were interfering with her therapeutic treatment. Puzzled by a dream that dealt with the appearance of a scarab, also known as a beetle, she shared her dream with Jung. Just after explaining that a scarab is the Egyptian symbol for rebirth, both he and his patient heard something tapping on the window of his office. As he opened his window, a beautiful golden-green scarab, very rare in Vienna at that time, flew into his office. The synchronicity, or "too coincidental" timing of events, deeply moved the woman, causing her to change course in her therapy. She released her need to rationalize and met with greater therapeutic success.[205]

Arnold Mandell, who continued Jung's work, expanded the understanding of synchronicity even further. Not only are synchronicities meaningful, but "they occur at peak experiences, times of transformations, births, deaths, falling in love, psychotherapy, intense creative work or even changes in profession."[206] I have found this to be absolutely true in the research and interviews I have conducted since 1990. Take a moment, if you will, and consider the timing of your own extraordinary moments—the ones that you never can forget!

Morse, in *Where God Lives,* supports Jung's belief of a state of interconnectedness that binds everyone together. He notes that Niels Bohr, the father of quantum physics, supported Jung's theory. The idea of interconnectedness was a concept of primary importance for Bohr.[207]

It makes sense that if one is thinking of someone or something, such a thought may become a part of the collective unconscious which, in turn, provides one with an appropriate response from this pool of knowledge—or what is called by some the Universal Mind. Renowned biologist Rupert Sheldrake, author of *Dogs Who Know When Their Owners Are Coming Home,*[208] explains such experiences using his morphogenetic theory. The collective unconscious is, I believe, essentially the same as the morphogenetic field—or Universal Mind.

The quantum physicists and physician, Larry Dossey, explain the concepts of collective unconscious, morphogenetic field and Universal Mind using the term **nonlocal mind,** a state of consciousness that exists without attachment to time, place or person.

When Synchronicity Touches Us Personally

What does synchronicity feel like? To me personally, it is a sense of my being aligned with my soul. It is as though all the pieces of the puzzle of my life are fitting together perfectly. Each time I have asked for specific help or assistance with a particular issue or project, and then received it almost immediately, or I have thought of someone (a loved one, a patient, a friend) and then heard from them within hours or days of such thought, I have always marveled at the wisdom of the universe. These events have happened frequently rather than just occasionally.

Synchronicities are revealing of our extrasensory or psychic relationship with one another and with the universe. Sometimes viewed as the little miracles in our lives, they appear to serve as indications of being a part of a greater collective consciousness. The following story, I believe, clearly demonstrates coincidental synchronicity.

After the death of my mother in 1993, my dad was determined to continue living in the home he and my mother had occupied for close to half a century. To make this happen, I needed to search for individuals who could continue caring for my father and his home. After some frustrating months of placing ads in local papers and interviewing many women who had responded, I had the good fortune to meet and employ two wonderful and elegant women, Mary and Delores, both highly skilled in housekeeping and cooking, and both wishing to continue the traditions of my mother.

Dolores was hired as the housekeeper and Mary was hired to prepare dinners and be a part-time companion for my dad. However, Dolores and Mary had never had an opportunity to actually meet with one another—though they had spoken briefly by phone on occasion.

According to Delores, while she was working at the house on a warm fall day she recalled hearing the doorbell ring. As she opened the front door, she found herself gazing at the face of someone who looked extremely familiar. Mary had come to put away some groceries she had just purchased at the market. In the moment of introducing themselves to one another, there was an instant sense of connectedness.

Looking at each other, Delores recounted to me, they broke into enormous smiles as they experienced a mutual sense of astonishment. These two women had, as children, grown up just a block or so from one another. In the circle of life, time had brought them back together, working for the same man.

What is especially amazing is that they both grew up in South Carolina and were now living and working for my dad in Pennsylvania. Had they met anywhere else, one might have thought the event to be a coincidence. But to have met while working for the same person removes the element of randomness from the picture and serves as a testament to the synchronicity and connectedness of life.

I encourage you to take time to note in a journal or small notebook any happenings or events that on the surface appear to be coincidences, but which, after examining the context in which they occur, are recognized as meaningful experiences. You will be surprised at just how many of these psychic moments are occurring. The numbers, I believe, will be far greater than you may have ever imagined!

I have been noting such experiences occurring in my own life, as well as in those of my patients, for over a decade. However, it has taken me years of practice to learn to be fully aware of my environment—including the people, types of communication and events. Once you begin the process, it is exceptionally satisfying and comforting.

A Touch of Hawaii

Several years ago, while my husband and I were having dinner in a local restaurant, we discussed where we might go for a much needed vacation. Since this was to be a special trip in honor of our thirty-fifth anniversary, I spoke of my wish for a week or two in Kauai and/or Maui. As we sat and talked about this possibility, I suddenly noticed that a young girl of about 14 or 15 was seated almost directly in front of me at the next table, and she was dressed in a Hawaiian blouse. (Probably the only Hawaiian blouse in the restaurant!) I recall that I smiled to myself as I registered the significance of this. *How wonderful,* I thought to myself. *The universe is listening.* I shared this with my husband who would not normally have noticed such an occurrence. I remember going to the restroom and, when I returned, I found my husband engaged in conversation with the family of the girl in the Hawaiian shirt.

As it turned out, my husband knew the family. Furthermore, after telling them of what had just taken place (the coincidental synchronicity regarding our conversation and the Hawaiian shirt), they shared with him a story of their own that also served to reinforce the idea that psychic or extraordinary events, including synchronicities, are a part of our existence.

Such experiences, such moments, are occurring frequently. They take place everywhere, always carrying messages for us. We need to be open to ways in which we are being spoken to and in which we are receiving some form of communication. Some people call them *signs*. Open your heart and allow yourself to be touched by them. They are often stunning expressions of your place in the universe.

Dr. Orloff's Perspective on Synchronicity

Physician and author Judith Orloff, in *Second Sight,* also stresses how important it is that we take time to notice the psychic happenings, or coincidences, that take place ubiquitously and at just the right moment. She writes that synchronicities can and do occur when you are not expecting such events, such as at the beauty parlor, the laundromat, while waiting in line at a market or bank, and at business meetings, school and special events. She writes, "Some synchronous meetings are serendipitous and can be harbingers of good fortune. When you take advantage of these golden moments, your life can change for the better. . . . If you stay on the lookout, they won't slip through your fingers. Synchronicities are enmeshed in the fabric of the ordinary."[209]

Orloff, in *Second Sight,* provides a superb example of synchronicity from her own life. She uses the example to emphasize that the universe enables those of us who are closely bonded with individuals we love to experience the bond of friendship and love anywhere we may be.

She writes of a dear friend from New York who, while on vacation in Boulder, Colorado, found himself browsing in a bookstore. He realized that he was thinking of Judith and the times they had shared in the past, as he had meandered into the science fiction section of the store, something that he loved to do. While he was still thinking of Judith, he selected a book that caught his interest, *A Wrinkle in Time,* by Madeleine L'Engle. Upon opening to the title page, Orloff's friend discovered the handwritten name of the child, ten years old at the time, who had owned the book. There it was, Judi Orloff, and the date, November, 1961. Orloff admits that she was deeply moved, even to tears, by the beauty and intimacy of the synchronicity that involved an old, dear friend. According to Orloff, the incident serves as an affirmation that "we are all bound together by such love. If we only look for it, the evidence is everywhere."[210]

Orloff continues: "The smallest of synchronicities, when you view them from this perspective, have meaning, if only to reinforce the understanding that we are all related to one another in some way." Just a few lines later, Orloff states: "Synchronicity is a sign that we are psychically attuned, not only to our immediate friends and family, but to the greater collective."[211]

Special Synchronicities

Many times patients have shared with me amazing stories of communication with loved ones. These stories often represent coincidental synchronicities in their lives. For example, a patient of mine, whom I shall call Ann, has shared numerous stories with me about the manner in which she now realizes that her father communicates with her. It appears that her dad uses a feather as his unique way of saying hello when she is thinking or talking about him.

Yes, a feather. A small white feather has frequently and unexpectedly drifted down—out of the blue—and landed on or in front of her or, on occasion, has been underneath something that she had to lift up. This has occurred in a variety of settings, including at home, the beach and while traveling in Europe. Dubious initially, Ann recognizes the meaning of the feather and smiles knowingly and confidently each time she describes a feather incident. The feather, she believes, is her father's way of conveying his loving presence.

Feathers can be magical, mystical and spiritual. They not only speak to us in many ways, but they also have the power to heal, teach, comfort, guide and convey the presence of spirit. As I write this, my thinking is that feathers serve in the same capacity as angels—as messengers. Their appearance in the most unexpected places, at the most significant moments, reinforces our sense that we are not alone and that we are indeed all very much connected at some level.

Further on in this book, I share some of my own experiences with feathers that have appeared at especially meaningful moments, indicative of extraordinary synchronicities. In fact, I am looking at one of the feathers I have written about as I write this very paragraph, and, as it comes into my vision, it fills me with warmth, joy and love. That's the power of feathers! If you would like to experience more wonderful stories dealing with feathers, I recommend a lovely and special book, *Sacred Feathers,* by Maril Crabtree.[212] This is a book in which you will be introduced to the stories of many people who have been blessed and touched by the gift of a feather at the most meaningful of times.

There are many other examples of special synchronicities. For example, another patient of mine, whom I shall call Mia, would often tell me that while on her way to my office, she would pass a large truck bearing the name of her father. She found this to be extremely comforting because much of our work had to do with grieving for her father and her mother. For her, there was a sense of connection with her father in the most meaningful way and at extremely special times. This is surely the essence of synchronicity.

Another example of synchronicity comes from my cousin, Leah, whose son, Gad, a young medic in the Israeli army, died in Lebanon in the early nineties and whose stories are presented in a later chapter. When I asked if she had experienced any sense of her son's presence, she emphatically responded that things drop from their shelves, landing directly in front of her, unexpectedly and frequently. Coincidental synchronicities? As far as Leah is concerned, they represent her son's way of letting her know he is with her. This occurs both in her home in Israel as well as in other countries in which she may be traveling. The phone also often rings repeatedly—with no one on the other end when she answers the call. These also she views as coincidental synchronicities.

One story Leah told me especially touched me. She had needed to have a biopsy taken for a possibly problematic skin condition. After the biopsy was performed, Leah was understandably anxious about the results. Thanks to a family friend and physician, news came quickly that she was fine and need not worry. This came just before her trip from Israel to the United States at the end of August of 2002.

Leah told me that she had run to the market immediately after receiving the good news from her doctor the day they were to depart for New York. It was between the market and home that her mobile phone rang and rang, with no one on the other end. However, she felt great comfort because she knew that the timing of the calls indicated that her son, Gad, was also aware of the good news and that he shared both her joy and her relief.

The truth is that the majority of stories presented in this book can be labeled coincidental synchronicities. I originally wished to write a book to comfort those in need, recognizing that the events occurring in people's lives after losing loved ones were being perceived as nonrandom events and, therefore, important. Had they been perceived as random occurrences, those I interviewed would, I believe, never had found them worthy of being remembered, nor would they have been so touched and moved by them to remember to share them with me.

The Timing of Mrs. Schwartz

One of my favorite people, and a highly-esteemed mentor of mine, is Dr. Elisabeth Kübler-Ross. Not only did Kübler-Ross present the world with her understanding of the death and dying process, she conducted research regarding life after life that closely parallels that of Moody, Morse and others. She has always adhered to the belief that there are no coincidences. For example, she believes that it was not a coincidence that she was born one of three triplet sisters. Being a triplet, she feels, forced her to work hard to prove that she had every right to life. This fact also likely contributed to her many achievements. (She weighed only two pounds at birth).[213]

She also believes that it was not a coincidence that she was unable to go to India, as she had planned, to study with Dr.

Albert Schweitzer. She knew that her presence in New York City, where she did not wish to be, was for a specific purpose. It was there, while working with psychotic patients, that she learned the symbolic language which she would use in her work with not only the psychotic patients but also with those who were dying, as well as very young children.[214]

One of the most incredible stories presented by Dr. Kübler-Ross, which reinforces her belief that there are no coincidences, deals with a former patient, Mrs. Schwartz. One can only imagine the disbelief and shock that Kübler-Ross experienced the day she ran into Mrs. Schwartz in the hospital as she was exiting the elevator. The woman who was standing before her as the elevator door opened, who had been her first patient to have a NDE, *had died ten months before this meeting.* Can you imagine the confusion and surprise that the doctor experienced at that moment? The meeting occurred just as Kübler-Ross had decided to end her work at the hospital and her research in death and dying. During the course of this meeting, Mrs. Schwartz revealed that her purpose in coming was to ask the doctor to continue with her work.

Kübler-Ross was so taken aback by Mrs. Schwartz's reappearance that she kept touching the other woman's skin. She also asked her to write a note, which she did. Kübler-Ross so treasured it that she had the note framed and hung it in her office. Rather than immediately disappearing, as Kübler-Ross expected, the woman asked her, in the clearest terms, to promise not to give up her work. Only after achieving her goal did she disappear.[215]

The arrival of Mrs. Schwartz at such a critical moment in Kübler-Ross's life confirmed the doctor's belief in Jung's concept of coincidental synchronicity. The meaningfulness of the encounter, regarding both the person and the situation, negated any possibility that this was a random event. In fact, the meeting of Mrs. Schwartz and Kübler-Ross had such a powerful effect on the doctor that she decided to continue with her research. However, her focus changed from death and dying to life after life, something for which I, as a psychologist and researcher of extraordinary or psi activity, am most grateful.

It was, and is, the meaningfulness of the events that affected Kübler-Ross. She had always believed that in order to survive, one must have a sense of purpose, or meaning, in life. She and Viktor Frankl, a psychiatrist and survivor of the holocaust, thought much alike. Frankl, who had survived the brutal experiences of four concentration camps, wrote in *Man's Search For Meaning* that having a purpose, "creating a work" or "doing a deed," and experiencing love, contribute to one's having meaning in life.[216]

The coincidental synchronicity of Kübler-Ross's meeting with Mrs. Schwartz validated the researcher's sense of purpose: to bring her findings regarding death and life after death to the public. By informing people that death does not exist, Kübler-Ross hoped to remove the fear of death and to enable life to be experienced positively.

For Dr. Morse There Are No Coincidences

In *Parting Visions* and *Where God Lives,* physician and author Melvin Morse, cites numerous examples that come from his research that have reinforced his belief that there are no coincidences. Indeed, in his work with children who have had NDEs, the message they convey is that the loving light they experienced comes from God and unifies all life. The result of hundreds of children sharing their near-death experiences with Melvin Morse, as well as the research he has conducted, have resulted in his belief that we are all connected physically and spiritually. We do not have to go far to find indications of this connection.

Morse has dedicated much of his time and research to understanding the nature of what it is that connects all of us.

It is his belief, based upon his research, that these connections may be a function of electromagnetic energy. In fact, in *Parting Visions,* he cites as an example of this belief an episode in which he encouraged a neighbor, whose father was a dowser, to use his own intuitive ability to find water on Morse's property. Drillers found an artesian well at the very spot to which his neighbor had pointed.

This was not a coincidence, according to Morse. He states: "I believe that his ability to find water on my land was not a coincidence, but a dramatic illustration that all life is physically connected through patterns of electromagnetic energy." To support his thinking, Morse points out that "scientists recently found magnetic particles in our brains that may act as sensors of these unseen forces."[217]

Morse takes coincidental synchronicities seriously, believing that his thoughts on the subject are similar to the thinking of such scientists as Albert Einstein and Steven Hawkings. From Melvin Morse's perspective, to label something as a meaningless coincidence is to deny the significance of a divine spiritual element, which is our connection to the divine, that brings meaning to our lives.[218]

Like Orloff, Dossey, Jung, others and myself, Morse believes that we need to stay open to the meaning of events by trusting our intuition and listening to our instinctive hunches. We need to listen carefully and be alert for the many ways in which the universe lets us know that it is lovingly providing for us.

Finally, Morse provides an anecdote I especially like of an incident that occurred at a time when he did believe in coincidences; that is, he believed they were only random events to which man assigned his own meaning. He writes about his meeting in Holland with Dr. Von Lommel, a Dutch cardiologist and NDE researcher who believed that there are no coincidences.

After returning home from Holland, Morse found a set of medical texts written in Dutch and sent them to his new friend, believing that if it were simply a coincidence, the books would have no meaning for him. As it turned out, the books were especially meaningful for his friend not only because they were written in his native language, but also because Von Lommel knew the author.

After the books had been validated as being extremely meaningful, Morse wrote in *Parting Visions,* "I agree with Dr. Von Lommel that when we dismiss these events as mere coincidence, we are dismissing and trivializing our own spiritual beings. We cut ourselves off from a rich source of knowledge that we can use to understand our lives."[219]

In the following pages, I share with you stories deemed to be meaningful and purposeful by my patients and others I have interviewed over the past decade. These experiences, which may be dismissed and trivialized by others, have deeply impacted the lives of these individuals, not only enriching them with meaning and beauty, but also providing them with a sense of connection with their soul.

I believe that everything in life is about meaning and purpose and that the meaning we give life events determines the quality of our lives. I emphasize, as does Viktor Frankl, that it is in man's best interest to know that life has meaning. In fact, Dr. Frankl found that survival in the concentration camps during World War II was nearly impossible unless prisoners could hold on to some sense of purpose or meaningfulness regarding their existence.[220]

In *Man's Search for Meaning,* Frankl wrote that experiencing love is one of the three ways in which we arrive at a sense of meaning in life. In other words, the more we can view a situation as one that expresses love, caring and empathy, the more meaning we can subscribe to our lives.[221] Interpreted another way, the more love we bring into our lives, the more satisfied and at peace we are and the more joy we experience.

Intention is everything. If your intention is to find meaning in your life, then your life shall be filled with an enriched sense of purpose and satisfaction. May you enjoy and discover a sense of identification, meaning and connection with the people and events in the stories that follow, and may they bring you comfort, joy and peace.

Two

THE STORIES

There are only two ways to live your life. One is as though nothing is a miracle. The other is as though everything is. I believe in the latter.

ALBERT EINSTEIN

God does not play dice with the universe.

ALBERT EINSTEIN

Introduction to Part Two

When you have learned to think with your heart instead of with your brain, You will have taken a great step forward. The humanity of the future will think with the heart-mind, For intuition is the next sense which will be developed in humankind.

WHITE EAGLE

Part Two is a collection of unique and exceptional encounters that either I have personally experienced or that others have shared with me. I invite you to bring your expanded consciousness and knowledge regarding extraordinary events, along with a healthy critical perspective, to each of these stories.

Perhaps the reading of this material will not only help to "normalize" the extraordinary for you, at least to some extent, but also enable your mind and heart to be more open to the possibility of the impossible being possible. Here's to a truly enjoyable experience!

CHAPTER **5**

Hellos, Goodbyes and Synchronicities

When it comes to the last moment of this lifetime, and we look back across it, the only thing that's going to matter is, "What was the quality of our love?"

RICHARD BACH

Miracles and the meaningful coincidences of our lives are evidence of our immortality. They prove that we are "soul" and not just "stuff."

PAUL PEARSALL, *Miracle in Maui*

A Poem for Grampa

His warmth touched your soul; his smile touched your heart; even his sense of humor had a sweetness that always made you feel good. My father-in-law, Herb Apollon, who was affectionately known as "Grampa Herb" to his grandchildren and "Dad" to his children and their spouses, dearly loved his grandchildren, a point made obvious to them by his presence at their baseball, basketball and football games and other important school events. In fact, it was through his presence that he was able to convey his feelings of pride regarding their various accomplishments. That was the way it was with Herb Apollon. He had no intention of letting the fact that he had died stop him from being present one more time when his grandson, Matthew (Matt), spoke at his funeral on a warm September morning in Miami, Florida in 1995.

Matt, then a handsome, strapping seventeen-year-old football player, had adored his grandfather. Their relationship had been a special one. Although Dad did not have favorites, he and Matt certainly had enjoyed a precious relationship as grandfather and grandson. With his heart filled with the pain of the loss of both friend and grandfather, and with the ability to beautifully convey in words what he was feeling within his heart, Matt was eager to share with the world his feelings about his "Grampa Herb's" uniqueness. And so it was that Matt spoke to the large crowd that attended his grandfather's funeral.

A tall, extremely handsome man with a full head of light gray hair, Herb Apollon's appearance had belied his seventy-four years of age. He had possessed a fantastic smile, big brown eyes that really twinkled, and a firm, secure handshake that assured you of his good nature and sincere intentions. It is no surprise, then, that he was genuinely likeable and, indeed, lovable. It seemed that everyone liked doing business with my father-in-law. He made you feel so good that you wanted to be around him. If it weren't for his heart, he would still be rooting for his grandsons at their sporting events as well as attending Miami Dolphin football games, and celebrating holidays and special occasions with them.

The event I am about to describe took place during Herb Apollon's funeral. I wish I could honestly say I witnessed it, but I must admit, much to my own disappointment, that I missed this wondrous event. Fortunately, however, my brother-in-law, Mark, and a friend of the family, Susan, witnessed the event I am about to describe.

I was totally caught up in wanting to comfort both my husband, who still could not believe that his dad was gone, and his mom, Molly, who was also having difficulty dealing with the situation. The three of us sat in the first row, closest to the podium where the Rabbi and Matt addressed the guests. While I sat holding the hand of my husband, to my left, and my mother-in-law, to my right, my eyes were focused only on my nephew, Matt, who was speaking about his grandfather. His casket was located to the right of the podium where Matt was speaking, in front of a large, beautiful window. I do not recall taking time to notice the window for any extended time, other than to perhaps glance at it. I do wish that I had because, according to my brother-in-law, Mark and Susan, I missed quite a show.

It was not until after the funeral had concluded and all the guests had returned to my sister-in-law and brother-in-law's home to sit shiva with the family that I heard the following story. Susan approached Matt to tell him that not only had she been moved by the poem he had written and read at the funeral about his grandfather, but that she believed that his grandfather was there and that he was also extremely pleased with what Matt had written.

According to Susan, a "strong shaft of light came through the window, spread onto the casket and over it." The light was striking, unlike any other light she had ever experienced (reminding me of the light described by those who have had near-death experiences), and appeared to cover the entire casket. Furthermore, the light seemed to remain there during the entire time that Matt spoke of his grandfather and only receded when Matt had concluded his poem. Susan went on to say that she remembered looking around the room to see if anyone else had witnessed what she had seen. When she found no one sharing her experience, she was quite surprised and even wondered for a moment if she had really seen what she thought she saw. But, deep within her, was a validation that her experience had been truthful and genuine.

While Susan was speaking to Matt of her observations, my brother-in-law, Mark, overheard the conversation and was visibly shaken. In fact, he said that he reacted to hearing her story by suddenly experiencing "goose bumps." Why? Because he, too, had experienced something quite similar.

According to Mark, it was while the Rabbi was speaking about my father-in-law that Mark first noticed an intense, bright, magnificent light that came through the enormous, grand window in front of which the coffin had been placed. The light spread across and around the coffin. A glowing, pulsating type of energy, similar to the energy of an aura that surrounds all living things, seemed to envelop the entire casket. Mark used words like "shiny" and "beaming" to describe the light. Mark, like Susan, noticed that this took place as Matt began to read the poem that he had written about his grandfather, and that the casket continued to glow during the reading of his poem.

Mark and Susan were in agreement concerning the meaning of the light. I have always believed that it is the meaning we give events that determines the impact they have on our lives. In this situation, the light was especially meaningful because, from Mark's and Susan's perspective, the light represented Herb Apollon's presence and conveyed to them just how delighted, touched and happy he was with Matt's words. The light was, in effect, an expression of his love and a good-bye as well. The light was so much like my father-in-law, in that it gave off a warm, golden glow that conveyed a sense of his gentle, special soul.

My gut feeling, based on many years of research and inter-views I have conducted, was that Susan and Mark were not the only ones who had witnessed this. However, I am will-ing to bet that, like Susan and Mark, those who did view the light probably questioned the reality of their own experience and were afraid to share it with others. Fortunately, thanks to Susan and Mark, Matt was given the gift of knowing that his loving words had actually reached his "Grampa Herb."

A Sister Says Hello

Adam,* an old, dear friend of mine, and his wife, Anita,* were busily working outside along their property line in the back of their home. It had been a relatively comfortable spring day and Adam was eager to dig holes in order to prepare the ground for posts for a wooden fence he was planning to install. His wife was standing by his side, chatting with him as he worked.

Suddenly, while he was bent over, his head facing down, a quarter fell and landed heads-up on the ground where he was digging. This stunned both Adam and Anita because the quarter appeared to come "out of the blue." One might have said that it fell from the sky. They looked up and around the area as well as at each other, quite puzzled by what had just happened. Before they even had a moment to comment, another quarter came falling "from the sky," landing just a few inches from where the first had fallen. This second quarter also fell into a heads-up position.

Again, they looked to see if someone could have thrown it, but they believed that to be impossible since they were at a distance from anyone or anything. Furthermore, the tall blue spruce trees that bordered the property would have prevented this from occurring. Adam also checked his clothing but quickly realized that he had no pockets from which the quarters could have fallen.

Unable to find a reasonable explanation, the couple looked for some sort of meaning connected with the unexpected gift of quarters. They considered many possibilities, including the thought that the quarters were a sign of some future blessings. They simply could not make sense of the event.

Several weeks after Adam told me this story, while visiting with him in his place of business, I had an intuitive experience. I had quieted myself for a few moments and unexpectedly found myself receiving a name that began with A. In an instant I realized that the name I was getting was Alice.* When I asked Adam about this, he informed me that Alice was his sister with whom he had been very close and who had died a few years earlier.

With this small but important piece of information, I then intuitively saw Alice in a garden, actually in Adam and Anita's charming garden, located in the back of their home in Pennsylvania. Adam informed me that the garden was one of Alice's favorite places and that, while alive, she would often spend time there with Adam and Anita. I smiled because I had not known this.

And, then, the best part came forth. Suddenly, I was shown the scene of the quarters falling from the sky while Adam and Anita stood in front of their huge spruce trees preparing the ground for the fence posts. I knew immediately that Alice had been responsible for the quarters. It was her unique way of sending her brother and his wife her love and her own special hello. Both Adam and I smiled as we reflected upon Alice's persistence, creativity and determination to connect with her loved ones.

A Visit from Molly

"Susan, do you know a Nancy? Or a Dori? Also, is there someone named Harry that you know? Does he have problems with his back?"

With these questions, I once again knew I was in for an interesting half-hour or so. Harry was my father and he had been having back problems. Dori is the name of my father's dear friend. While I did not recognize Nancy at first, I did about an hour into my visit with Samantha. My heart beat a bit faster; my interest picked up. This was usually how the visits began: Loved ones coming to me through my good friend, Samantha,* and bringing messages they felt I needed to hear.

Before continuing, I would like to introduce Samantha to you. A deeply sensitive and empathic soul, Samantha genuinely feels the pain of others and is a healing presence for those who are fortunate enough to know her. In addition to being a loyal, caring and true friend to me for more than two decades, she has also been a mentor of sorts in the area of intuitive wisdom. I smile almost every time I am with her because, while I have been engaged in formally developing my own intuition, Samantha's intuitive abilities are already exquisitely developed and finely tuned. In fact, Samantha's ability to intuit whatever energy may be present is as natural to her as is breathing. I feel blessed to have had her in my life as both friend and teacher all these years.

"I am getting a woman with reddish blonde hair. A Molly? Do you know a Molly?" My heart took off as I told Samantha, "That's my mother-in-law. That's Molly!" And with this, I quietly said hello to her. I remember feeling very surprised and honored by her visit. She rarely chose to come on her own to me.

"Your husband is working very hard, she says, and she is worried about him," said Samantha. "He has to slow down," continued Samantha. "He needs a break—a vacation. He is working much too hard. She repeats how worried she is about his health." As Samantha spoke, I sat there shaking my head in agreement, saying, "I know, I know."

I had recently been discussing the same concerns with our daughter, a medical student at the University of Pittsburgh School of Medicine. Both of us had been very concerned about the stressful conditions surrounding my husband's work. He had been working nonstop for several months, having recently sold his practice, merged with another and then moved into a new office. My mother-in-law's comments came as no surprise.

"She's saying that you haven't been to the ballet or the theater recently. You used to go to the city, to New York, to see shows?" asked Samantha. I told her that we had, but that recently we just hadn't been able to get away. "You *both* need to make time to get away and relax. She's saying that she is worried about *you also,* Susan. She is really emphatic about you both working too hard. Now is the time, she says, for you to have fun and enjoy yourselves."

I knew that my mother-in-law was completely on target. My own schedule had been filling up so much that whatever free time I had carved out for me was nonexistent at that point. And I was tired, very tired. *Mom is so right,* I thought to myself. *I just don't know what to do about it.*

"How is she doing?" I asked Samantha.

"I get the feeling of her being sad, Susan," said Samantha. "Is she buried in Florida?" As I nodded my head, indicating that she was, Samantha went on. "She is telling me that no one has been to her grave recently." I felt badly for my mother-in-law, believing that she thought she had been forgotten and was feeling hurt by this.

"Did your mother-in-law like pink roses?" asked Samantha. Though I did not know definitively whether she did or did not like such roses, I knew that I had to do something that would comfort and soothe her pain. I said to my mother-in-law, "Mom, in just four weeks, we will be in Miami, and we will bring you spectacular pink roses."

I wanted her to know that we would not forget her. I also made a mental note to telephone our family in Florida in order to share with them my mother-in-law's feelings. When I did this later that evening, Sharon, my sister-in-law, informed me that she and Casey, my nephew, had recently been to her grandmother's grave (that of my mother-in-law's mother) and had brought her—You guessed it!—pink roses. I smiled inwardly when she told me this.

"Is Molly with Dad and her mother?" I asked Samantha. I was curious, as I always am whenever loved ones come to me. Samantha continued, "She says that she was with them when she first crossed over and that she has been at times. But, she is telling me that they are where they need to be now, just as she is. 'It is different here,' she says. 'It is not as it was where you are. I am happy here,' she says. She wants you to know that."

I was grateful for the information Molly had shared with me. Essentially, she was validating my belief, based on my research, that loved ones are there for those who die, but for the purpose of easing the transition from physical to nonphysical—or to spirit. Once through the stages of transition, the spirit moves on to continue the journey of its soul.

Molly had come for several reasons. In addition to voicing the concerns she had for her son, as any loving mother would wish to do, and expressing her desire for company at her grave as well as flowers, she wanted to share some information with me about our children. What makes this rather extraordinary is that the information was being given to me because she had been listening to my daily prayers.

Yes, our prayers are heard. They are heard by not only the Divine to whom we pray, but also by all loved ones who live in the fabric of the universe. Like so many others who have come before me, I adhere to the belief that there is a Universal Mind. God, the Holy Ghost, Brahman, Universal Mind—they are all one and the same. They all represent the collective mind. Our prayers are thoughts and, when yielded to the collective mind, they are heard by not only God, but by all, including God, guides, deceased loved ones, Masters and angels. In this way, Molly had heard my prayers.

She came wanting to comfort me by providing information regarding the well-being of our children. Though caught totally off guard by this gift, I was extremely grateful.

Before leaving, Molly returned again to her worries about both my husband and myself. We needed to stop and enjoy life now, she emphasized, before it was too late. I knew her message was important and carried with it a sense of urgency. "Thank you, Mom, for coming and for watching over us," I said to her as she finished her visit with me. Her love and concern had touched me deeply.

Within the hour, I scribbled notes to help me recall the details of her visit. I also began planning the vacation that we had talked about for so long but had not made happen. Thanks to Molly, it was to become a reality!

A Winning Catch That Says Hello

Though the afternoon had been one of the hottest of the summer, we could actually feel a slight breeze as we walked the few blocks from the parking lot to the new baseball stadium in downtown Pittsburgh. We trooped across the bridge that had been closed for the game in order to allow fans to make their way safely to the field. It was early evening and the sun was beginning to go down.

We were genuinely moved as we noticed the city skyline with its many towers that glistened and gleamed against a backdrop of billowy clouds that looked as though they were ablaze with radiant shades of pinks and yellows. I recall feeling both exhilaration and excitement as I gazed upon the view down the river, with the city's skyline off to the left of us and the stadium and field off to the right, filling up quickly with thousands of fans. The sky was perfectly clear, actually quite beautiful, and I remember feeling a joyful sense of peace and serenity.

We had come to Pittsburgh to visit with Rebecca, our daughter, who was in her fourth year at the University of Pittsburgh Medical School. It was Rebecca's birthday and we very much wanted to help her celebrate her special day, especially in light of the stressful week she had just completed. Earlier that day, she had finished her fourth consecutive night shift in the ER, and she was feeling depleted, physically and mentally. She certainly deserved a break and being treated to a baseball game, a sport that she loved, seemed perfect. We were delighted that Rebecca's good friend, Phil, also a fourth-year medical student, was joining us for the evening.

Knowing that we were going to be with Phil, I thought that I might be able to help him, and perhaps his mom, on some level. Phil's mom had died within the last year and a half. He had, with generosity and considerable personal sacrifice, taken a leave of a year from medical school to go home to California to be with his mom, Connie, who was actively waging a battle for her life.

Though Connie had fought valiantly, she eventually died from cancer. This, of course, was emotionally devastating for Phil and his family. Yet Phil felt a sense of peace knowing that he had been able to share the last months and days with his mom. My heart went out to him during this time, particularly because of my own work with cancer patients and their families.

Not long after picking up Phil on our way to the game, I began thinking that perhaps I might use my intuitive training and connect with Connie. My hope was that if there was something she wanted Phil to know, she could use me in some way to convey the information to him. It has been my experience that those who are deceased and who leave family members behind want their loved ones to know that they continue to be around them, still present and going strong while watching over them. However, for the time being, I stilled these thoughts.

We made our way through the crowded corridors of the new stadium, filled with great positive energy of fans who were scurrying around for snacks or trying to find their seats. I could not get over the aura of excitement that permeated the stadium. Despite the hectic hustle and bustle, I felt exhilarated and truly loved being a part of it all. We found our seats and we sat down. Once again, the view of the field, the surrounding stadium filled with fans, and the radiant, distant skyline of downtown Pittsburgh that surrounded the field simply took our breath away. It was all so thrilling!

It was shortly after finding our seats, which were fantastic, that I allowed myself to take several deep breaths and go into a quiet meditative state. I have learned to do this even in the midst of what some may term chaos. I quieted my mind and, mind to mind, spoke to Phil's mom, Connie, to see if there was something she wished me to know. I went straight to my heart, visualized it opening, filled with love, and then waited to receive whatever might come forth.

First, I was shown a dog, a brown dog, with a bit of white in it, and one that I felt might have had a broken leg because it appeared to be injured and bandaged. That was it for a little while. I remained quiet, but mindful, always focusing on my breath and my heart.

My initial sense was that Connie was next to Phil. However, we had empty seats in front of us. I shortly saw Connie directly in front of me, quietly looking at me and telling me how grateful she was that Rebecca was in Phil's life as his friend. I immediately responded that I felt grateful, too, that Phil was in Rebecca's life. And we smiled at one another. There were a few more moments of silence.

Quite unexpectedly, Connie took both my hands in hers and looked at me with great love in her eyes. I filled with such emotion that tears came. I was moved and touched by this gesture of gratitude and affection. Feeling her warmth and love, I sat there in a blissful and rapturous state as though I were floating on an unearthly and sacred plane. Not knowing for sure whether what I had experienced was really Connie or my imagination or both, I explained to Connie that it would help me tremendously to have a sign from her that she had, indeed, actually come to me. At the same time, it would be something that I could offer Phil as a validation that all that had happened had not been solely a manifestation of my imagination.

I spent the game looking straight ahead at a huge monitor displaying the game and the scenes the officials chose to show the fans, sure that Connie would give me a sign via the monitor. I found myself gazing steadily at the mammoth screen before me. But there was nothing that appeared to be a meaningful indication of her presence.

Then it happened. Naturally, it came as I noticed myself relaxing more and not paying so much attention to the monitor. The batter who was up to bat hit a foul ball and there it was, coming directly at (guess who?) Phil. Yes, it went to Phil and, much to Phil's own surprise, he caught it! We were all so surprised and happy that we began to yell and clap.

It was after I had started to clap that the thought hit me, *Oh my God, that was the sign, wasn't it? Oh my God!* I smiled to myself and thought, *She really was—and is—here.* I was filled with more joy than I can possibly describe. And I clapped harder than I can ever recall clapping. I thanked Connie, mind to mind, for her creative and delightful way of making her presence visible.

The evening had been made perfect as a result of Phil's catching the foul ball. We took our time leaving the park. We went the long way, going down to the field, across the stadium and again climbing up the bleachers. This gave us all time to rehash the events of the game as we laughed, joked and took lots of photographs of Rebecca and Phil taking turns holding the foul ball.

Our little celebration continued as we joined throngs of spectators and walked across the bridge, now lit with a soft golden glow, towards our parked car. There was joy both in and all around us. However, I had some conversational ulterior motives.

Wanting to check out what I had received, I talked nonchalantly with Phil as we walked. I asked him if he had ever had a brown or brown and white dog. He seemed hesitant at first. Within a moment or so, he remembered having a brown dog that his family had rescued from the SPCA, but he did not recall its having a broken leg at any time. I tucked this little bit of information away, believing that I would retrieve it at a future time, when needed.

Since that evening, I have thought of the image of the brown and white dog with a broken leg or a leg that was damaged and bandaged. The pictures I receive can be interpreted as we interpret dreams, either in a straightforward manner or symbolically. I have come to realize that the picture I received from Connie was probably that of Phil who, in many ways, is like a puppy without his mom, and who is feeling damaged and in pain, as he grieves her loss. As a psychologist, this makes perfect sense to me.

I return now to our evening. Following the game, we continued our celebration, buying ice cream and taking it home to top our cake. Once again, I attempted to satisfy my curiosity while, at the same time, validating what I had experienced. While we were kidding around and cleaning up, I turned to Phil and asked if he happened to have a picture of his mom, something that some people carry with them, though not everyone. While obviously surprised by my question, he responded that he did not, but that there happened to be one of both his mom and himself on Rebecca's refrigerator—something I had not noticed.

Though the picture was small, I felt a great sense of pleasure as I gazed at the woman in the picture, believing her to be the woman who had been seated in front of me while at the game. Her hair was similar in style (short) and color (light) and she appeared to have the same gentle presence. *I believe that's Connie,* I thought to myself. *I do believe that is really her*! Once again, I experienced a warm, good feeling.

The following morning, just before Rebecca had to leave for the hospital, I asked her what she thought the odds were of anyone, let alone Phil, catching a foul ball at a game. They were ridiculously small, we both agreed, and with that, I told her a little about the events of the previous evening. It was comforting for me to not only share my story with my daughter, but to also feel her genuinely perceiving Phil's catching the ball as something more than a mere coincidence, especially as it followed the request I had made to Connie.

Obviously, I cannot prove that Connie was there at all. However, the fact that Phil left the stadium with the ball not long after my request for a sign is, for me, something that feels like a real connection with her. That feels wonderful. Actually, the events of the evening simply confirmed for me that deceased loved ones connect with us in the most creative ways, especially when asked to do so.

If Only They Had Listened

Den's sister-in-law, Theresa, affectionately called Tootsie by her family and friends, had an uncle, a priest in Mexico, who had gone to a conference in Mexico City. Since the hotel room he was originally given was on a lower level, exposed to street noise, he had asked for a different room. That evening, he was murdered. The police believed that whoever murdered the priest thought that he was someone else who should have been in that particular room.

After the police had finished their investigation, the family had the body sent back to Cleveland for a viewing, service and funeral. Several of Tootsie's family members, including the priest's two sisters (Tootsie's aunts), had to travel from Pittsburgh to Cleveland for the events. En route to the funeral home, the car in which they were traveling was involved in a terrible accident. Another car hit their car head-on. Unfortunately, the priest's two sisters who were seated in the front died. However, another family member who was in the back seat was taken to the hospital.

When Tootsie's brother and his wife went to Cleveland to bring back the bodies to Pittsburgh, the funeral director asked them to call the paramedics who had worked on his aunt because they had important information to share with them.

According to Den, when Tootsie's brother called the paramedics, the story they told him was astonishing. While the paramedics were working on the highway, attempting to save the woman's life, a man approached them from behind. He said, "I can help you. Please let me help you."

The paramedics responded, "We are professionals, sir. We know what to do. We'll do the best we can. Just give us room." They continued working on the woman, giving her mouth-to-mouth resuscitation, ignoring him. However, he insisted. "I can help you. Please, let me help you."

They turned back to him and once again repeated that they were professionals and that it was their intention to save her and get her to the hospital as soon as possible.

One can only imagine the amazement of the paramedics who read the obituary page of the newspaper the following day. As they peered at the photograph of the priest, they found themselves looking at a picture of the same gentlemen whom they had seen less then twenty-four hours before, trying to help them save the woman's life. They were shocked—as would be anyone in their situation.

Den emphatically stated that this threw Tootsie, a clinical psychologist. She had not experienced anything similar to this during her many years of clinical experience.

I must admit that I found this story to be a wonderful example of what others have shared with me during my many years of research. My observations have taught me that those who die do attempt to help save and protect their loved ones who may be in need of their help. Unfortunately, in this situation, the assistance was denied, despite the persistent and pure intentions of the priest.

Mom Is Always There

After their mom died several years ago, one of the most difficult things to pull off, it seemed, was to get Isabel* together with her siblings. Isabel had adored her mom and very much loved her brother and sister. Unfortunately, with everyone living in different parts of the country, the chances of time together were few and far between. Her sister, Leah,* and her family lived in California and her brother, Jim,* in Texas. Isabel lived in Pennsylvania, where she had been raised since childhood.

Isabel's mom, Robin,* had been a dear friend of mine. From the time she had been diagnosed with breast cancer, she fought for every moment of her life with great courage, persistence and determination to live every moment to the fullest. Robin taught me so much, especially about how the universe speaks to us. Her faith in something greater than any of us enabled her to find joy in the most unusual situations. "Look for signs," she would so often remind me. "They are everywhere. Just keep your eyes and your heart open and you'll see them." And she was correct. She was truly my first teacher of how spirit, loved ones, God or the universe speak to us.

After Robin died, which was several years after her initial diagnosis, I would frequently visit and lunch with Isabel. Isabel had rarely left her mother's side in the weeks, months and year that led up to her death. And it was Isabel who had so lovingly guided her mother through her last moments of life. She was there with her mom every moment of the journey. I knew that Robin would continue to be close to her daughter, even after her death, so I was not surprised when Isabel shared this story with me.

After months of anticipation and excitement, Isabel and her husband Jack,* Leah and her family and Jim were all finally getting together in Pennsylvania, in their family's original home.

Their plan was to meet and divvy up among the three adult children what had been their mom's special treasures, including her linens and Christmas decorations. Their plan was to do this first and then spend the remainder of their time together vacationing as a family at the Jersey shore.

On the morning after Leah's family and Jim had arrived in Philadelphia, they met with Isabel in the living room of their parents' home in Bucks County, Pennsylvania. Since Jim was not yet married, let alone engaged, he lacked the enthusiasm that his sisters were feeling. The young women had been looking forward to this meeting because it would enable them to finally begin using their mom's special linens and treasured pieces that she had collected during her lifetime—all of which had been buried away in storage since her death. Leah and Isabel actually bubbled with excitement as they thought of sharing their mom's precious belongings with their own families, and of being able to touch and hold those items that held endearing memories of their time with their mom.

According to Isabel, it was while they were beginning the process of deciding which tablecloth was to go to which person that the lights suddenly blinked. "What's happening?" asked both Leah and Jim, almost simultaneously. Before Isabel could answer them, the lights blinked again. In fact, the lights blinked on and off several times.

Aware of no problem with the electrical wiring either in the home or in those particular lights, Isabel responded, quite confidently, "Oh, that's just mom." Leah and Jim looked at each other and, not knowing quite what to make of the situation, just shook their heads in disbelief. "Sure, Isabel. Whatever you say," said Jim.

Isabel, on the other hand, had experienced her mother's presence many times. In fact, there were times when the sense of her presence would be accompanied by the blinking of a lamp or light in the room. She was familiar with her mom and the ways her mom chose to communicate with her. The fact that Isabel's siblings did not believe her really did not bother her.

The following day, everybody gathered in the kitchen. This time the purpose of their coming together was to divide the Christmas ornaments that their mom had gathered and saved. Even Jim was looking forward to this. As they pulled a bright red and green velvet Christmas pillow from a rather large and slightly tattered carton, everyone broke into laughter, each recalling a favorite Christmas associated with it. Almost instantly, the overhead light in the kitchen blinked. Once again, it blinked several times.

Leah and Jim looked at one another again—and then at Isabel. "C'mon, Isabel. That can't be mom!" Yet, something, they knew, was peculiar. And perhaps, just perhaps, they were acknowledging that mom might have been there, right there in their kitchen, where they had all been many years before, laughing and playing with them.

Isabel just looked at them both and smiled. She knew that mom was letting them know that she was there with them, enjoying the gift of being with all her children at one time. This was a delicious moment for Isabel because it was that special and needed validation that her mom continues to be with her and her siblings. She quietly thanked her mom for joining them on this particular weekend.

Isabel and her husband recently moved to Chicago. Isabel's face radiated warmth and joy as she explained her reason for believing that her mom continued to be present in her life. According to Isabel, the street near her home is called Angel Alley, something that would have thoroughly delighted her mom, who not only believed in, but adored, angels.

Was this just a coincidence? Not as far as I am concerned. *After all,* I thought, *Robin was angelic in so many ways. What a wonderful way, and such a perfect sign, for Robin to convey her ongoing loving presence in her daughter's life: to move to a new home in a new city on a street named Angel Alley!*

$\mathcal{T}$ wo Bits and a Hello and a Goodbye

Can you imagine how it might be for you to start married life, the second time around, with your beloved new husband, only to find that you are spending many of your days with his deceased spouse as well?

This had been the situation for Sara,* who frequently has experienced the presence of her husband's first wife, Judith.* Having battled cancer for about a year, Judith died several years ago. Her husband, Russ,* had spent the last year of Judith's life caring for her every need. He also devoted the two years following her death to actively processing his grief, coming to terms with his loss and to healing his emotional wounds. Russ eventually felt that he would like to marry again if the right woman came along. It was not long after this that he met Sara, and the rest, as they say, is history.

Sara is a bright, successful, down-to-earth, gentle, spiritual woman whose essence is one of caring compassion. She has struggled to feel what it might be like for Judith who, having unsuccessfully waged a mighty war with her cancer, still succumbed to the disease. Sara recognizes that it might have been difficult for Judith to leave her husband and family and that she was not ready to leave. Consequently, Sara believes that Judith has chosen to remain close to her loved ones, especially her husband. Sara has tried her best to understand the situation. However, everyone, even Sara, has a limit.

The situation seemed to become more substantial on the first Mother's Day that Sara celebrated with her husband. Sara and Russ had invited her mother and grown children, and Russ had also invited his grown children, including his new grandson. As in any group of people, there are always some who are more sensitive to energy than others. On that particular Mother's Day there were at least three other family members who, noticing or sensing Judith's presence, took Sara aside and quietly shared this information with her. Up to this point Sara had indeed been sensing Judith, but the Mother's Day happening and the feedback she received from the others served to validate her own experience.

Understandably, the events of Mother's Day were upsetting for Sara. She had wanted the day to be special for both her mother and for Russ's daughter who was there with her husband and family. Though Sara tried to feel for Judith and imagine how she, if she were deceased, would still wish to remain a part of the honoring of motherhood, Sara was feeling as though Judith was vying for some of the attention. This just did not feel right or appropriate to Sara.

Judith smoked a lot. Sara had begun to notice the scent of smoke throughout the house. Since neither she nor Russ smoked, Sara believed that the scent of smoke was a telling sign of Judith's presence. Sara was feeling more uncomfortable each time she sensed Judith.

What has made it more difficult for Sara to cope with the situation is the increased pain she suffers as the result of a work-related accident that is responsible for her having to be out of work and on disability. Once able to bring forth her ability to compassionately understand and tolerate Judith's spirit, Sara's patience had begun to wear thin as her level of pain increased. Because she was on disability, she was home more often, and thus more aware than ever of Judith's presence.

Sara had began to talk to Judith, requesting that she leave their home. However, this, Sara knew, would be hard for Judith. After marrying, Sara had moved into Russ's home, which had been Judith's home. Despite the fact that Sara and Russ had spent the better part of a year redoing and recreating a home for their new life together, this was Judith's home while she had been married to Russ. She did not appear willing to leave it or him.

Since talking nicely to Judith did not seem to make a whit of difference, Russ and Sara went to Russ's priest, who visited the home and did his own form of exorcism. *Ah, that must have done the trick,* you might be thinking. But that was not so. Though things seemed to quiet down a bit, they began to pick up again shortly after a close friend of theirs became ill.

The friend, Ann,* had been a childhood friend of Judith's and then a dear friend of both Judith and Russ. After Judith's death, she became a special friend to Russ and Sara. It was Sara's sense that Judith has been around much more, especially after Ann became extremely ill. This is typical of relatively recently-deceased loved ones. When something is not going right, they remain close to their physical loved ones to bolster and support them. It could also be that Judith wished to be here for Ann, her life-long friend.

And so we come to the second half of Sara's story.

After valiantly struggling to live for several months, Ann finally lost her battle to cancer and died peacefully. She was known and loved by the entire town. According to Sara, as they entered the church where the service was being held for Ann, they found the church overflowing with those whose lives had been touched by her, including the shoemaker, druggist and plumber. Sara recognized familiar faces everywhere she turned.

Arriving early gave Sara and Russ the opportunity to find seats that provided them with an excellent view of the actual ceremony and the ability to hear the eulogies prepared by good friends of Ann, including Russ. As Sara slid into the bench row, she found herself staring at the kneeling bench just in front of her. It was raised up, and as she glanced down at the floor, she noticed how clean and spotless it was.

Since there was no one sitting in front of them, their view of the proceedings was excellent. There were several places in the service that required everyone to kneel down on the bench for just a brief time. After each kneeling, the seat would be lifted back up again, causing Sara's gaze to rest on the same place on the floor.

According to Sara, about a third of the way through the service she happened to glance at the floor and, to her astonishment, she spotted a quarter with the head face up. She was stunned. The quarter seemed to have appeared out of nowhere. She knew that there had been nothing in the area just minutes prior to the appearance of the coin. Furthermore, since there was no one seated in front of them and she had not heard any coins drop or roll down the seat or floor, the appearance of the coin made no sense.

Sara's first inclination, she told me, was to pick up the coin. However, she suddenly and intuitively felt the need to pull back and leave the coin in its place. As she became absorbed in listening to the stirring eulogies being given for Ann, she forgot about the quarter on the floor. There was at least one other kneeling on the bench that meant that it was lowered and raised again.

While the service was concluding, Sara's eyes once again fell upon the space occupied by the quarter, and what she saw, she said, took her breath away. She was flabbergasted to see another quarter lying next to the original and, again, with the head face up. She said that she was entirely "spooked by this." Sara instantly knew that Judith had found her childhood buddy and that they were once again together. It was comforting for Sara to know that Judith was no longer alone. She believed that the two souls had chosen to speak to Russ and her through the use of the quarters.

In telling me this story in session, Sara could not get over the fact that, for her, this incident represented the first concrete, material proof of something extraordinary having taken place.

*U*niversal Connections

While listening to my cousin Leah's story, I could not help but think that it would be perfect for this book. It demonstrates so well the manner in which we are woven together, thread by thread, in the fabric of life.

A relative of Leah's who lives in the United States had retired and written a book that included quite a bit of informative and interesting material about Leah's mother's family. Her mother, Fanya, was a favorite relative of my own mom, who had gone and visited with Fanya in Israel on several different occasions. Fanya's children include my cousins Leah, Ami and Uri, all of whom live in Israel with their families.

According to Leah, the son of her relative (the writer), Michael, was in medical school in the United States. However, he had wanted to study abroad and had decided to study in a hospital in Tel Aviv, Israel, for one year. At the very same time, Leah's son, Yoav, had started a program in the same hospital as part of his training to be a doctor.

Despite the fact that Michael and Yoav had not known one another initially, and each had chosen a different roster of medical rotations, as luck and circumstances would have it, there were opportunities that brought the two students together. As the two young men came to know one another better, they made the inevitable discovery of their families knowing one another. After Michael spoke to Yoav of his father having family in Tel Aviv, and that his father had included stories of his Israeli family in the book he had written, Yoav quickly realized that the family Michael's dad had written about was his own family who lived in Tel Aviv.

Needless to say, Michael and Yoav were moved by the synchronicity of circumstances. They could only imagine the wisdom of a higher power that brought them together. From there, Michael and Yoav went on to become exceptionally close friends.

Again, I emphasize that there are no coincidences. The universe works in its own way to join those of us who need to be connected. Both of these young men share common interests. But even more important, they are grounded and rooted in a lineage that seeks to bring together the past and present.

On a warm but extremely pleasant summer evening several years ago, my husband and I were returning home from visiting with Leah, her husband and their daughter in New York City. No more than fifteen to twenty minutes after saying our goodbyes to my family, we had stopped to pay the toll for the Lincoln Tunnel. What took place as we pulled up to the tollbooth will be with me forever. My eyes zoomed in on the license plate of the car just ahead of us. It read GAD 36. Gad was my cousin Leah's son who had been killed four years earlier in Lebanon. Not often seen on a license plate! And, in the Jewish faith, 18 is chai, symbolizing good luck. Any multiple of 18 is also considered to be good luck.

I was highly moved by this sighting. It was, for me, a communication from Gad, letting me know that he had been with us in New York. Let me explain. After dinner, Leah, her husband, my husband and I had decided to take advantage of the incredible summer evening by taking a walk. The men walked behind us as Leah and I walked and talked. We had spent a good portion of our time talking about Gad and ways in which she felt he was still with her. While I felt strongly that Gad was probably with her even as we talked, I had no way of really knowing.

It was the license plate that confirmed my sense that Gad had been right there with us. Essentially, the license plate validated my feeling regarding his presence. ***This cannot be a*** *random event,* I thought. ***There was nothing random about the timing, location and the actual name on the license plate. Everything was too meaningful.***

As far as I was concerned, this was coincidental synchronicity at work. Gad not only wanted me to be aware of his presence, but he also sent me double wishes of good luck!

CHAPTER 6

Intuitive and Precognitive Wisdom

Every step of the spiritual journey, no matter how small or when we begin, leads us closer to the intuitive wisdom of our hearts and to love. We can't help but grow stronger. Love gives us the power to transform any seeming calamity into an asset and source of comfort.

JUDITH ORLOFF, M.D., *Second Sight*

Through his or her intuition, the multisensory human comes to understand and to experience truth consciously.

GARY ZUKAV, *The Seat of the Soul*

A Child's Legacy

Life is filled with many difficult, painful moments, but I am convinced that the greatest pain is caused by the loss of a child. Sharon's story is heartbreaking and stirring. Like several other women I have known who have lost a child, Sharon* is a strong woman whose courage and perseverance have earned my admiration and respect.

According to Sharon, her memories of June 20th, 1970, though blurry at first, have crystallized over time. She recalls that it was a delightful, balmy summer day and that she had left work earlier than usual. Sharon was looking forward to a sociable family dinner since her daughter, Sarah*, was home from college and the piano lessons for both her daughters, Sarah and Ellie*, had been canceled.

As Sharon drove into the driveway of her home, she could not help but notice how tall the shrubs around the house had become. In fact, everything looked full and colorful, probably due to the heavy rains that had recently fallen. Sharon was delighted with the growth of everything that she and Todd,* her six-year-old son, had planted. *The geraniums, begonias and impatiens are all off to a good start,* she thought as she pulled into the garage. *Todd is going to be so excited when he sees how high the geraniums are!*

As Sharon began preparing for dinner, she thought of the skirt she planned to make for Sarah's school wardrobe. While she was washing lettuce for the salad and considering whether a plaid or plain fabric would be best for Sarah's skirt, her two daughters ran into the kitchen and announced that they were going strawberry picking with their dad. Todd, right behind them, begged to go too; he craved strawberries from the day they ripened in June.

As Todd was leaving, he called out to Sharon, "Mom, come look! My flowers are starting to bloom!" These were flowers that he had actually started from seeds, and he was proud of them. Sharon joined in his excitement, giving him a hug and a smile. "I see them blooming, Todd! They look wonderful! Now, hurry! Daddy's waiting." And with those words, she waved goodbye to her family as they drove off.

This is perfect, she said to herself. *Now I have time to make dinner and work on Sarah's skirt.* She quickly mixed together the chicken and rice casserole and then sat down at the sewing machine, eager to make some headway in the time she had just acquired. She put a favorite tape in her tape player as she sighed and thought how rare it was to have some moments of quiet and precious solitude. She had been an hour or so at her sewing machine before she heard sirens, but thought nothing of it. Warm weather always seemed to increase accidents—people got careless, she guessed.

At about seven thirty, not long after hearing the sirens, there was a knock at the door. Sharon had no idea that upon answering that doorbell, her life would be forever changed. As she opened the door, she found standing before her both Sarah and Ellie, sobbing uncontrollably, and with them a rather tall, middle-aged man. "There's been an accident," he said. "Your son was hit by a car while crossing the street—but I believe he will be all right." Perhaps it was that Sharon was not able to hear what she could not bear to hear, but she later remembered that she thought, *Oh dear. Todd will have a broken leg this summer.*

Within minutes, Ed,* her husband, arrived home. He came in quietly, his head down and his eyes puffy, red and filled with tears. "Sharon," he almost whispered, unable to bring himself to look directly at his wife. "Todd is gone. He's dead! We have lost our Todd. He's gone!" He repeated it over and over as he fell onto the sofa, shaking violently and sobbing. Sharon was stunned.

In that moment, time seemed frozen. She stood, shocked for some moments, thinking, "This can't be! *Can't* be!" She screamed, "This *can't* be! I want my son! Please, God, please!" As she screamed and sobbed, she fell to the ground, pounding her fists into her lap. Life seemed to have come to a standstill for Sharon. She was traumatized and in shock, but she had to know what happened.

According to Sharon, Todd had loved nature. In fact, the family often went into the fields to pick daisies and wildflowers or to find frogs. So it was no surprise that on the way home from picking strawberries, Todd and his sisters had stopped to pick tiger lilies, knowing how much Sharon loved them.

While picking the lilies, Todd had recognized poison ivy mixed in among them. Seeing more tiger lilies on the other side of the road, he had darted across. Just then, a woman driving down the hill, not seeing Todd in time to stop, hit him. He was tossed into the air like a limp weed and then was hit again. Though an ambulance had arrived shortly, Todd was pronounced dead on arrival at the hospital.

As the tragic news of Todd's death spread, good friends came by, offering hugs, sympathy and support. When Sharon and Ed's oldest daughter, Michelle,* arrived, she too was sobbing. She, like her sisters, had adored and loved Todd. He had brought such joy to the family. Even in her pain, Sharon found the means to comfort her daughter.

The months that followed were pure hell for Sharon. She often found herself choking with intense anger and overwhelming sadness. With each passing day, Todd's death was becoming more real. As she was forced to confront the reality of his death, she found that she was unable to tolerate people telling her that they knew just how she felt. That was simply impossible. She found herself especially short tempered and impatient with church representatives who came quoting the Bible. She was enraged with the way the police and the township had handled the accident.

But there were some people with whom Sharon was able to find comfort. Her sadness was alleviated by people who had endured a similar loss and who took the time to write or call, and she was very touched by those who took time to cook a dinner for the family. She especially recalled someone from her church cooking them a big ham dinner.

According to Sharon, it was in the weeks shortly after Todd had died that she remembered an incident that had taken place about six weeks before his death. Actually, it had had such a stunning impact on her that she could not believe that she had forgotten it. She recalled one evening when Todd had come downstairs after dinner.

Sharon and Ed, both exhausted, were sitting and talking about the events of the day while having coffee. As they talked quietly, Todd walked over to where they were seated, looking very sad and troubled. His large eyes filled with tears that gently rolled down his cheeks as he spoke. His words completely shocked both Sharon and Ed as he announced, "I am going to die, Mom and Dad." And, handing his parents three sheets of paper, he said, "This is my will."

Sharon and Ed were flabbergasted. Neither of them had a will—nor, to their knowledge, had they or any of the girls ever discussed the idea of a will with Todd. Regaining his bearings, Ed took the copy of the will away from Todd, crumpled it up and threw it away. Sharon gathered Todd into her arms and, hugging him, said, "Oh, what a lot of nonsense!"

Todd, upon hearing his mom's words and noting his dad's reaction, seemed to experience a sense of relief. Comforted by Sharon's hug, Todd ran outside to join his friends in play. Sharon, however, remained very much frightened by what had just taken place. In fact, she said that it seemed to have been some sort of omen. An uncomfortable, anxious feeling remained with her for many days following the incident, though she tried to put it out of her mind.

Because it is always hurtful to go through the possessions of loved ones who have died, it was six months after Todd's death before Sharon gathered the courage to go through his desk. It was bittersweet for her as she cleared out each of the cubbyholes. Touching his many small treasures brought tears to her eyes. One of the many discoveries she made was a draft of Todd's will. She remembered being impressed that in addition to making a will, Todd had actually made two copies. She could not help but think how extraordinary this was for a child of only six.

Todd's will, including the manner in which he detailed and described his belongings and to whom he was leaving them, was a reflection of his compassion, sensitivity and genuine sense of caring about others. Todd had thought of everyone when he wrote his will. He wanted his sister, Elle, to have his treasured coin collection. Knowing that his good friend, Danny, did not have a bike, Todd left his precious two-wheel bike to his friend. His special furry blanket ("fery blankit") went to his sister, Sarah, and his homemade rockets he left to his friend, Bill, nearly two years older than he.

Todd had made sure that he left something of his to each of those friends and family members with whom he had a loving connection while alive. And Todd had truly been connected to his family. He had loved writing to family members, telling them how much he loved them. Letters often arrived to members of the family with no postage stamps, and postage due. But they would come with messages such as, "I love my sister, Michelle," or "I love my brother-in-law." A letter from Todd was always viewed as a special token of love and a treasured gift.

In thinking about the events that preceded Todd's death, Sharon knew that something extraordinary had taken place with regard to Todd's precognitive or intuitive knowledge that he was going to die, and that he needed to prepare for his death by making a will. She desperately wanted to discuss the significance of these events with family members or church representatives. However, she met with avoidance and resistance each time she attempted to initiate any discussion of the will or Todd's sense of his impending death. She was terribly disappointed, frustrated and angered by what she considered to be a cowardly response by others. She searched for reading material to help her make sense of both her loss and the meaning of the will. But, at that time, there was none available. This would not be the case had it happened more recently.

When anyone dies unexpectedly, especially a child, the death traumatizes loved ones. Traumatic events take from us our sense of control, our sense of security (leaving us feeling totally vulnerable), our self-esteem and our belief in the world that things are as they are supposed to be. Family members feel the effects of the traumatic event for years and, often, for a lifetime. In this case, Sharon has observed the aftermath in the over-protectiveness of her daughters with their children. She shared with me her feeling that the whole family would have benefited from counseling and the processing of their grief, but that, unfortunately, did not happen.

The grieving process took its toll on Sharon and Ed. Though both returned to work almost immediately, weekends were usually spent at home alone, with no company. They were always exhausted emotionally and physically. In fact, they would be so tired that they were usually in bed by 8:30 P.M. When Sharon thinks back on the year following Todd's death, what stands out is the unbelievable state of exhaustion she experienced. Getting up each morning was agonizing for her, as was mustering the energy to enable her to get through the day.

However, Sharon, unable to share her pain and thoughts, knew that she had to find her own ways to heal her grief and broken heart. She took up journaling, spilling her heartache out onto the pages of her diary. Unable to locate the group support she intuitively knew she needed, she sought out the writings of others who had lost children. She would spend hours in libraries and bookstores seeking the works of authors and writers who had endured similar tragedies. It was with these individuals that she most closely identified and found the support she most needed.

The majority of parents who lose a child have strong feelings of remorse or regret about not having spent enough time with their son or daughter. This was not the case with Sharon and Ed. Their life with Todd had been filled with joy—many, many simple joys. If they were not out picking daisies, gardening or looking for frogs or caterpillars, they were visiting museums, libraries and the planetarium, sharing countless moments together. Todd had brought warmth, laughter and love to their family, making his loss grievously hard to accept.

One other extraordinary note needs to be added here. In the same way that Sharon felt Todd knew he was going to die, she experienced a sense of the date of the birth of her son, Bill.* Bill was conceived after Todd died. It was Sharon's feeling that Bill was going to be born on July 14th, a Friday. Oddly enough, Todd had been born on a Friday and on the 14th–August 14th. Though Bill was actually due on July 18th, he was born on the 14th, just as Sharon had believed he would be. She admitted that she thought she had encountered some inner guidance regarding the date.

It has been my experience that individuals do have a sense of their approaching death. Though this, at times, may be an unconscious awareness, it still has the ability to influence behavior. This explains why many people seem to achieve closure with loved ones in weeks and months preceding their death. My research of works written by hospice workers and doctors indicates that this is the case, as has also been the case with many individuals whom I have interviewed. How this takes place is unknown.

Perhaps, with the assistance of our intuition, we are able to connect with the wisdom of our higher power, perhaps that of the soul, or that of our guides, angels or God. Clearly there is a connection with a higher wisdom. This connection, I believe, is what Todd experienced and acted upon by making his will. It was his way of continuing to care for his loved ones and thoughtfully saying goodbye.

A Grandmother's Intuitive Gift

My patient, Allison,* grew up being impressed by her grandmother's intuition. And for good reason: it may have saved her mother's life!

Allison recalled one extremely cold winter evening. It had been snowing heavily all day and into the evening. Neither she nor her sisters had gone to school that day, though their father had gone off to work earlier in the day. She remembered being inside, cuddled up in a warm comforter and, with her mother and sisters, waiting for their dad to come home. They had been listening to the radio and were concerned about the conditions of the road that, according to the news, were making driving very difficult.

Allison and her sisters had just finished reading a chapter in a favorite book when suddenly they heard a knock at the door. It surprised all of them because they knew their dad had a key and, since the weather conditions were so terrible, they did not think anyone would be out at a late hour in such heavy snow.

Looking out one of the windows, Allison and her sisters glimpsed a gentleman, heavily dressed in a long, dark brown coat and sweater. He was signaling to them as he pointed to his car, which seemed to have gone up and over the curb, that he needed to use their phone. Allison described her mother as hesitant and nervous as she opened the door.

"May I use your phone, ma'am?" the gentleman asked. It was obvious to Allison that her mother sensed something was not quite right and that she did not wish to allow the gentleman, who appeared to be in his late thirties or early forties, into their home. However, wanting to help someone who was in a difficult place, she ignored her own internal guidance and permitted him to come into the house.

As Allison's mother guided him into the kitchen to make his phone call, it became immediately apparent to all of them that he was inebriated and that she had become alarmed by his inappropriate behavior. According to Allison, her mother abruptly turned to her daughters and ordered them to go immediately upstairs to their rooms. This surprised Allison, and she had a queasy feeling that something was very wrong. At that point, she began to worry for her mom.

What was stunningly amazing to Allison and her sisters was that at the very moment they were heading for their rooms, the telephone rang really loudly, as if it meant to interfere with whatever was going on. Allison recalled the sense of relief she experienced when she heard her mother answer the phone with "Hello, Mother, I am so pleased that you called."

What Allison could not hear—and neither could the gentleman—was her grandmother questioning her mother about what was going on. Allison's grandmother later told them that she had been walking around, thinking about all of them, and had strongly sensed that her daughter might be in danger. With these feelings and thoughts, she called and asked her daughter if she were in danger and if she should call the police. Without the gentleman being aware of the contents of the conversation, Allison's mother confirmed her mother's fears by answering "Yes."

In less than twenty minutes, the police arrived and took the man away. Allison recalled both the relief and the exhaustion that she, along with her mom and her sisters, experienced following this incident. She remembered how grateful they were to their grandmother for trusting her intuitive feelings.

Given the fact that intuition is about receiving information and knowledge, something that every human being frequently experiences, the choice becomes ours as to whether or not we honor the incoming information we receive. As this story demonstrates, those who choose to respect this intuitive wisdom, which sometimes directs us to immediately listen and take action, may be making life-preserving decisions.

A Loving Connection

While there are times when a loved one has the sense that he or she may be close to death, it is not uncommon for others to also experience a sense—intuitively or precognitively—that someone they love is nearing death. A close friend of mine, Colleen,* shared a story with me about her husband Rob's* aunt, whom she loved very much.

Aunt Beth,* who was in her late sixties, had the most wonderful ways of expressing her affection for Colleen. She never forgot a birthday or anniversary and loved to make Colleen and her family feel special. Aunt Beth had, in earlier times when she was in good health, enjoyed visiting Colleen, Rob and their boys, Charlie* and Danny.* The kids, in particular, enjoyed her warmth and delightful sense of humor. Unfortunately, she suffered from numerous medical problems, including diabetes, arthritis and a cardiac condition, all of which made it impossible for her to make the journey to visit with Colleen's family.

According to Colleen, one spring morning she had a particular conversation with Aunt Beth that left her feeling rather uncomfortable as she hung up the phone. "Something is wrong," she said to herself. "Something is very, very wrong." It had been more than two years since Aunt Beth's last visit to their home. While she could not put her finger on what contributed to her feelings, she strongly felt the absolute necessity of going to see Aunt Beth.

It was not their custom to take their children out of school, especially with the year soon coming to a close and with their older son in honor classes. But after talking with Rob about her phone conversation and her strong gut feeling that they needed to see Aunt Beth immediately, Colleen and Rob made the decision to take the children and visit with Aunt Beth in

Virginia. As it turned out, the visit went incredibly well and provided them with the experience of a wonderful family reunion.

Unexpectedly, Aunt Beth's son, his wife and their baby daughter, who were visiting from Panama and were supposed to have left for home the week before, had been told by their pediatrician that they needed to stay in the United States for a longer period. The baby had developed mild tremors and needed to be treated before their departure. Consequently, the two families were given an unanticipated opportunity to get to know one another. This turned out to be a beautiful gift for everyone. They dined and played together, shared favorite stories and memories and took lots of photographs of each family member, especially of Aunt Beth with each of her grandchildren and her nephews. Colleen and Rob treasure these photos, photos they would not have if Colleen had not listened to her inner wisdom.

There were many times when Colleen found herself musing about the coincidental nature of the two families being able to visit with one another as well as saying their good-byes. Was this just a coincidence? Or might one consider the circumstances leading up to these events as coincidental synchronicity?

The following events appear to confirm that the universe had a role in arranging the visit of Colleen's family with her Aunt Beth. According to Colleen, while the families were dining at a casual Italian restaurant the evening before they were to leave for home, Aunt Beth, finding it difficult to walk, asked Colleen to walk with her to the ladies room, which was on the other side of the restaurant and quite a distance from where they were seated. As they walked, hand in hand, Colleen observed that Aunt Beth maintained a positive and uplifted disposition, despite the fact that she was obviously suffering. Noticing this, Colleen shared her feelings of affection for her aunt, saying, "I wish you were my mother-in-law."

Genuinely moved by Colleen's remark, Aunt Beth replied, "I love you for that, and I want you to know that if I die tonight, I will die a very happy woman." Colleen, in turn, was deeply touched by her aunt's loving words.

Early the next morning, Aunt Beth, dressed in black silk slacks and a stunning pale pink blouse, managed to come with Colleen and her family to the airport, in spite of her pain. She said that she just wanted to look at them until they had boarded the plane and she could no longer see them. Colleen, Rob and the children kept peering behind them as they headed for the plane, "not knowing it was to be the last time, but knowing."

As you may have guessed, two weeks to the day after their departure, Colleen received that call that she had both dreaded and anticipated. Aunt Beth had passed away in her sleep. Fortunately, according to her doctor, she had experienced little, if any, pain.

Colleen has never doubted that there was some higher guidance that urged her to drop everything and make the trip to Virginia with her family to see her aunt. She recognizes that had she not listened to her intuitive wisdom, which spoke to her of Aunt Beth's approaching death, goodbyes and closure would have been an impossibility. Furthermore, by honoring her intuition, Colleen felt that both she and her aunt were able to be at peace. Knowing this brought Colleen a sense of serenity and joy.

An Anticipated Good-Bye

My patients repeatedly share stories with me in which their loved ones say or do things that clearly appear to be indications of their having an intuitive or precognitive sense of their impending death. As indicated in several other chapters of this book, numerous hospice doctors and nurses have written of such experiences.

A good friend of mine, whom I will call Ellen, believes that her mother had such an intuitive sense of her own death. According to Ellen, her mother and Ellen's sister were returning home late on the evening before her mother's death. They had been out for several hours that evening and were both exhausted and anxious to get home to their families. It was only after Ellen's mother had died that her sister recalled the incident that occurred while they were traveling home that night and which, they felt, was revealing, considering that she died within hours after it took place.

As Ellen's sister was parking her car, the loud screeching of tires pierced the night, followed by the sound of a car gunning its motor and accelerating. Ellen's sister recalled that at that moment both women turned to look at one another and, with a terrified look on her face, her mother exclaimed, "Oh my God! Did you hear that? That is how people get killed!" According to Ellen's sister, her mother was terribly shaken by what she had just heard.

Could she, at some level, have known that in less than twenty four hours she would be one of those to whom she had just referred: a woman, quietly walking, minding her own business, suddenly struck by a hit-and-run driver just a few days before her sixty-first birthday?

As with so many grievances, it is the looking back after a loved one dies and noticing the "little things" that were said or done that point one in the direction of believing there really was a sense or knowledge at some level of death being relatively imminent. For Ellen and her sisters, the feeling that this was the case comes with remarks that they recall their mother made with regard to retiring. While she enjoyed her work, she often spoke of looking forward to her days of retirement. However, it was her mother's tendency to couple those thoughts with the comment, "If I ever get there!"

"If I ever get there" never felt right for Ellen and her family. They were obviously uncomfortable with the comment. It came too often, and after their mother's death, it contributed to their wondering if she knew, at least unconsciously, what they were unaware of consciously.

The example of the mother-of-the-bride dress for Ellen's sister's wedding further reinforces Ellen's belief of her mother's unconscious awareness of her forthcoming death. According to Ellen, her mother and her sisters had been searching extensively for the "right" dress for the wedding. Like any proud mother, Ellen's mom was filled with excitement and enthusiasm as the plans for the wedding were being made.

The search was somewhat difficult because her parents were not wealthy. They had five daughters and tried to live within their means. In spite of this, Ellen's mother eventually found an elegant dress that she adored and could see herself wearing to her daughter's wedding. Unfortunately, it was, of course, ridiculously expensive! But her mother absolutely loved this dress.

While they continued to look elsewhere, searching for something equally as appealing to her mother but less expensive, they had no luck. So what was a mother supposed to do in such a situation? As you might imagine, Ellen's mother yielded to her own desires and decided to buy the expensive dress.

If you are wondering how she managed to justify this decision, it was really quite simple. The decision to purchase her beautiful dress was made with the following comment: "We'll just bury me in it!" And this is exactly what took place. She was buried in the dress she absolutely loved. Ellen is convinced that her mother not only had a sense of her impending death, but that she wanted to go out in style!

Grateful to Be Alive

A few years ago, an old friend of mine, Don,* experienced a truly remarkable incident that he graciously shared with me. Don, who is a dentist, said that he had been working in a clinic in downtown Philadelphia for several years. Since he and his wife lived in the suburbs, he would customarily take the train into the city.

Don established a specific routine that he followed each morning upon arriving at the station, which was just a few minutes from his home. He would arrive at a designated hour, being sure to greet the ticket master, purchase his ticket and quickly walk down the steps to the train, entering the same car and taking the same seat each and every day. He made a point of purchasing his newspaper only after arriving at the station in center city. Don actually loved his morning time; it gave him an opportunity to do some serious reflecting and even meditating on problems and issues that he could not have done otherwise.

According to Don, on a crisp, beautiful fall morning, after a particularly pleasant drive to the train station, he pulled into the parking lot and, to his surprise, immediately found a parking space. As he turned off the engine, he looked up and was pleased to see that his train had just pulled in. *Terrific!* He thought. *I should be able to make it on time for my first patient!* He recalled going to the window, greeting Mike, the ticket master, and buying his ticket. Then the strangest thing happened, something he could not explain.

Don found that as he turned around to go down the steps, he began to experience the most uncomfortable feeling. He did not know what to make of it. He felt the need to turn around, go back up the steps and go to the newsstand for the morning paper. Don knew this was totally out of his ordinary routine, yet he felt compelled to follow where his body and his legs were taking him. It was as though he was being driven by his intuition rather than reason. He admitted to me that at the time he was thoroughly confused about his own actions.

Don went on to say that after buying his paper, he folded it, tucked it under his arm, quickly turned around and began to descend the steps to get to the platform for his train. However, upon turning around, he was completely unprepared for the scene that lay before him. Essentially, "All Hell had broken loose." He could not believe what had taken place.

Everywhere Don looked, there was pure chaos. His mouth dropped open, his eyes tried to take everything in, but the reality of what had just occurred was too much to be absorbed. The train he would normally have taken had just pulled out of the station. Having gone only a few hundred feet, it then had jumped the track.

It was painful for Don to hear the cries and screams of those who had been in the cars involved in the accident As he headed towards the scene of the accident, he could hear the sirens of approaching ambulances and fire engines. It was apparent that many had been injured and, sadly, there had been at least one fatality.

Probably the most disturbing part of this whole situation was Don's realization that had he been sitting in his usual seat and car, he would have been one of those who were significantly injured or perhaps killed. Unfortunately, the individual who had died had been sitting close to where Don usually sat. Though unable to explain the unusual circumstances of that memorable day, Don continues to be grateful for the inner wisdom that guided him to safety and out of harm's way.

The Wisdom of the Written Word

At the time of the events that are about to be described, Annie*
and her sister, Alisa* were both sophomores at a prestigious
Ivy League university. Though they have now graduated, I
spoke with them when they were in their junior year. Having
had a very close and loving relationship with their grandfa-
ther, David,* they were eager to share their special experiences
with me with the realization that by doing so, they might be
able to help others who are dealing with the loss of a loved
one. It may be that they recognized that the process of talking
about the events would assist them and others to find a sense
of meaning in the events, perhaps relating to matters of the
soul and to the purpose of life.

Annie and Alisa had always been very close. Being able to
attend the same university and pursue an education was a gift
they had not taken for granted. They grew up in an especially
loving and nurturing family. While they each had their own
friends, their own interests and pursuits, Annie and Alisa genu-
inely loved being with one another and with their family. They
had spent much of their summer visiting their grandfather after
finishing work each day, not only wishing to distract him from
his discomfort, but to express their affection and concern. Each
time they came home for a weekend visit, they never failed to
visit their grandparents, especially to check on their grandfather.

According to Annie, it was during their midterm exami-
nation week that both she and Alisa had gone to the library
to study, something they often enjoyed doing together. They
found a relatively quiet niche on the second floor, made them-
selves comfortable and began the long process of reading,
reviewing and studying for their exams. They each worked
quietly, sometimes sharing a thought or two or asking a ques-
tion of the other. After sitting for about an hour and a half in

one place, Annie felt that she needed a break. She stretched and headed for the restroom.

On the way back to her desk, Annie found herself glancing quickly at the books on the shelves. Suddenly, she noticed one book in particular. For some reason she could not explain, a book had caught her eye. Reaching up to take it off the shelf, she saw that it was a book of poetry.

The moment that Annie lifted it off the shelf, she recalled thinking to herself, "I'm going to turn to a poem in this book, and the poem I choose is going to be really meaningful for me." As she thought these words, the poem to which she opened included the lines, "My grandfather died today," and "I am awfully sad about that."

In reading through the poem, Annie saw that these lines were often repeated. Not only did the poem strike Annie as strange, but, given that her grandfather was not in the best of health, it also made her feel uncomfortable. Annie returned to her desk and decided not to discuss the incident with her sister, knowing that it would most likely disturb her and interfere with their studying.

It was often their custom to talk before going to bed. Annie remembered that their conversation that evening seemed different than usual. They usually talked about the day's events, events coming up in the next day or two and about family and friends. That evening, Annie and Alisa spoke about the film they had lovingly made for their grandfather. They had spent many hours filming their friends, the campus and the favorite places they loved to visit at school.

Annie and Alisa were excited about sharing it with their grandfather on their visit home the following weekend. Yet, that evening both seemed to sense that something was not right. Annie, in particular, could not stop thinking about the poem she had come across in the library earlier that day.

Unfortunately, the sisters' premonition came true: in the early morning hours their mom called to tell them that their grandfather had died during the night. Though neither girl had shared with the other her thoughts or feelings, Annie believed that they somehow intuitively knew that this was about to happen. My research has shown that in the days and weeks preceding death, people seem to have an intuitive or precognitive sense of the timing of their death.

In fact, the authors of *Final Gifts,* by Maggie Callahan and Patricia Kelley (both hospice nurses),[222] and Pamela Kircher, M.D., a hospital physician and author of *Love Is The Link,*[223] have confirmed this. According to these writers, we need to listen carefully to ill or dying patients if we wish to be present at the time of their death. They have found that those who are dying have knowledge, actually an intuitive wisdom, often unknown to them at the conscious level but frequently demonstrated in their words and behaviors.

If you find yourself questioning why or how it is that both David's granddaughters and his wife would be given indications of his death, perhaps it has something to do with the extremely close relationship David had with his family. My experience has been that it is not unusual for loved ones who have a genuinely close and special relationship with the individual who is dying to have such experiences. There are some who believe that the soul makes a contract with other souls to come into physical form together in order to heal those aspects of the soul that are in need of healing. It may be that the intuitive and precognitive communication occurring at the time of one's death is on some level a demonstration of the soul's desire to say goodbye and seek closure.

CHAPTER 7

Answered Prayers

When we investigate prayer scientifically, we show that "it works," not "how" or "why" it works. This means there is a threshold beyond which science cannot pass

LARRY DOSSEY, M.D., *Prayer is Good Medicine*

When I find myself taking my own prayer and meditation too seriously—feeling as if I should be more disciplined and "pray better"—I remind myself that I am still learning. . . . The Universe doesn't depend on whether we get it right in prayer.

LARRY DOSSEY, M.D., *Prayer is Good Medicine*

A Gift for the Sabbath

Leah, a small but strong, beautiful woman, is a dear relative of mine who privately grieves the loss of her seventeen-year-old son, Gad. While serving as a medic in the Israeli Army in 1993, Gad had been killed as he went to the aid of another soldier in Lebanon. I recall how heartbroken I was upon hearing the news of his death. *This just can't be,* I thought. *He was too young to die!* My heart filled with sadness for Leah and her family. While we all realize that life is filled with loss, the loss of a child is beyond the ability of most of us to wholly fathom.

Naturally, I immediately thought of my visit with Gad just months before his death. During a family get together with Leah and her family at a local restaurant in Tel Aviv one evening, I had had the pleasure of getting to know him. The handsome young man that I remembered was filled with hopes and dreams for his future. As he spoke of his plans to go on with school, I was genuinely touched by his warmth, vitality and love of life.

Over the years, Leah has struggled to come to terms with the loss of her son. The loving support of family and friends has enabled her, her husband and her other three children, all of whom have been deeply hurt by Gad's death, to grieve and to go on with life. As with any mother whose son dies much too soon, she has tried to make sense of his death. But the wounds are so deep that even a lifetime is not enough time to heal the intensity of the pain a mother feels for the loss of her child.

Leah has continued to visit Gad's gravesite regularly, where she prays and talks with her son. Although she no longer goes as frequently as she did in the months following his death, she does continue the practice to maintain a connection with her son. Her visits provide her with an opportunity to feel a sense of closeness to Gad. It brings her pleasure to be able to sit, pray, and speak with Gad at the cemetery. However, this is not enough.

There have been times when Leah would struggle emotionally with her loss. It would become unbearably painful for her to think of life without being able to see, touch and hug her son. Frankly, as with all women who have lost a child, this is something that still continues. It is during such moments that Leah may ask for a sign from Gad to let her know that he is truly with her.

Leah recalled for me one Friday afternoon when, upon leaving the cemetery, her pain was so intense and her desire to experience Gad so great that she asked both God and her son for a sign that would enable her to know that he was really with her. *Please, God,* she prayed silently to herself, *give me some type of sign that will enable me to know Gad is with me.*

According to Leah, she had gone directly to the supermarket upon leaving the cemetery. It was about to be Shabbat, the Sabbath, and she needed to prepare for her Shabbat dinner, something she took great pride in doing for her family. This was a different market than the one in which she normally shopped. Not quite sure of where everything was, she took a little longer than usual shopping for dinner on this particular Friday. She was also feeling more drained emotionally because of missing her son so dreadfully.

Because this was a Shabbat dinner, she needed a challah, the traditional braided egg bread made for the holy day. Having finished the rest of her shopping, she headed for the bakery to purchase her challah. *There it is,* she thought to herself, with some excitement. It looked like the perfect challah. One can only imagine how astounded she was by what followed. As she picked up the bread, she found that her hand fit perfectly into a molded indentation that took the form of a hand on top of the challah!

Tears came to Leah's eyes, but they were tears of joy. Stunned by what had just taken place and moved by the meaning of this for her, she smiled as she continued to rest her hand in the molded hand formation in the bread. *He truly is with me,* she thought, *Gad is with me,* she repeated over and over to herself. *This is the sign I have waited for. Thank you, thank you, thank you!*

And what an appropriate sign this was. The hand carries great significance in Israel. It serves as a symbol of protection, especially from evil. Those who visit Israel often return with a piece of jewelry in the form of a hand. Leah wears a hand-shaped piece of jewelry on her neck. Thus, for Leah this incident was an obvious answer to her prayer for a sign that Gad was with her. She felt that her prayer had been answered and, because of this, her heart filled with gratitude and joy. The memory of that day continues to touch her.

Leah shared another experience with me in which she felt that her prayers had been answered. She described a visit that she, her husband and her daughter, Ofra, had made to New York. It was springtime, and she and her family were enjoying the exquisite pear and cherry trees that were blooming while they took in the sights of the city. One very important sight-seeing activity included the United Nations. Though this was their daughter's first visit, Leah and her husband had brought Gad there on a previous visit to New York. Gad was just thirteen at that time.

As they walked through the corridors of the United Nations, Leah found herself reflecting on their last visit there with Gad. It was difficult for her to stop thinking about the things that moved or interested him on that visit. As hard as she tried not to think about those memories, they came anyway. Then, suddenly, she found that she was in a state of both anxiety and panic.

She realized that she was becoming immobilized by a feeling of fear, irrationally connected to the thought that, given the similarity of the situation, perhaps what happened to her son would also happen to her daughter. Though she knew this made no sense, the feeling of fear continued to grip her, with her chest feeling tighter by the moment. She started to pray: *Please, God. Give me a sign that I have nothing to fear and that everything will be fine.*

She continued on their tour through the United Nations. According to Leah, it was not long before they were provided with a guide, a handsome young man with dark hair named Yoav, who was also an Israeli. It was with this, the meeting of the guide, that Leah allowed herself to relax and breathe more easily. She no longer felt a sense of dread and concern. She absolutely knew that all would be well. Why? Yoav happens to be the name of one of her other two sons. Her prayers had been answered.

Like Leah, I have come to believe in the value of prayer. I always recommend to my patients when they are feeling help-less, powerless and alone that they consider prayer. Experi-ences such as those of Leah and others, including myself, have taught me that prayers are heard and, if nothing else, there can be great comfort in prayer.

For those of us who are curious about issues regarding the spirit and the soul, the fact that prayers are answered and that loved ones find ways to let us know they are still with us serves to validate our sense that perhaps we continue to live, though not physically. Perhaps we can allow ourselves permission to go a step further and consider the meaning of why we are here, as well as the purpose of our existence, both physically and spiritually. I believe we are more than physical beings. We have a soul, a soul that lives, and a soul that is immortal. Then what is our relationship with our soul? These are just a few of the issues that stories similar to Leah's push us to consider and, by so doing, move us a notch or two higher in our own spiritual evolution.

A Little Prayer Goes a Long Way

My friend Adam* has the best luck, though I have come to believe that his good fortune is more than simply good luck. After returning home from work one evening, Adam and his son, Jon,* were relaxing in the family room while Adam's wife, Anita,* prepared dinner. As so often is the situation, when this father and son are tired and hungry, they begin to have differences of opinion.

According to Adam, in the middle of an argument they were having he could hear the television airing a commercial that dealt with the day's lottery. He said that he suddenly had the strongest urge to go and buy a lottery ticket. He grabbed his car keys and called out to Anita that he was running out to the convenience store to buy a ticket and that he would be back in a few minutes. Then he practically flew out the door.

It did not take long to get to the local convenience store and purchase a ticket. On the way home, Adam reported, he passed the Church of Chestehova in front of which stood a radiant statue of the Virgin Mary. Believing in the power of prayer, Adam wasted no time uttering a short prayer. *Bless me, please,* he prayed to the Virgin Mary. While praying, a glorious rose bush near the Virgin Mary caught his attention. As he drove further, he again noticed roses, this time on a large banner that was hung across the street on which he was driving. *Perhaps the rose is a sign,* he thought to himself. *We'll see.*

After arriving home, Adam had dinner with his family. Following dinner, while relaxing and talking with Jon, Jon noticed that the lottery winners were being announced. Suddenly, he yelled out, "Dad that's your number!" They were bursting with excitement about this turn of events. Though the winning number did not pay a huge amount of money, Adam was still thrilled that he had listened to his intuitive sense urging him to buy a ticket for that evening's lottery. In fact, Adam felt very comforted by the thought that this was an indication or sign that his deceased loved ones and the universe are lovingly watching over him and his family.

An Answer to a Mother's Prayer

The sister of a patient of mine wanted to share her story not only with me, but also with the readers of this book. Here it is.

My son, Matthew, died in April, 1994. He fell asleep while driving home from work, and his pick-up truck hit a wall. He was twenty-seven. I didn't know how my life could go on. For weeks a terrible panicky feeling would come over me, and I felt as if I couldn't breathe. I would feel sick. I felt like I just had to run somewhere. I wanted to help him. I would picture myself standing in front of his truck, trying to stop it from going off the road, or trying to wake him up before he hit the wall.

I had always believed in a life after death. I had believed that a person's soul or spirit lived somewhere for all eternity after they left this life. But I began to wonder about this place now. Where is this life? Where was Matt now? Was he safe with God? I had so many questions. As a parent, I had to know: it's the protective instinct. If a child moves away from home, the parents can still be in touch with him. They can phone. They can look at a map and know where their child is. But where was Matt? There is no map of this place where spirits go. And was he really there or is this belief in an after-life not true? I had to know. So I prayed and prayed for an answer. "Please God, let me know that Matt is with you. Send me a sign, so that I know he is safe."

I began going to a support group, The Compassionate Friends. On the first night that I went, I mentioned how I was feeling. A woman there told me that after her son had died, she was in a religious shop, and she had purchased a picture of God standing in the clouds embracing a young man. She said the picture brought her great comfort, and she asked me if I had ever seen it. I told her, "No, I have never seen the picture."

The next day at work, I decided to go home for lunch, which I didn't often do because I had lunch with a friend every day at work, but she was leaving early that day. I went out to my car to go home, and the feeling of panic came over me again. I put my head on the steering wheel and cried. I prayed again, "God, please send me a sign to let me know that Matt is with you."

When I got home, there was a package wrapped in brown paper lying at my door. I didn't notice whom it was from. I didn't even pick it up, but as soon as I saw it, I knew it was the picture that the woman had told me about the night before. I took it in the house and opened it, and it was that picture.

My sister had sent it to me, along with a note that said that since Matt's funeral she had been thinking of us and of Matt. She said that she was in a religious shop and this picture caught her eye. Something kept drawing her to the picture, and when she looked at it, she had a strong feeling that Matt was with God and that she had to "send that message to me." When I saw the picture and read her note, I felt as though something heavy was lifted off of me, and I said, "Thank you, God. Now I know where Matt is. I know he is with You."

Comforted by an Angel's Words

It was just two weeks after 9/11, and Rosalie could not stop thinking about all of those who had died or who had lost loved ones in the collapse of the World Trade Towers. Seeing the rescue efforts at Ground Zero that were being televised daily continued to break her heart. She clearly was not in a celebratory mood, and the last thing she felt like doing was going to a billiards competition in Chesapeake, Virginia. But because that is what she and her husband, Lou, had planned to do that weekend, she loyally accompanied him to the match.

According to Rosalie, the tournament was held in a large gymnasium. She was seated in the back towards the end of a row, with two empty folding chairs next to her on her left.

Rosalie was feeling sad and was finding it quite difficult to stay focused on the competition. Her mind frequently wandered to the events of 9/11, and she found herself praying for both those who had died and for those who grieved loved ones lost in the World Trade Center. Her heart was heavy.

Suddenly, a gentleman who slid into the folded chair next to her caught her attention.

"Hi. My name is John," he said in a warm, pleasant voice.

"Hi. I'm Rosalie," she quickly replied, wondering where he had come from. He seemed to just appear out of the blue. *Who is this young man?* she wondered. She observed that he was dressed in a brown shirt and trousers, was fair-complexioned and about thirty-five years old. His features, however, she still cannot recall.

She distinctly recalls asking him, "Where are you from?" and his answering, "From everywhere." *What an unusual answer*, she thought.

They began talking. Somehow, the young man seemed aware that Rosalie was upset, sad and feeling as though she did not belong there. She explained that given the events of 9/11, she did not feel up to clapping, cheering and having a good time.

Rosalie clearly remembers John's words: "Rosalie, there are some things over which you have no control and about which you can do nothing—except pray. He looked her directly in her eyes and said, **"You can pray, Rosalie. You know, Rosalie, don't you, that your prayers are heard?"** The fact is that Rosalie, who is an extremely intuitive and spiritual woman, has frequently been given indications that her prayers are heard. At the time, she recalled saying to herself, *this man is talking to me as though he knows me and has heard me praying.* Hoping that she was not being rude, she found herself staring, almost with disbelief, at this gentle, kind man who seemed to have appeared out of nowhere.

They talked a bit more. Rosalie found that she was experiencing chills, but not fear. She knew deep within her soul that something extraordinary was occurring. Somehow, she knew that John's appearance was not a coincidence.

She also realized that she was beginning to feel a sense of calm and serenity that she had not felt in some time. "Yes, I can help them. I can ask God to watch over them and help them, if nothing else. They need my prayers, and that is something I can offer them."

"Good, Rosalie," he reiterated. "Remember, your prayers are always heard. So, please, do not be afraid to pray."

Rosalie turned her head away for just a moment to see if she could see Lou at the pool table. When she turned back to John, he was gone. He seemed to have disappeared as easily and quickly as he appeared. She looked everywhere but there was no sign of him anywhere.

This is too strange, she thought, *just too strange.*

Feeling so much more at peace than she had in weeks, she looked for Lou. She could not wait to tell him about John. However, she knew that it would be difficult for him to fully accept her position regarding John. "Who do you believe he is?" asked Lou.

She replied, "Why an angel, of course, Lou. He is an angel."

Though her husband felt that if she looked carefully around the gymnasium she would definitely find John, Rosalie knew that he was nowhere to be found. Knowing how troubled and upset she was, her angel had come to help her find peace. Having accomplished his intentions, he was no longer needed. He then disappeared.

Touched by the Light

A number of years ago, Bonnie,* the aunt of a patient of mine, shared the following story with me. She had come in for a special visit with her niece, knew of the research I was doing for this book, and agreed to tell me her story. While I was moved by the events that she had shared with me (probably because I could personally identify with her), her story is especially meaningful for anyone who wishes to pray for a loved one who has died, no matter what his or her religious preference.

Bonnie and her husband, Steve,* had been completely devoted to one another. They not only shared raising their four children, but also enjoyed working together. They were a team in every sense of the word, their unspoken love obvious even to strangers. Thus, Steve's death devastated Bonnie. Only her faith sustained her in the following weeks and months.

A member of the Jewish faith, Bonnie found comfort in the ritual of going to synagogue every morning in order to pray and say Kaddish, a prayer that is recited for a loved one who has died. Each morning before dawn, Bonnie, still emotionally and physically exhausted, would awaken with a heavy heart. She would ready her children and take them to synagogue to pray, arriving by 6:30 A.M.

According to Bonnie, something strange would take place during every visit as she and her children began reading and chanting their prayers. While the beauty of the prayers, many of which she and Steve had recited together, initially moved her, she found herself being distracted by an unusual light coming from one of the light bulbs that represented the Eternal Light. *What's happening here?* she wondered. Confused, she re-examined the bulb from several different angles, to be sure she was not imagining the unusual glow. But no matter how she checked out the bulb, the light was always present and radiant.

Bonnie also noticed that as she and her family continued praying, the light bulb would glow more intensely, giving off a vibrant light that almost seemed to be conversing with her. There was definitely something unique and special about this light. *Could this be Steve?* Bonnie wondered to herself. She knew that she had not experienced this pulsating light effect when she had come to say Kaddish in synagogue prior to Steve's death.

Bonnie was convinced that the glowing bulb represented her husband. This was his way, she felt, of making his presence known to her. Because of the manner in which the light appeared to be pulsating, she found herself conversing with it. Intuitively, she knew this was Steve!

Of course, the children could not help noticing their mom talking to the light. Bonnie's daughter commented on how weird it seemed that her mother was actually holding conversations with a light bulb! To this Bonnie responded, "Okay, so you're thinking that I am losing it because I'm talking to a light bulb! Well, I can't help that. It just feels like it's your dad!"

Somehow, this weirdness filled Bonnie with optimism and bliss. How difficult it had been for her to go on without Steve. Yes, she was aware that her interpretation of the glowing light was being determined by her loss and her extremely close relationship with her dead husband. She recognized this and saw the light as confirmation that Steven had not left her and that he remained near and wished to communicate his presence to her via the glowing bulb. Getting up early each morning to go to synagogue was no longer a chore for her. Knowing that Steve's spirit would come and be with her was, as she said to me during our interview, "one of the things that really kept me going when I did not think I could go on at all!"

Bonnie's personal experience has been one that has supported the research of physicians and scientists who study prayer. Not only has prayer been a comforting experience for her, it has also enabled her to feel a sense of connection with her husband. Her commitment and dedication to carrying out the rituals of her faith, with regard to daily prayer in synagogue, have brought Bonnie a heightened sense of serenity and peace because she feels so close to Steve during prayer.

Finally, when one ponders the meaning of Bonnie' story, the idea that something transcends the physical experience called life must surely be considered. What brings Bonnie comfort is the knowledge that though her husband died physically, she is able to maintain a sense of connection with him or perhaps with his soul. It is the recognition of the meaning of this that we need to tuck away in the back of our mind for the sake of further consideration when we are ready to explore such matters.

CHAPTER 8

Extraordinary Encounters and Connections

If you would indeed behold the spirit of death, open your heart wide unto the body of life. For life and death are one, even as the river and the sea are one.

KAHLIL GIBRAN, *The Prophet*

I feel such a sense of solidarity with all living things that it does not matter to me where the individual begins and ends.

ALBERT EINSTEIN, *The Born-Einstein Letters*

Dolphin Medicine in Hawaii

What was it about her connection with dolphins? Was it their sweet, gentle disposition? Or their way of expressing their support, love and acceptance while gently nudging her during their aquatic dance of joy? Sylvia* knows only that, for reasons she cannot explain, she has always loved dolphins. She has especially felt the need to swim with them in times of emotional crisis.

Like several of my other patients, Sylvia has found great comfort in swimming side-by-side with the dolphins. She began swimming with them in 1989. Over the years, they have helped to heal her pain, especially the pain stemming from the loss of both her husband and her son.

Hawaii, by far, is Sylvia's favorite place to swim with these playful, loving beings. On several occasions she has made the long and arduous trip to Hawaii to swim with the dolphins "in the wild," but she especially recalls her trip there in 1991. Many other people with whom she swam were extremely ill, physically as well as emotionally. They came because they knew something remarkable took place when they swam with the dolphins: they forgot that they were sick. While they were swimming, they were one with the dolphins. Problems seemed to slip away, leaving only the joy of the present.

What was it like to be there, swimming with the dolphins? "It was sheer bliss," according to Sylvia. "Our days would begin at six. By nine we would be in the water, swimming, playing and laughing with the dolphins until late afternoon. Day after day, for five days at a time, we would swim with them. Yes, it was exhausting, but wonderful."

In Sylvia's words, "We would eat, we would laugh, and we would simply be with the dolphins." Her sense of connection to the playful, docile mammals sometimes overwhelmed her. When she was not in the water with them, she would frequently meditate on them as well as listen to their sounds, something she loved to do. Sylvia loved to talk about her adventures with the dolphins. "You cannot chase dolphins," she told me. "You cannot swim as fast as they swim. They choose to circle you; you don't choose them."

Recalling one extraordinary encounter in particular, she said, "It was just the two of us. I was sitting there in the water and when I looked down, there he was, glistening in the sun, absolutely still and just looking at me. I was so moved by his eyes. It almost seemed that they were speaking to me. Feeling a sense of gratitude for his being there with me, I said, 'thank you!'

"He turned in the water and began to swim away, and I started to swim, slowly, with him. I remember that we were conversing telepathically with one another. Suddenly, he started to pick up speed and I told him that I could not swim that fast and asked him to please slow down, which he did. He was so patient with me. I had snorkeling equipment on and had to come up for air. He waited for me one more time, and I thanked him again.

"Suddenly he went down, and I found myself in a pod. What a glorious experience this was! I counted eleven dolphins, including two precious tiny babies. One of them was on his back and all he had was this white belly and little tail that sticks out. He was flipping up the tail of the baby swimming just beneath him. I had never seen a dolphin upside down."

The dolphins Sylvia swam with were spinner dolphins, unique in Hawaii because, according to Sylvia, they don't come out of the water in the same way as Atlantic bottlenose dolphins. They begin with their noses pointed upwards and actually spin as they come up and out of the water.

For twenty-five minutes that day Sylvia remained with the dolphins, lazily swimming with them and watching them swim and play. She felt they were enjoying her as much as she was enjoying being with them. Unfortunately, her time with the dolphins was coming to a close. Suddenly, she saw that they were beginning to swim much faster and were, sadly, moving on. She thanked them for the gift of their presence as they swam away. Though they were out of sight in just a moment or two, she knew that the memory of their time together would be with her for the rest of her life.

The dolphin has always been associated with love, joy, intelligence and spirituality. Gary Zukav, in *Seat of the Soul*,[224] writes painfully of the dolphin species someday becoming extinct because it is unable to fulfill its purpose for being on earth. Zukav writes that the dolphins came to serve as a bridge between the aquatic kingdom and the human kingdom. The human species has responded to these loving, gentle beings with brutality, daily killing great numbers of them that get caught in tuna fishing nets. According to Zukav, the dolphins are exhausted and are leaving the Earth, by disease or by beaching themselves.

I have observed in my own work that there are some individuals who have an affinity with the dolphin, and it may come as little surprise that these tend to be very spiritual people. I have also observed children who, about to lose a loved one, tend to draw dolphins happily playing in the ocean. The children wisely recognize the spiritual connection a dolphin has with their dying family member.

As for Sylvia, she believes that the dolphins have the ability to know humans as they truly are at their core. She is also familiar with the research dealing with dolphins, including their ability to know that a woman is pregnant, even before she does herself, and their ability to be instrumental in easing a person's pain. On a personal level, she knows that when she swims with them, the emotional and physical pain she may be experiencing at the time is significantly alleviated. With the dolphins she finds great peace, joy and well-being. Swimming with the dolphins has become a matter of nourishing and healing Sylvia's soul.

$\mathcal{B}$ecoming One with Our Loved One

I admit that I continue to be amazed by the creative manner in which loved ones who have died choose to come to us and indicate their presence. There is one method, in particular, that I have found to be especially extraordinary. I have found that it appears at times when our loved ones are desperately trying to give us an indication that they are with us, providing much needed support and comfort. They do this by becoming one with the person; they merge with the individual who is grieving the deceased loved one. As amazing as this may seem, several patients and friends whom I have interviewed shared similar stories with me.

Rosalie has been a friend of mine for many years. Her bubbly enthusiasm, warmth and wisdom have touched not only my family, but also all of her neighbors. Besides baking the best chocolate cakes and apple pies that I have ever tasted, "RoRo," as those who know her call her affectionately, feeds all of our souls with compassion and love.

Furthermore, since Rosalie has served as a testing subject for some of my psychological assessment classes on several occasions over the years , I am able to substantiate that she is a mentally, emotionally and spiritually healthy woman. I feel it necessary to establish this information, given the unusual nature of the story that follows.

The year 1991 was notably difficult for Rosalie, because in a span of nine months her world essentially fell apart: she lost not only her parents, but also her brother. The death of her mother occurred first. I recall how Rosalie would frequently travel to Pittsburgh, her hometown, to visit with her mom in the weeks preceding her death. Losing her mom was especially tough because Rosalie idolized her and they had been so close.

Before she could absorb the reality of the loss of her mother, she was faced with the loss of her father.

I remember how much Rosalie doted on her dad, who had come to stay with her. Since she had been the caregiver of both of her parents, who had been ill for several months leading up to their deaths, Rosalie was emotionally and physically weary and burned out in the months following their deaths. To make things even worse, the unthinkable happened. Rosalie's brother died only seven months after the death of her father. The third death in less than a year left Rosalie empty and exhausted. Yet, it was with the third loss that she could finally begin to grieve for all her loved ones.

A month or two after the death of her father, the following incident took place. Rosalie recalled that on a fresh spring day in April, she awoke feeling unusually good. Something, she felt, was different about this particular morning. Having been accustomed to awakening with a terrible, sick feeling in her stomach and a sense of gloom and deep sadness, she knew that she was in a different place, a better place. For the first time in many, many months, she did not think, *Oh my God, did this really happen? Are they really gone?* In fact, she actually felt refreshed and full of energy, and she could not get over how good she felt.

Rosalie remembered that she almost leaped out of bed that morning and bounded into the bathroom to wash. She was amazed at her own vitality. She told me that, as she examined her face in the bathroom mirror over the sink, she was delighted by her own appearance. *Wow! You look unusually good today,* she thought to herself. What really surprised her was what she saw when she went to scrub her hands. They bore an uncanny resemblance to those of her mother. *My God, girl,* she thought, *you have your mother's hands! Just look!* While this made quite an impression on her, the thought slipped away into oblivion as she thought about what she felt like doing that day.

Wanting to take advantage of her sudden burst of energy, Rosalie decided to go to the mall. She knew that she needed to get clothes for the holiday and she finally felt like shopping. She dressed hurriedly in one of her favorite cotton sweaters and a pair of navy slacks and rushed downstairs. Her husband, Lou, who happened to be just coming in as she was preparing to leave, commented that she looked especially pretty and so much like her mother! *How odd,* thought Rosalie. *Lou rarely compares me to my mother.* However, she was feeling so up and was so much looking forward to shopping and having lunch at the mall that she ignored the remark.

Saying goodbye to Lou, she closed the front door behind her and proceeded down the steps to the sidewalk level. As she did this, she took her customary glance at her reflection in the large family room window that faced the sidewalk. What she saw will remain with her in her memory, and soul, forever. She found herself observing her mother, who was just a step behind her, coming up behind her and striding into, or actually merging, with, her. *Oh my God!* she thought. *Mom, you're really with me—and a part of me! I can't believe this, but I know what I saw—this was real!*

It was in the moments following this incident that Rosalie was finally able to accept her mother's death. She found herself experiencing a surge of energy and great excitement. At the same time, she felt a sense of warmth and comfort as she realized that her mother was really with her. As she climbed into her van, she once again noticed her hands and how they resembled her mother's. But this time, she was not surprised.

Rosalie had such an enjoyable day at the mall that she actually forgot about her early-morning encounter. However, she recalled that upon arriving home and pulling into her driveway, her neighbor, Jean, who lives across the street, called out to her to wait a moment. "Rosalie," she exclaimed, "you're never going to guess what happened! I saw you getting into your van earlier today, but honestly, I thought it was your mother—not you! Isn't that strange?"

Rosalie just smiled at Jean. She knew what she herself had seen and that she was of sound mind. However, she admitted that while she knew she was not losing her mind, it certainly felt good to have someone who could reinforce the events that had taken place.

Rosalie also knows that this is an incredible story, one that most people would have a hard time believing. Consequently, she has not often shared it, because she fears that most people will pity her and think that she misses her mother so much that she needs to fabricate such a tale. She continues to rely gratefully on Jean's observation as the key validation of her experience.

While Rosalie's mother was alive, the two women always had a loving and close relationship. As far as Rosalie is concerned, it would be typical of her mother to continue being worried about how her daughter is doing and to find a way to help her feel better. Rosalie grew up believing that loved ones are always there for us—in death as well as life. This was, for Rosalie, just her mother's actions backing up her words.

Comforted from the Inside Out

Penny* stood immobile by her husband's hospital bed, trying to protect him from everyone and everything. Having been diagnosed with colon cancer just a few years before, Stan,* her husband, now found himself fighting for his life. Overwhelmed by her own fatigue and by the scent so typical of hospitals and illness, she looked to Stan for some sign of his usual strength, perhaps a squeeze of her hand, just something that would assure her of his presence. But Stan had little strength left. He had lost so much weight that he no longer resembled the man she had married.

Standing next to Stan, her mind raced with a myriad of thoughts. *I don't know how I can go on without him! How can this be happening? Please, God, don't take him yet. Please, not yet. I just don't think I can manage without him.* But within hours, Stan was gone. Despite her prayers, Penny was left alone to raise their two children as a single parent.

I had come to know Penny, Stan and their children in the years following Stan's diagnosis of colon cancer. He wore his devotion to his family on his sleeve. I could feel his strength and his desire to protect his family at all costs. Stan, even in death, had no intention of abandoning his family. He continued to provide his wife and children with ongoing indications of his presence, protection and comfort.

As for Penny, she admitted to me that since Stan's death, her basic character and personality have undergone a transformation of sorts. She has found herself doing things that reflect more of her husband's qualities than hers. For example, before Stan became really ill, he would often work ten to twelve hours a day and then return home smiling, in a good mood and with energy to spare. This amazed Penny. *How does he do that?* she would ask herself. What has amazed Penny even more is that this is exactly what she now does every day and, to use her own words, "without batting an eyelash."

The more Penny finds herself carrying on in a manner similar to Stan's, the closer she feels to her husband. She often wonders where this enthusiasm and energy are coming from, since it was certainly not typical for her to function like this in the past. Could it be that Stan, like Rosalie's mother in the previous story, finds ways to share his energy with his wife?

Penny also shared an incredible incident involving her good friend, Grace.* Penny recalls a particularly hot summer day in 1993 when she was feeling especially close to Stan. She was both working and attending classes at the local community college at the time, and the day felt as though it would never end. In need of a cold drink, she went to the cafeteria and found a comfortable table where she could relax for a few minutes. As she sat, catching her breath, she felt as though Stan was with her, not simply next to her, but within her. She could actually feel his energy and his love. While she was experiencing this strange but wonderful sensation, her friend, Grace, came into the cafeteria, looking for Penny. At one point, Grace actually walked right past Penny, not noticing her at all.

How strange! thought Penny. *She was looking directly at me and did not stop or call my name.* Feeling perplexed, she called out Grace's name. Grace turned around and exclaimed, "Oh my God!" Grace explained that she had seen a large-boned person with a ponytail in Penny's seat. Penny knew instantly that Grace was describing Stan (a large-boned man who always wore a ponytail). It is important to note that Grace had never seen or met Stan. At the same time, Penny intuitively knew what had taken place. Stan had actually merged with her. What an unbelievable thought, let alone reality!

As Penny and Grace reviewed what had just occurred, it became apparent to Penny that there were other similar moments when she had experienced the same kind of sensations. For the first time since Stan's death, Penny understood the source of her strength and her transformation. It was as if a light had been turned on; suddenly, everything began to make sense. Grace's observations of Penny's moments of strength, confidence and assertiveness further served to validate Penny's belief that Stan was with her.

After all is said and done, it is the commitment of love that transcends time and space. So often, we seek answers in places where there is little light. It is when we choose to go within that we find all that we need.

$\mathcal{D}$ena Comes Home

Moving from one home to another is often stressful. For a six-year-old German Shepherd named Dena,* moving from Colorado to Pennsylvania, in a crate, and to an apartment from a house, was particularly difficult.

Dena's owner, Alice,* an active, vital and gifted artist and sculptor in her late eighties, had moved back East in April of 1997 in order to be closer to her children and grandchildren. Dena went from a house in Boulder where she could run free, to an apartment in an assisted-living facility, where she could only be walked. It was a very tough adjustment for Dena.

Dena did not handle the change well at all, and she did not enjoy being left alone for any extended period of time. Frustrated, she actually worked her way through several walls in her new home, including the bathroom, bedroom and the living room. Within two months, Dena had destroyed much of Alice's new apartment.

Cat,* Alice's daughter, was so concerned about the situation that she brought in a dog psychologist, a dog trainer and a dog sitter. Unfortunately, nothing helped. Alice was actually considering the idea of pretending to be blind in order to be allowed to bring Dena into the dining room. However, the idea did not go over very well with her daughter, Cat. Everyone, including the residents of the assisted living facility, was worried about Dena. In addition, Alice was disturbed about what was happening to Dena's personality.

Dena and Alice had been together for several years. Cat had found Dena, who was just six months old at the time of adoption, at the SPCA. Dena was a gentle dog, and she looked much like the other four German Shepherds that her mom had owned in the past. Each of the dogs had been sable colored, female and with black points. All were delightful dogs, and all were called Dena. Cat thought that this dog would be perfect for her mom, who was 84 at the time. No one, of course, had anticipated that Alice's life would change dramatically and that she would need to come back East.

As difficult as it was, Alice realized that her beloved Dena needed a new home. Cat began her search for just the right family for Dena. Shortly after contacting Hope for Animals in Bucks Country, PA, a new family that seemed promising was found. Her new parents were a retired couple who enjoyed traveling. Their plans included taking Dena with them whenever they traveled. A trial period of two weeks was established.

Parting with Dena was not easy for Alice, but knowing that her beloved dog would finally have a home where she could run and be free brought Alice a sense of comfort. The arrangements were made, with an agreement that Alice would not see Dena for two weeks unless a problem developed.

Two weeks later, to the day, Cat's daughter, Ann,* and her two children picked up their grandmother, and they all went to visit Dena in her new home. It was a beautiful summer afternoon, just the kind of day that Dena loved to spend outdoors. Alice was not sure what her visit would yield. *Would Dena recognize her?* she wondered. They knocked on the front door and almost immediately Dena and her new owner came to the door.

Seeing Dena warmed Alice's heart. Obviously happy to see her beloved old friend, Dena wagged her tail, looked at Alice and barked happily. After an exchange of greetings, Alice's granddaughter and children sat down in the living room, but Dena had other plans for Alice.

Nuzzling her face into Alice's hand, Dena appeared determined to show her dear friend her new home. Dena took Alice's hand in her mouth and began to walk her former owner through the entire home, room by room. She wished Alice to see where she slept, where she ate, where her leash was and even where she went to the bathroom. She also actually took Alice by the hand and walked her completely around the perimeter of the property. Alice was pleased to see a chain-link fence that she knew Dena would not be able to jump surrounded the property. Dena even guided Alice down into the basement, continuing to joyfully show off her new home.

While this was taking place, the new owner, Dawn,* watched Dena with absolute amazement. Dena had chosen to take only Alice, and no one else, on the house tour. When the tour was completed, Dena guided Alice back into the living room, led her over to one specific comfortable chair, and pretty much suggested that Alice sit down there. She did this by nudging Alice with her face.

According to Dawn, after Alice had taken her seat, Dena then planted her body right between Alice and Dawn. Alice felt that this was Dena's way of expressing that she had indeed found a new home. With this, Alice finally felt a great sense of peace, knowing that Dena was truly content.

Alice died several years later, in September 1999, of a massive stroke at the age of 90. Dena had died in February 1998. Cat truly believes that the strong bond between animals and people is an eternal experience. Thus, though Cat had never told her mom of Dena's death, at the time that Alice was dying, Cat told her that Dena would be there in heaven to take her hand and show her around again. Their journey together, she believes, continues.

Interrupted Prayers and Rosaries

Having lost both his dad and his mother-in-law in a two-year period, Den never passed up an opportunity to say the rosary for his beloved family members. Saying the rosary was as comfortable for Den as breathing, and it represented a way that he felt he could help the souls of his loved ones.

Den had been raised in a strong Roman Catholic tradition. His faith and his religion were notably important to him. Furthermore, his Catholicism brought him comfort and contributed to a sense of healing for him, especially when dealing with death.

Knowing that life is hard and that we all would benefit from prayers being said for us at the time of our death, Den felt genuinely good about saying the rosary for his mother-in-law and his dad. Since his work with the state police required that he travel extensively investigating crimes nightly, he spent long hours in his car, which allowed him plenty of opportunities to recite the rosary.

In fact, according to Den, it was not unusual for him to say the rosary as many as thirty or forty times a week, sometimes even more, depending on whether he was working or not. (This was due to the fact that as a state trooper, he and his team were sent to investigate any suspicious deaths or accidents, requiring that he sometimes put three or four hundred miles on his car during a shift.)

One night, while on his midnight shift (the busiest of all shifts), he noticed that while he was saying the rosary, on the very rosary beads that his father had held at the time of his death, the strands of beads went limp and fell apart in his hands. "While holding it, it actually came apart for no reason," he said. "I would not be pulling it and I would not be squeezing it. Instead of a circle of beads," he continued, "I would have a straight line of beads. Then this turned into two lines of beads. I would be holding the cross and the medal and maybe the one decket and the other beads would fall on the floor.

"Years ago, I helped the priests at the local monastery make rosaries for the poor. I knew how to do it. I had a pair of eyelet pliers that you could use to put the beads back together, turn the wire and tighten it up. And I would think, *fine, now it will stick together.* And I will be darned, I would be going down the road and it would happen again! Actually, it happened forty, fifty, sixty times.

"At first, I thought, *this is just a coincidence.* However, after so many repetitious events, I felt differently. It kept getting worse and worse. A few years ago, after coming home from a part-time job at about seven A.M., my daughter-in-law had brought the grandchildren to our home, and I was looking forward to seeing them. I recall carefully leaving my rosary on the seat of my truck (a bench seat, so nothing could fall off). I even put a moving pad inside in the middle, near the gearshift, so the rosary would not be able to move about.

"I recall going inside and coming out several hours later. I could not believe what I saw. The rosary was in forty different sections. What amazed me was that the chain was not broken, there was no sign that it had been pulled apart, and the loops were still solid, rather than being stretched open, (which they would have been, had they been pulled apart). The beads were in small clusters of two and three beads. This really threw me.

Den remembers thinking to himself, *This is weird. I know I locked my car. There is no sign of tampering. This has to be the work of something evil.*

"That was the worst time," he continued. "Since then, it aggravates me. I get mad, not afraid, just mad. But it seems to happen while I am saying the rosary in the middle of traffic. It is as though it—this evil force or the devil—I believe in the devil—wants me to stop. It feels as though it is throwing roadblocks in my path to get me to stop saying the rosary. But I do not stop. I continue to say the rosary, and it has never been as bad as it was that time it was in forty sections."

Another strange thing that occasionally occurs is that the rosary gets knotted up, Den reports. It can be so tightly knotted that he has to sit down and try to work out the knots. According to him, the coming apart of the rosary continues to take place with his original rosary as well as his back-up rosary. But Den says he has no intention of letting anything or anyone stop him from praying for his loved ones.

Den admits that he did not like having to say the rosary as a child, but that as an adult he has come to really love saying his beads for his loved ones. "When I do it, I feel comforted and good inside. It is similar to when you do a charitable thing, you do it and feel good just doing it and not expecting anything back." He has made it clear that his determination to pray for the blessing of his loved ones will not be stopped by any force whatsoever—no matter how many times his rosary beads may be intentionally broken.

Two of a Kind

Glancing at her new neighbor, Kim* did a double take. If she had not known that her own mom had recently died, she would have sworn the woman was her mother. *What is going on here?* she asked herself. However, the movers were just behind her, and as she found herself needing to direct where boxes were to be placed, she quickly forgot the incident until a few days later.

As exciting as it was to move, moving into her new home without the loving support of her mom had been especially difficult for Kim. The two women had been so close. It had only been a few months since her mother had died. Furthermore, though Kim's mom had been seriously ill for some time, neither she nor her family were prepared for the intensity of the grief they experienced after her death.

On a cool fall day, just two days after moving in, Kim needed to run to the hardware store for some paint for the bathroom. As she closed the front door behind her, she caught a glimpse of her new neighbor, who was sitting on her porch reading the newspaper. Once again, she felt the same sense of astonishment that she had experienced on moving day.

The woman could have been her mom's double. The woman's frame was identical to her mom's. She had white hair neatly tied in a bun and a cheerful facial expression. As she rose to go inside, Kim noticed that she also had the same walk and gestures as her mom. She even bent over and held her hands on her hips, as her mom had so often done.

I have to go and meet her, thought Kim. She walked over to the woman's home and introduced herself. "Hi, I'm Kim, your new neighbor. It's so nice to meet you."

The woman flashed a big smile and greeted Kim warmly. "Hi," she said. "I'm Lynne.* Welcome to our community. I apologize for your coming over to meet me before I welcomed you. I had been planning on doing that later today."

As Kim was telling her not to worry about that, she noticed that Lynne's eyes were the same crystal blue as her mother's. Not only Lynne's eyes, but also her gestures, the way she would talk with her hands, her speech and, as Kim was to find out, her behaviors and her interests were much like her mother's.

In the months following the move, Kim and Lynne became very close. The more time they spent together, the more Kim was reminded of her mother. Lynne loved to go to Atlantic City to play the slot machines, as had Kim's mom. They spent many a day at the shore, talking about their families and getting to really know one another.

Thinking that she wanted her mom's clothes to be worn and enjoyed, she decided to offer them to Lynne. When Kim saw how perfectly her mother's pants, blouses and dresses fit Lynne, she experienced "goose bumps." It seemed so unbelievable to Kim, so strange, but in a good way.

This is amazing, Kim would think to herself. *How can two women who did not know one another be so alike?* Kim, who was always looking for more similarities, noticed that the two women were not only built alike, but also did things in a similar fashion. For example, Kim's mother had pierced ears, but could not put the earrings in herself. The same was true of Lynne. Lynne even lost her temper and yelled at her granddaughters the way her mother had with her own grandchildren. And, like her mom, Lynne loved to tell Kim stories that she had already told her.

Talk about coincidences! However, these were not coincidences for Kim. There were just too many similarities, all of which negated the idea that moving into a home just two doors away from Lynne, who was so much like her mother, could be a random occurrence.

The universe seemed to have provided for Kim's needs. Having recently lost her mom, her heart had not wholeheartedly embraced the idea of moving into a new home and new community. Given the heaviness of her grief, she had had little motivation, desire and energy for such a move. Yet, provided with the most unlikely of neighbors, Kim found the support and comfort she so desperately needed literally in her own backyard.

Being and talking with Lynne was as close to being with her mother as she could possibly be. Though Kim certainly could not explain the similarities, all that truly mattered was the wonderful sense of connection with her mom that she experienced whenever she was in Lynne's presence. Is it possible that Kim's mom had found her own unique manner of connecting with her daughter? Perhaps.

Whether Kim's mom managed to pull this off using Lynne as a conduit of sorts or the Universe assisted her, Kim has no way of knowing at this point. What she suspects is that she clearly benefited from the assistance of some special divine intervention. For this she is eternally grateful.

CHAPTER 9

Watched Over with Love and Protection

As for myself, I am content with the conviction that God's eyes are ever upon me, and that his providence and justice will follow me into the future life as it has protected me in this.

MOSES MENDELSSOHN

The most beautiful thing we can experience is the mysterious. It is the source of all true art and science.

ALBERT EINSTEIN

A Father's Special Protection

Sometimes, in telling their own extraordinary stories, patients share with me one that is not their own but that deals with the life of a family member or good friend. Because the story is so unusual, they remember it. It connects with a part of them that registers the need, to try to understand the meaning of the experience. The tale of Alexa,* my patient Reba's cousin, is such a story.

A slender, attractive woman in her forties, Alexa was blessed with a father, Richard,* whom she adored and revered. He was a stately gentleman, both admired and respected in his position as police chief of the township in which they lived. As an only child, Alexa had an exceptionally close relationship with him. He was always been there for her on weekends, holidays and vacations. They loved going places as father and daughter, whether it was an outing to a museum, the city, the theater or the park. After Alexa's father retired, they had even more opportunities to be together.

Thus, it surprised no one that, upon learning of her father's sudden death, Alexa had a great deal of difficulty coming to terms with the loss. Dealing with the pain of his absence proved enormously hard for her to bear. She missed speaking to him, hearing his voice and his laughter. She missed his hugs and his gentle reassurance that she would be all right whenever she was feeling especially low. Alexa's grief was overwhelming her with unbelievable pain. Rather than dealing with her grief head-on, by working with someone who could have helped her process the loss of her father, she chose to run from her pain, to escape her lonely existence by drinking, and drinking heavily.

According to Reba, on one cold, frosty evening, dealing with the reality of her father's absence was too much for Alexa to tolerate. Wanting to be able to pick up the phone and call her dad, and not being able to, she called her friend, Bobbie* instead, with the intention of meeting her at a nearby bar. Alexa wanted nothing more than to bury her broken heart in glass after glass of an alcoholic beverage. She wanted to numb herself, and she very nearly succeeded. Bobbie, concerned about Alexa, had tried unsuccessfully to limit her friend's drinking. However, on this particular night, Alexa would have nothing to do with putting limits on her alcoholic intake.

Bobbie noticed, with a bit of apprehension, that a man sitting only a few tables away from them kept watching Alexa. He was perhaps in his sixties, wearing a compassionate, concerned expression and dressed casually in a navy blue sweat suit. While nursing a large cup of coffee, he had been eyeing Bobbie and making her more nervous as she tried to coax Alexa away from her drinking. From his facial expression, observers might have thought that this was exceedingly painful for him to watch. Indeed, it was.

Finally, after an hour and a half, Alexa had reached her limit and had decided to leave. After putting on her coat, gloves and hat, and weaving her way to the bar to pay her check, the man stood up and reached out, touching Bobbie's coat sleeve. "You mustn't allow your friend to drive herself home tonight," the man said quietly, but firmly. He was obviously distressed by the thought of Alexa driving in a drunken condition.

Bobbie, who was surprised that this stranger would express concern for Alexa, said, "I'm also concerned, but she's done this many times before and I really can't stop her. Believe me, I've just about given up trying."

Frustrated that he might not be able to keep Alexa from driving herself home, the man blurted out, "Please, stop her! If she drives home alone, something terrible is going to happen to her!"

There was something about this stranger's concern for Alexa that impressed Bobbie. She also was genuinely worried for Alexa. Unfortunately, by the time he and Bobbie had left the bar and walked to the parking lot, Alexa had already gotten into her car and was pulling out of the lot. They were both powerless now to prevent her from driving off.

Before the two even had a chance to comment on what to do next, they heard a crash coming from a block or so down the highway. They rushed to the scene of the accident. It was just as the gentleman had warned. Alexa's car had hit an oncoming vehicle. They found Alexa trapped in her car, dazed. The gentleman worked rapidly to jiggle the door lock open and pull Alexa from the car. Though initially stunned and unable to say very much, she was coherent and seemed to be relatively uninjured. By this time, the police had arrived on the scene.

After pulling Alexa from her car, the stranger directed her to the back seat of a police car, instructing her not to move. During the rescue Alexa had been too intoxicated to notice anything, much less the face of the gentleman who had removed her from the car. He had also asked Bobbie to sit with Alexa in the car while the police were writing up the report. In fact, Bobbie insisted that her friend stay with her that evening because she was worried about any possible problems resulting from the accident and wanted to be sure that Alexa was all right.

It was not until later the following day, around noon, that Alexa felt better and stronger. After returning home and feeling a little more settled, she decided that she wanted to know more about what had actually taken place. To do this, she needed to see a copy of the police report. Even though a searching look in the mirror told her that she looked awful, she ran out the door and rushed to get to the police station, just a few blocks from her home.

As Alexa approached the station, she was flooded with memories of her father, of visits to this very station and of the many shared moments of laughter they had enjoyed in this building. Once again, feelings of loneliness, sadness and desperation filled her whole being. She wanted so much to be with him, wherever he was.

Opening the door to the first floor office of the police administration office, Alexa reminded herself that she had to pull herself together, which she did. She hurried up to the main desk and asked for a copy of the report of the accident of the previous evening. As soon as it was given to her, her eyes jumped to the signature at the bottom of the report. She was jolted. It was her father's signature, in his own distinctive and unusual scroll!

"There must be some mistake." She waved the report at the policeman who had handed it to her. "This simply cannot be correct," she said, pointing to the report. "This is my father's signature, and he has been dead for several years."

The police officer looked startled by Alex's comments. He seemed to sense that she was not able to be think clearly. He responded that the gentleman who had been at the scene of the accident had written up the report and had taken care of everything. In fact, the officer described him as an older man, wearing a navy blue sweat suit. Because she had been so intoxicated, none of this information was very meaningful to Alexa.

Alexa left the administration building in a state of great confusion. *Something is very wrong here,* she thought to herself. *How can this be?* She knew that her father had died, but also that the signature was his. Hoping that Bobbie could help her clear up the situation, she called and arranged to meet her friend for lunch.

"Yes, yes," Bobbie responded affirmatively to Alexa's question about whether or not an older gentleman dressed in a blue sweat suit had been present at the accident. Bobbie also confirmed that this was the same man who had urged her to try and stop Alexa from driving home alone while intoxicated. Even when Bobbie provided Alexa with a detailed description of the man and Alexa realized that it matched that of her father, Alexa still refused to believe that the signature really was his.

Several other events were to take place before Alexa agreed that the gentleman in question was her father, Richard. First, she went to see her mother, who verified that the signature was her father's. Second, she questioned Bobbie further and learned that some of the things the stranger had said, as well as his style of speaking, were typical of her father. Finally, she learned that the police had not charged her with drinking and driving. Her driving record was still intact, much to her amazement.

He really is here with me, Alexa thought, and as she allowed the meaning of this to register, she smiled in huge relief. Just the thought that he could be there with her, watching over her, protecting her, was incredibly comforting for Alexa. Knowing that her father had been at the bar that evening because he was worried about her, Alexa made the decision to stop drinking. Unfortunately, sobriety did not come easily for her. Along the way, especially during tough times, she would occasionally regress and slip back into her old ways. However, at such times, Richard made a point of re-emerging, and by doing so, he would reassure her that he believed in her and in her ability to maintain her sobriety and quality of life.

Love accomplishes so much. Somehow, despite the small detail of dying, Richard had found a way to continue to love, guide and protect his daughter. Alexa did not choose to spend needless additional hours debating how the stranger could be her father. She knew that even with her father having physically died, she could still feel his presence. She knew that she would never again be truly alone.

At some point, when we have been blessed with profoundly moving, touching and special moments, it is important to stop questioning and to begin accepting the gift of the experience. Such moments add only richness and great joy to this journey called life.

Believing in Angels

The reality of losing her mother and then, not long after that, losing her brother, David,* was a lot to process and it certainly did not feel real to Cat!* David had been such an active man, always puttering and fixing anything he could get his hands on. He had also been a successful golfer who often played with Jack Nicklaus and whose last score was a 69. It had been more than a decade since David had traded in his golf clubs for his boat and fishing rod. David and his wife had made their home near Sanibel and Captiva, on the island of Useppa, off the western coast of Florida. He had loved boating so much that he had attempted to sail up the East coast to attend his mom's funeral.

The last thing that Cat had expected to hear was that her brother was very ill and dying. Unfortunately, despite catching a plane to Ft. Myers and arriving there in less than 24 hours, David died before she could see him. Though desolate, Cat and her husband, Jake,* decided to stay and help the family with funeral preparations.

Cat was desperately in need of a sense of connection with David. The place closest to her brother was definitely the beach. On a clear, radiant day, Cat and Jake decided to drive to the beach where they could sit and watch the sunset together.

Suddenly, Cat had a desire to run on the beach, something she loved to do. In fact, what she really wanted to do was to run with the porpoises feeding nearby. While Jake was curious about the fishermen and their catches, she laced up her running shoes and began her run. Several miles up the beach, Cat spotted the porpoises feeding along the sand bar. She knew that she wanted to be much closer to them. To accomplish this, she kicked off her running shoes. She also felt a need to remove her earrings and necklace, as well as the ring her mom had given her just before she died. Cat had been wearing her mom's wedding ring on her middle finger but removed it because it had been slipping a little, and she feared that she might lose it while swimming. She carefully placed everything in her running shoes before entering the water.

Cat's goal was to get as close as she could to the porpoises and to attempt to swim with them for just a little way, something she thoroughly enjoyed. She slipped into the water, and as she did, noticed the magnificent sunset, something that she knew that her brother would have appreciated. This was just what she needed to soothe her broken heart. How refreshing it was to swim in the cool, blue-green waters of the Gulf!

Sensing that it was time to get going, Cat left the water and walked over to where she had left her shoes, jewelry and towel. Sitting down on a small mound of sand, she began taking her jewelry out of her shoe. First her earrings, then her necklace and, finally, the ring. But just as she was taking the ring out, it suddenly bounced off her left hand and away from her.

In a flash, her precious ring was gone. Cat frantically looked everywhere. *It is lost!* she thought. She kept looking, fearful of leaving the area and forgetting where she was seated. Much to her chagrin, she began to cry. She was angry with herself for crying over a piece of jewelry, something material, but the ring, she knew, was a powerful connection she had with her mom. Fearful of not being able to return to the same location, she felt she must locate the ring. In great distress, she searched everywhere and for quite some time.

According to Cat, there were two families who, upon seeing her search for the ring, joined into help. As for her husband, she knew that he was used to her very long runs and being gone for long periods of time. She felt that he would not be too worried. But as darkness fell, the families had to leave her alone on the beach.

One woman, however, who was renting a condo nearby, had a huge spotlight and had remained to help Cat in her search. Drained and physically exhausted, Cat knew she had to leave. She put on her shoes, grabbed her towel and was about to say something to the woman, when the woman turned and introduced herself to Cat.

"Hi. I'm Abby," she said.

Cat also introduced herself and was about to thank her for spending so much of her time in the search, when Abby asked her, "Do you believe in angels?"

"Yes, I do," she replied.

"Then, Cat, if you believe in angels, the ring will be here at sunrise. What time do you leave tomorrow?"

"My flight leaves around 3 P.M.," answered Cat

"Cat, if you believe in angels and you also believe that your brother has become an angel, he'll have your ring for you, because your mother's wedding ring belongs to both your brother and you. And, he truly knows how much the ring means to you, especially now that both your mom and he have died."

Cat repeated that she did believe strongly in angels and that she felt a strong sense of connection with her brother. With that, she again thanked Abby and headed back to her husband.

The next morning, after a night of almost no sleep, Cat was awakened at 7:20 A.M. by the telephone. The caller identified himself as Harry,* the gentleman from one of the families who had joined in the ring search the previous day. "We found your ring!" he exclaimed, his voice filled with excitement. He had remembered that her last name rhymed with boot and was able to locate her at her hotel in Ft. Myers.

"My daughter and I awakened at seven this morning," he said. "She wanted to come down to the beach with me to see the sunrise. It was my daughter, Lisa,* who found your ring. But you must be exhausted. How about getting some sleep, and we'll hold your ring until you get here."

Several hours later, Cat and her husband returned to the beach. There they met Lisa and her dad. Lisa was so excited that she raced to Cat, clasped her hand and pulled her over to the spot where the ring had been found. Lisa had placed a small stick in the sand to mark the location. According to Lisa, the ring had been partly buried in the sand, about a quarter of an inch down. Somehow, while swiping the sand back and forth with her hand, as children often do on the beach, Lisa's eye had caught a glimmer of something shiny—and there it was! Even Harry, her father, was visibly shaken, surprised and in a state of disbelief. After all, it had not been Harry who had told Cat to believe the ring would be there if she believed in angels. It was Abby, the woman from the other condo.

Cat was gratified that Jake had gone with her to the beach. She wanted him to meet Harry and Lisa because, she knew, there was no other way he would believe what had happened. He was, after all, a dentist, a left-brained man of science and logic. She knew that without meeting them, he would view the whole thing as ridiculous.

In fact, upon meeting Harry and Lisa, Jake was initially speechless, and then said, "Honestly, I have never really believed in either miracles or angels before, but I certainly do now. This is a miracle!" He was so amazed by the sequence of events, Cat said, that he told me I had to write about the story and that I had to share it with my family."

As Cat was finishing, she put out her hand to show me her mother's ring. "Here it is," she said. "It actually looks shinier now than it did before. And it also feels better and more comfortable."

Cat continued, "You know, this whole thing blows my mind. My mother was not a diamond person. The ring is a simple ring, but it has become even more special to me than my own diamond because it has been with the angels."

The primary angel, in this case, according to Cat, is her brother. She believes that it is important that this story be told so that her brother's children and his family all know that their dad and loved one is an angel.

$\mathcal{G}$rampa's Lifesaving Love and Protection

Cat's daughter, Ann,* burst into the house, shouting, "Mom, you will not believe what I have to tell you! It's about grampa. It is so unbelievable, but at the same time, it makes sense."

Ann had just come from a party held at the home of one of her college friends. A medium had been hired to entertain guests, and though Ann did not believe in mediums, she had agreed to sit and talk with this particular woman. Evidently, the message the medium gave Ann made the party one she will never forget.

According to Ann, the medium told her that her grampa was present and that he had a message he wished his granddaughter to give to her mom, his daughter. Despite Ann's skepticism, she knew that the medium was legitimate because of the manner in which she had described her grandfather: "He is a little man with a big nose, dark hair and glasses, a well-fitted suit and a tailor-made shirt." The description fit Cat's dad perfectly.

"What is it?" asked Cat. "You seem so excited!"

"Mom, grampa wants you to know that he is always looking after you and that he is always taking care of you. And, he is always protecting you."

"That's really special and nice to know, especially if I get into trouble," said Cat.

Cat's daughter laughed. "Yes, Mom, it really is since you are the kind of person that gets into all kinds of situations and does need protection." They hugged and talked about the party, letting go of the news they had just received.

The following day, Cat left to go on her usual six mile-run. It was a cool but sunny fall afternoon, and Cat was looking forward to getting into the run, hoping to release some of the tension she knew was plaguing her. As she began her sixth mile, on her way back home, she noticed that two large German Shepherds were chained to a tree in a yard and barking ferociously at her. Obviously, they did not care for her. Though anxious at first, she thought she would be fine since they were chained.

Unfortunately, however, one of the dogs pulled so forcefully on its chain that it broke loose. The dog ran across the street and, in mid-air, grabbed Cat's jacket with its teeth. Luckily, the shepherd managed to tear through only the jacket, sparing her skin. Terrified, Cat ran even faster. However, she knew that she could not outrun this dog. Then, as she looked back over her left shoulder, she noticed the dog, preparing to attack her once again. This time, the dog was already in midair, aiming directly for her neck.

I am done for, she thought. *I do not see how I can outrun this situation.* Suddenly, she heard a screech and a scream. Then a cry, and a gurgling sound. She turned around and was astonished to see the German shepherd lying dead in the middle of the road. She was thoroughly confused by what she saw, but just for a moment. Then it made sense.

A car seemed to have come out of nowhere. Cat had not seen the car, and its driver—the postmaster's wife, accompanied by her daughter—had not seen the dog. The car had miraculously hit the dog in midair just as it was about to lunge again for Cat. The dog had flipped in the air and fallen immediately to the pavement, and had died instantly. There was pandemonium everywhere. The owner of the dog came running out of her home accusing Cat of aggravating her dog—though, obviously, she hadn't killed her dog. The owner of the car and her daughter could not stop crying, because the dog had been killed.

As for Cat, she was numb. She knew that her being alive was miraculous. Remembering the words of her daughter earlier that morning, Cat knew that she was alive thanks to the loving attention of her father. "Thank you, Dad," she whispered quietly to herself, "for watching over me, just the way you said you would. I really love you so much." And with that, she withdrew from the commotion and began her walk home, still pondering her close call with death and still marveling at the incredible series of events.

Ongoing TLC

Some women have the ability to touch their loved ones, spouses, children and grandchildren in ways that stay with them forever. They are often thought of as angels who have taken physical form, perceived as ever-present, ubiquitous caretakers and protectors of those they hold dear. These are precious souls who are dearly missed following their deaths. It is specifically their tender loving care that is missed. But there are apparently a few souls who are determined to continue administering their special TLC. Elena,* the mother of a patient of mine, is such a soul.

According to my patient, Anita,* Elena had been diagnosed in January 1996 with lung cancer. Though devastated, the family immediately responded to the crisis by taking an active role in helping Elena research the best treatments available for her specific type of cancer. They supported her through her chemotherapy and radiation treatments, hovering over her with great care and attention.

However, despite all of their efforts, they could not prevent the cancer from spreading and ravaging Elena's body. Elena lost her valiant struggle with cancer in March 1996. She was sixty-five years old: too young, as far as her family was concerned, to be leaving them. As one might expect, her husband, children and grandchildren were heartbroken.

But Elena wasn't gone forever. She was one tough cookie and, even without a physical body, she was determined to keep a watchful eye on her husband just as she had in life. According to Jay,* her husband, before Elena had been diagnosed with her cancer, he had walked at least fifteen to eighteen miles every other day. He did this, he said, to keep his diabetes and high blood pressure under control. However, after Elena's diagnosis, he stopped walking. He wanted to spend every moment with his wife, knowing that he might not have those moments ever again. Before dying, Elena had made Jay promise that after she was gone he would continue to take care of himself, watching what he ate and being sure to walk every day. Little did Jay realize that his wife intended to stay on his case, even from beyond.

As it happens with grieving people, in the weeks and months following Elena's death, Jay had little energy or desire to care for himself as he had promised. Like the majority of spouses who have been married for many decades, Jay fell into the throes of a deep grief depression. Feeling fatigued, totally unmotivated to do anything, wishing to be left alone to drown himself in memories of his life with Elena, Jay totally gave up his walking regimen and paid little attention to eating healthy meals. However, several events took place that represented wake-up calls for Jay, enabling him to sense that perhaps his Elena was still with him.

The first event that took place occurred about three weeks after Elena's death. Jay had fallen asleep in his lounge chair late in the afternoon while watching television. He suddenly felt a strong burst of energy that ran through his body, jolting him from sleep. It was Elena; he was sure of this. He clearly felt her presence, though he did not actually see her. But he did hear her call his name and he had a sense of a vision of her as well. He was delighted to find that the blonde hair she had lost during chemotherapy had grown back

Her words were sharp and clear. "Jay, I am so disappointed in you!" she said. "You promised me that you would get back to your walking and you have not even started to walk. Furthermore, I can see that you aren't keeping your promise. You are not taking care of yourself!" Jay heard these words as he was attempting to become more alert and figure out what was really going on. He recalled reaching out for Elena, wondering where she had gone. He would have given anything to be able to touch and hold her.

It is Jay's belief that Elena had come back to him, if only for a brief moment or two. As a result of this experience, he resumed his walking routine. In fact, Jay has not missed a day since Elena's visitation.

In the second incident, Jay feels certain that it was Elena's intervention that saved his life. Though she did not make direct contact with him, it was what he believes she did that reinforces his sense that she is with him, always watching over and protecting him from harm.

Jay recalls a brilliant fall day when he decided to go for a drive in the country. He had actually been feeling a bit more positive and lighthearted than in previous weeks. While driving along a rather expansive thoroughfare some twenty to thirty minutes from his home, he remembers thinking how wonderful it was to be feeling good enough to even notice the flaming oranges, reds and yellows of the sugar maples. He was driving at a speed of about fifty miles an hour when suddenly a small silver sports car came from what seemed to be nowhere and whizzed right in front of him, cutting him off and just barely missing him by a fraction of an inch.

Jay was stunned! "Oh my God!" he whispered to himself, shaking so badly that he had to pull over to the side of the highway. Several drivers who had happened to catch the whole thing also pulled over, wanting to check and see if Jay was all right. Everyone agreed that it was a miracle that his car had not been hit. Clearly, it should have been. "I was sure we were going to crash into one another," he said, his voice low and unbelieving.

Jay also has no doubt that the only reason he is alive today is because Elena intervened to save him. As far as Jay is concerned, it is as though Elena had commanded the driver, "Thou shall not touch my husband!" Since that day, Jay has kept a picture of Elena hanging in his car. He is convinced that she is not only with him, but that she continues to keep him safe, as well.

In the last incident that Jay related to me, Elena once more made her presence known to her husband when she appeared to be concerned about his well-being. During the time that Elena was very ill, it was Jay's custom to cook for her every night. Since she loved pasta, Jay cooked a number of pasta variations for his wife, often including spaghetti. Following her death, he found it difficult to cook pasta. However, he was in the habit of going into her room, imagining that she was there in bed, and asking her if she were hungry and wanted some pasta for dinner. He would then say, either verbally or non-verbally, "Good night." (This is something that many of us do after the loss of a loved one. It is our way of slowly coming to terms with the reality that our loved one is really gone.)

According to Jay, he returned home late one afternoon after attending a baseball game with his family. Having stuffed himself with all sorts of junk food at the game, he had no desire to start cooking a meal for himself, despite the fact that it was dinnertime. Totally exhausted, he collapsed into his lounge chair and immediately fell asleep.

While he was dozing, Elena came to him, bearing two messages. The first informed him that she was just fine and that he did not have to worry about her. She said, "I know you're having a tough time with my loss, but I want you to know that everything is fine, including me!"

"Jay," she continued, "every night you come into my room and ask me if I want pasta. Well, this evening, why don't we have a pasta dinner?" With that, Jay suddenly awoke. Without actually seeing Elena, he sensed her presence and knew what he had to do. He would make a pasta dinner!

When Jay walked into the kitchen, he nearly tripped over a box of spaghetti on the floor, some three or four feet from the bottom shelf where it was normally stored. *What's going on here?* he wondered. He looked around carefully, not finding any reasonable way the spaghetti could have gotten where it was. Seeing the box of spaghetti in the middle of the kitchen floor literally made his skin "start to crawl" and his hair "stand straight up on end," which is most unusual, since he sprays his hair!

Jay admitted that in telling the story to his family and friends, he, in his typical style, embellished things just a bit by adding that there was a jar of Prego next to the spaghetti. Despite his added touch of humor in describing this event, Jay contends that the one thing he is sure of is that he was not dreaming. This was definitely a meaningful incident for Jay. He emphasized that although he had been a disbeliever and he knew that there would be those who would not believe his story, he was absolutely sure that his wife, Elena, had been there with him.

Just think for a moment what it would mean to you if your loved one had, in some way after her death, let you know that she was still with you, looking over your shoulder as in life, to be sure that you were taking care of yourself. Events such as these push us to consider the possibility that the soul does not die when the body dies. Not only do we give more thought to taking care of ourselves, but what also often occurs is that we begin to open ourselves up to exploring the meaning of these events in terms of our soul. Each time we give thought to such matters, we push the evolution of our soul just one more notch up on the ladder of our soul's development.

Protected with Love

Judy is the mother of a striking young woman, Kim, who herself was both a wife and mother of two young children. Unfortunately, Kim died unexpectedly of cardiac arrest several years before my meeting with Judy and her husband. Though numbed and stupefied by Kim's unanticipated death, all of those whom Kim left behind have, according to Judy, continued to experience her presence in some way. She was a devoted mother, wife, daughter and sister while she lived and has maintained her devotion to her family even after her death.

On a warm fall day, Judy and her husband sat with me in my office and painfully but lovingly shared several stories which demonstrated Kim's ongoing need to protect and watch over her loved ones, especially in times of danger. I recall how moved I was by their sense that Kim continues to be with them, despite her physically leaving them at the time of her death. My heart went out to this couple as they joyfully, even in their pain, spoke of situations in which they had felt a connection with their daughter.

Judy recalled an incident that had taken place several years before, which had involved her son, Matt. According to Judy, Matt and his fiancé, wanting to make the most of the unexpectedly mild autumn day, had decided to go for a ride in his Jeep. However, they had not thought to fasten their seat belts.

While they were both enjoying the yellow and red leaves twirling on the road, the Jeep suddenly hit something in the road, perhaps a brick or a very large rock. In a fraction of a second, Matt was thrown from the car. To make matters worse, he somehow became entangled in another vehicle and was dragged a good twenty feet before being run over. The whole thing was so horrible that onlookers who were present at the scene were sure he could not have survived and that he must have died.

Fortunately his fiancé, though dazed and bruised, was not injured. With the help of those who stopped to offer their assistance, an ambulance was called and Matt was taken to the trauma center of a nearby major hospital. The situation was bleak and did not look promising for Matt.

One can only imagine the amazement of everyone—the doctors, nurses and witnesses—when Matt was examined and found to have no bruises, no broken bones, not anything that was indicative of the horror to which he had been exposed. Surely, between having been thrown out onto the road, dragged by another car and then actually run over, it was reasonable to expect that Matt's body should have experienced significant trauma. But there was no indication anywhere of anything.

The whole thing seemed quite miraculous, which is what everyone was thinking. Everyone, that is, except Matt. During the entire time that he was being evaluated by the doctors and nurses, he kept repeating, "Kim is here. Kim is here, and she is holding me." No one knew what Matt was talking about. Most of those present thought he was delirious.

Matt, however, knew that if it had not been for Kim, the situation would have been much worse. Realistically, he probably would have died. In fact, it was Kim who most likely had cradled him in such a way that he was physically unharmed by the accident. Matt was well aware of this and of Kim's presence in the hospital. Both he and his family knew that he was alive thanks to Kim and her devoted protection.

Matt recovered rather quickly from the traumatic event, but what has continued to stay with him is the sense that Kim is always there for him and his family. He knows that, even though Kim physically died, she is with him, keeping him safe and out of harm's way. Matt considers his sister's presence to be an extraordinary gift for which he feels blessed and grateful.

Judy also described another story involving Matt and Kim. As she spoke of how close her children had been, despite the fact that Matt was six-and-a-half years younger than Kim, Judy became quiet, sad and tearful. It was difficult for her to talk about how Kim tended to be a second mother to her younger brother, and how much they had adored one another. Once again, my heart went out to Judy, identifying with her on a mother-to-mother level.

In this incident, Matt was out driving by himself on a bitter cold day. There had just been an ice storm and the roads were in terrible condition. A thin coat of ice covered most of the highway on which Matt was driving, making it difficult for him to keep his car on the road. It did not take long before he lost control of it. The car skidded on the ice, veered onto the shoulder, and was on the verge of diving down a thirty-foot drop. That's when it happened!

Just as Matt's car was about to go over the side, he saw Kim. Everything seemed to stand still. *It's Kim! It's really Kim!* he thought to himself. She had positioned herself in such a way that she blocked his car from going down the ravine. Thanks to her, his car came to a complete stop. Matt closed his eyes for a moment as he sat at the wheel, silently thanking God and Kim for saving his life. When he opened his eyes, his sister was gone—visually gone, that is. Though he initially questioned himself about whether he saw what he thought he saw, he knew without any doubt that it was Kim who was responsible for the fact that he was alive.

For the second time, Kim had made herself known to Matt in order to save his life. While there is no doubt that these experiences have brought great comfort to Matt and his family, they have also served as a validation of Kim's presence. It is this validation that is probably the greatest gift of all.

As I think back on these stories Judy that shared with me, I think of my patients, and especially those who have lost children. I believe that if I were such a parent, I would want to know of other parents who have had these experiences, because it would provide me with a sense of hope and perhaps reassurance that my child was all right and, perhaps, still with me.

Judy shared one more story about Kim and how she demonstrated her desire to keep a watchful eye over her mother. Judy recalls that about six months after Kim's death, she had had a shower to attend for a relative who lived in New Jersey. It was to take place on a Sunday afternoon during the middle of the summer, and she was looking forward to taking her time and making the trip there a relaxing experience.

However, the night before the shower, Judy had a vivid and memorable dream in which her daughter, Kim, had come to her. Kim had come with a clear, distinct message: Judy was not to go her usual way to the shower. Her route had to be changed. There was no explanation of the reason for the change, just the sense of urgency that her mother not travel the route she normally would have taken. The implication was clear that a longer route would be safer for Judy.

Upon awakening, Judy thought only briefly about the meaning of her dream. She knew that if Kim had come to her in a dream, there had to be a good reason. Thus, she allowed herself even more travel time than she normally would have to get to the shower. The day was warm and sunny, the scenery lush, making the ride much more relaxing.

When she arrived at the shower, everyone seemed to be talking about a horrific accident that had taken place on the highway. In fact, several of the guests were late because the accident had caused a major backup on the road. Unfortunately, this was an accident involving several fatalities.

Judy felt a chill run down her back when she heard this. She immediately and intuitively knew that she would have been involved in the accident had she gone the way she had originally planned to go. "Thank you, Kim, thank you, thank you!" she whispered. She felt a rush of overwhelming gratitude for her daughter's caring protection.

Certainly, Kim and Judy had shared a very special bond before Kim's death. From the stories Kim and her husband shared with me (some of which appear in this book), thanks to Kim's determination to look after her family, their close relationship has continued to be maintained. I can only imagine the extent of comfort that these experiences with their daughter provide Judy and her family.

Respecting and Honoring Close Calls

The more Denny and I talked, the more he found himself recalling extraordinarily close calls he had endured during his lifetime. Here are two that particularly stand out and fill him with a sense of awe and recognition that there is something at work and offering him protection.

One day, while driving on the turnpike during Den's first ten years of working as a state trooper, he was told to pursue and stop a vehicle that was traveling westbound at a rate of eighty to one hundred miles an hour. He waited on the eastbound side for the designated car to go by, and when it actually flew by, he made a fast U-turn into the westbound lane.

"So I began chasing it," he said. "I could see that the car was filled with young people—there were four or five heads and a long-haired person driving. It was daylight and the roads were dry, thank God! The car was a late model Plymouth.

"I am in the fast lane, approaching the truck they just passed. Well, the truck ends up on the berm. I am doing one hundred ten miles an hour and there is no way I can hit the brakes in time. I see the truck come down off the side of the embankment, flip over, land in the right lane and slide over into the left lane in front of me. It was so fast!

"I got through the hole somehow. I do not know how because the truck banged into the medial barrier. And as I looked back into the rear view mirror, I could see nothing but dust and dirt. You could not see vehicles or anything. All this stuff was flying—and the trailer broke open and everything was flying out of it. So I hit the brakes and the car got away. And I backed up—and there were three people who had been killed who had run into the back of the truck.

"I knew I had come close to death. But I did not start to register what happened until the following day when I began to shake as I realized how really close I had come to losing my life." But, he noted, he had not died—and that amazed him.

The second close call came at another time when Den was working radar and found himself in intense pursuit of a speeding car traveling at a hundred miles per hour. "I had come around a bend on an uphill grade under an overpass. At that speed, if you are chasing anyone as the pursuit driver, you are watching the car to see if brake lights come on. Sometimes, they slam the brakes on and try and outrun you, going the other way. They could not get away on the turnpike.

"So, I was watching the car, and instead of being in one lane or another, I was in the middle of the road, going up the broken line—sort of like Mario Andretti, the racetrack driver. I was trying to bank the turn so I wouldn't skid or anything. It was dry and it was evening.

"Suddenly, I saw these brown streaks go by out of the corner of my eye, one on each side of the car. I looked and there was nothing on the road. When I looked again in the rearview mirror, I saw two deer lying on the road. A buck and a doe had jumped off the bridge. Had I been in either lane they would have come through the windshield. They were both dead. So, I broke the chase and backed up to get off the road. It was on a curve and I feared they could cause another accident.

"Then I thought again, this is the second time that this has happened to me." With this, Den allowed himself to admit that perhaps he was being watched over by someone or something. It was just a thought, but he could not help considering the possibility, especially since the circumstances appeared to be so incredibly extraordinary.

Clearly, he recognizes that his "time" has not yet come. The bottom line is that these two incidents bring Den some level of peace and comfort. And this, considering the numerous times his rosary beads had been torn apart, feels good.

CHAPTER 10

Stories from the Women of 9/11

Death is but a transition from this life to another existence where there is no more pain and anguish. All the bitterness and disagreements will vanish, and the only thing that lives forever is love.

ELISABETH KÜBLER-ROSS, M.D.

In order to be a realist, you must believe in miracles.

DAVID BEN-GURION

Stories from the Women of 9/11

A little over a year and a half had passed since their husbands had died in the events of September 11th, 2001. As they sat in my office on a bitterly cold winter morning in late January 2003, Fiona Havlish and Ellen Saracini reflected on the ironies of life that had brought them together. Had it not been for the deaths of their husbands, these two women, who lived only minutes from one another, might never have known the gift of a friendship that felt more like that of closest kin than that of friend.

Neither Fiona nor Ellen had hesitated for even a moment to share their stories for this book. However, I doubt that either one had actually realized how the experience of doing this with one another would contribute to her own personal and spiritual growth and awareness. Both have come to appreciate the finely-tuned nuances of their shared journeys of life.

While the stories in this section are those of Fiona (also called Mikki) and Ellen, there are moments when these two women talk warmly of their relationship with several other women who are also widows of husbands who died in the destruction of the World Trade Center. The stories of some of these women will be told further on in this book. What is important here is the manner in which these women have bonded and the meaning which they bring to their relationship. One might think of them as belonging to a unique sorority, one with extremely demanding rules for membership. Clearly, it is the nature of the circumstances that only they, and relatively few others in the population, share that have contributed to their bonding so tightly and powerfully.

While I worked with Fiona and Ellen, I realized they were gradually beginning to feel secure enough in their relationship with me to share some of their most precious moments in which they had experienced a genuine sense of connection with their spouses. They and Clara Chicherella and Tara Bane (yes, these are their real names), two other wives whose husbands died in the World Trade Center, sat down with me to make a recording of their stories so that others might find comfort, as they have, in learning of the innovative ways deceased loved ones find to convey their love and presence.

Clocks, Lights and Airplanes Communicate "I'm Here!"

According to Fiona, the first time she absolutely knew that Don, her husband of eight years, was with her occurred during the early afternoon hours of the 21st of September, just eleven days following the events of September 11th. She recalls that there were a number of people in the house who were suddenly surprised by the chiming of a clock. These included Don's closest friend, Danny, as well as Don's sister, Susan, and the house-cleaning staff. Since the televisions sets all over the house were on at the time the clock was chiming, Fiona thought that perhaps the chimes were coming from one of the sets. She walked into the den to check the television set for this.

She looked first at Susan and Danny, who were in that room, asking them if they had touched or wound the clock. Danny said, "Absolutely not. That's Don's clock. I would not touch it." Susan also responded that she had not touched it. At this point, all the cleaning staff stopped working and had congregated near Fiona. She then turned to them and asked if anyone had touched the clock. They answered that they had not even dusted it.

Fiona had been counting the chimes from the first chime on. There were ten chimes. Don had died at 10:00 A.M. Given that the only person who ever touched the clock had been Don, and that it had not been touched or wound in eight months to a year, Fiona knew that the chiming of the clock was her husband telling her he had died at 10:00 and, more important, that he was there with them. From then on, for the next seven days, the clock chimed every hour—always ten chimes on the hour.

The clock, she said, was immensely comforting for her. She would awaken daily and run down to see if the clock was still ticking. She cried when the week was over and the clock actually stopped. Why? Because she initially feared that Don had left, although she now feels that probably was not the case. In fact, she emphasizes that she had truly believed that he was there—in their home—with her and their family. This was the validation she needed. She had craved his presence, and the clock represented this for her. It was a precious gift, coming at the most crucial time in her life.

Hearing this, Ellen was reminded of the manner in which her husband, Victor, had let his family and her know that he was still with them. She recalls that during that first week following September 11th, there were many, many people in her home. Friends and family were busy working on the preparations for the memorial service. Lights were on everywhere in their home.

In the middle of their planning, they began to notice that the light bulbs were burning out throughout their home. The lights burning out were beginning to get in the way of their work, which is what led them to take notice of the fact that there were seven light bulbs that had burned out in two days. That was when Ellen realized that this was Victor's doing.

Victor had two favorite expressions: "Close the door," and "Shut the lights off." Their parakeet imitated only what was frequently said, and "Turn off the lights" was one the bird's favorite expressions, thanks to Vic. Everyone then knew that Vic was both present and upset by the lights being on. It was Ellen's sister, Joni, who took it upon herself to go through the house shutting off the lights while talking to Vic, saying, "Vic, you don't have to worry. I know that it's you. I know that this bothers you. I love that you are here but you don't have to worry. I will go around and shut the lights off for you." They then replaced all the bulbs and made a point of shutting off all the lights when not in use.

According to Ellen, during the same time period, Vic found another way to convey his presence to her. Victor had an alarm clock that he loved because it had sounds such as crickets, waves and wind, which would both comfort him and help him fall asleep. Ellen said that she would usually ask him to turn if off, because he would fall asleep while the clock kept her from sleeping.

A few days after September 11th, she recalled that she was trying to sleep. She was sharing the bed with her sister, who had not wanted to leave Ellen alone for the first few days. Suddenly they were awakened early one morning by the sound of crickets. Neither she nor her sister had set the alarm, and it had not been set in at least a couple of days. This, she knew, was Victor, finding his own way to connect with her. It felt good, very good.

About a month or two later, when everyone had finally left Ellen's home and she was able to be by herself, with her own thoughts, she again felt Victor finding his unique way to express his presence and love. On a warm, late fall day, she was sitting and having a cup of coffee in one of her favorite places, her patio in her backyard. She recalls that she was sitting, crying and thinking, *Victor, where are you? Why did you leave?* She recalls that she was trying to comfort herself and realized that he was actually more prepared for his death than she would have been. The bottom line: she was looking for something, a sign that represented a connection with him, because she was so lonely and so full of pain.

Suddenly, Ellen said, she noticed a plane coming from her right and going to her left. Before it left her view, another plane from the left came in, flying to the right. And before that plane was out of her view, another plane flew in from her right going to her left. In seeing the three planes, she was struck by the sense that the three planes had to do with her family—Ellen and her two daughters. She felt that the three planes were Victor's way of lovingly telling Ellen that life was going to be about a family of three and that he was no longer going to be a physical part of their lives. This was a bitter-sweet moment for Ellen because the meaning of the connection to her was actually one of disconnection. I recall that all three of us—Ellen, Fiona and I—were moved to tears as she shared this story.

Ellen's telling of this particular story reminded Fiona of a similar situation involving her kitchen light and Don. Evidently, just a week before September 11th, Fiona had asked Don to replace all of the eight fluorescent light bulbs in the kitchen. Even after replacing the bulbs, they noticed that the light failed to work without problems. There always seemed to be problems with the light—until September 11th.

Fiona, recalls coming home, after hearing of the planes crashing into the World Trade Center, and finding that she had absolutely no problems with the kitchen light when she flipped the light switch on. It was not until two days later that it dawned on her that the light had worked perfectly since September 11th. She even remembered quietly thanking Don for making the lights work, since she did not have the strength or patience to fix lights at that point.

A Club of Their Own

As Fiona and Ellen spoke openly of their experiences involving their husbands, they emphatically stated their shared belief that their spouses were together, just as they were. They went on to describe events that supported their belief. It was delightful to listen to their spirited conversation about these experiences. It was also moving to hear these two women state that they believed their connection was at the soul level, and that they felt their husbands had a lot to do with bringing them together.

Ellen went on to say that she believes that Victor planned for his death not only in terms of the normal logistical planning, but also for a support system for Ellen and his girls. They told a story that had some evidence that Don, Fiona's husband, and Victor, Ellen's husband, hung out together as spirits. This took place during Ellen's visit to my friend, Samantha, who is extremely gifted intuitively. The visit came during a time that Fiona had been hospitalized. Ellen, Tara and Suzanne (another wife whose husband had died in the World Trade Center) had formed a tight support system to assist Fiona, who had become seriously ill with complications from pneumonia. This resulted in Fiona having two surgeries within two weeks. It was in the days preceding Fiona's first surgery that Ellen had gone to see Samantha, hoping to connect with Victor.

As Ellen tells the story, much to her surprise, it was Don, Fiona's husband, who showed up initially. "I wanted so much to talk to Victor about my issues and who shows up? Don! Victor isn't even there! The first words out of Samantha's mouth are 'Do you know a Don or Donald?'"

Ellen said that she answered, "Yes," but was thinking, *It is all about Fiona! I still want Vic to talk to me about my issues and he isn't even there!* All of this was said with a smile but with a feeling of annoyance.

Ellen continued her story. "Well," Samantha said, "He needs for you to do him a favor. He needs for you to give Fiona flowers, specifically the color violet as well as multiple colors." Ellen went on, "And I had to give them to her, and I had to show her or kiss her in a certain way three times, on the forehead, the nose and then the lips.

"We continued on with this conversation. It is still about Don. Michael, Tara's husband, came in and said his typical few words. Vic also eventually arrived. So, the three of them did come during this reading. And Don comes back, knowing that I tend to forget things." Ellen shrugs and takes a breath. "Again, he asked if I would do this favor for him. I then went out to get these flowers and brought them to Fiona. When I went to the hospital, Suzanne and Tara were there with Fiona who was in bed, and I remember saying, 'Oh great, all three of them are there today.'"

Fiona picked up the thread of the story. "I needed to know that I was going to make it, and this was Don's way of letting me know that I was going to be okay. There was a part of me that was not so sure of this by the time the second surgery came around. That was such a hard experience for me that by that point, I was ready to quit."

The bottom line here, for these women, is that they strongly believe that their husbands are often together.

Fiona then went on to substantiate this by describing the first time she had gone to see my friend Samantha. She described the visit as something she would never forget. Samantha began to talk about seeing fire, about falling and about being hit on the head. At one point, Samantha put her hands up and made the motions of what appeared to be a window, causing Fiona to wonder if this might be the window in front of Don's desk. But Samantha stared at a point and described an almost circular motion. Fiona then thought, *This is the wrong kind of window. It's not flat. That's not the kind of window Don would be looking out of.*

Samantha continued on, sharing with Fiona the impressions she was intuiting or receiving. While some of the material Samantha discussed with Fiona provided absolute evidence that Don was present, Fiona was feeling some confusion because some of the information offered her did not seem to match up with Don's life, but rather seemed to belong to the life experience of Ellen's husband, Victor. Victor Saracini had been the pilot of the first plane that the terrorists flew into the World Trade Center.

I later learned from Samantha that she, too, had been extremely confused by the information she was receiving. Her intuition was telling her that something was not right and that she may have been receiving information that was not meant for Fiona but for someone else. Not having had any pre-knowledge of the circumstances surrounding Fiona or Ellen, Samantha was, herself, briefly befuddled.

The confusion was soon cleared up. Unknown to Fiona, Ellen had scheduled time to meet with Samantha in the hour following Fiona's meeting with her. Fiona later learned that Samantha had shared with Ellen almost the same material, which is when she realized that it had been Victor who had come in with Don and had shown Samantha what had taken place, **from his perspective,** as pilot of the plane that hit the Tower.

My belief is that Victor, being nonphysical, was aware that Ellen would be meeting with Samantha. Excited about the opportunity to communicate with his wife, he, to use a cliché that is appropriate here, beat Don to the punch in order to share his story with Fiona, Ellen's good friend. Don then stepped in to speak with Samantha, after Victor had finished, with details of his own story. This is what caused confusion for everyone. Samantha was receiving information from two different nonphysical beings.

What these women have learned from their experiences in talking not only with Samantha but also with others who are highly intuitive, is that their husbands are, without a doubt, together. They believe this because the information offered to them has been exceptionally meaningful and unknown to the rest of the world. It tickles them that their husbands appear to enjoy being with one another. In Ellen's words, "It is a very comforting thought for us to know that our husbands are together, just as we, their widows, are."

Ellen continued, "But it also validates for me that we are all together for a reason, too, and that this was our destiny, that this was preplanned long ago and that we probably chose this. Go figure why we would choose this! I believe my life is getting better and better. My life was great before, and I hope I will again be able to one day feel my life is great. I do believe, though, that I knew about this before and that this serves a purpose. Hopefully, we are learning lessons from this."

Both Fiona and Ellen agreed that the experiences of September 11th have changed them and have greatly enhanced their spiritual journey while here on earth. They sat thinking aloud how each of them has been impacted spiritually by their life changes. Both women acknowledged that Ellen had been fairly spiritual, as was Victor, before September 11th. Fiona, on the other hand, admitted that she had taken a hiatus of twenty some years from the spiritual pursuits of her late teen years. The result of being married to a husband who laughed at her interest in spiritual matters and was extremely logical was that she chose to put anything dealing with spirituality on hold. However, the events of September 11th have contributed to a rebirth of her passionate interest in all that is spiritual.

Timing Is Everything

One of my favorite stories regarding extraordinary connections with loved ones comes from Ellen. She shared this story during our session. According to her, she had an opportunity to be involved with APSA (The Airline Pilots Security Alliance), a new organization of pilots whose main intention is to handle security issues, with special attention to arming the pilots to protect them from terrorists who attempt to break down the door to the cockpit. Given that Ellen's husband died as the result of an unsecured cockpit, and the fact that she is in a position in which she has been the center of the public's attention as the surviving wife of a pilot who was killed by the terrorists, Ellen believes that she is obligated to assume responsibility for assisting the pilots in their fight to be armed.

"I wanted to, I felt that I had to and I felt that I should; so I chose to help them." These were her very words. However, she felt that she needed a sign from Vic as an indication that he not only approved of what she was doing, but that what she was doing was "good and right." She asked Vic to help her by giving her a sign.

She was to be interviewed on Fox television while in Washington. She recalls that as she was entering the lobby, she had to sign her name and the date. Not having a watch on because she believes time does not really exist, a thought identical to that of the quantum physicists, she looked over to the guard and asked for the time.

What followed were those two words that had changed her world forever. The guard quietly responded, "Nine-eleven." The words stunned her, causing her to stop, take a deep breath and register what she had just heard. She thought, *Nine-eleven. Thank you, Victor, Thank you.* She knew that this was the validation she had requested. *He is here,* she thought, *and he is definitely supporting our efforts.*

With this, she looked over to the other two pilots who were signing in and asked them, "Did you hear what the guard just said? Did you hear that?" She asked again. The two pilots had heard the words "Nine-eleven" but had not really been paying attention. When Ellen asked them again, they took note and they smiled.

Without saying a word, Ellen and the two pilots seemed to understand that the synchronicity of hearing those two words at that very moment was too meaningful to have been a coincidence. They were all aware that something extraordinary had just taken place. Ellen was filled with joy. She believed that Victor had not only chosen this way to convey his presence, but also to indicate that the pilots would meet with success in their fight to arm all pilots.

Later that afternoon, as the two pilots took Ellen to the train station, she recalled turning to them and saying, "This will happen. This may take some time, but it will go through. I know it will because I received a sign today from Vic." With this, she climbed onto the train with an enormous sense of peace and calm. Victor had spoken to her.

For Love of Bonsais

Ellen went on to tell us this delightful story that deals with bonsais. On one of his many flights to and from Japan, Vic had purchased and brought home a bonsai that he highly valued and cherished. Because he traveled so often, it was usually left to Ellen to care for the bonsai. Well, the bonsai died while Vic was away. Ellen was certain that the bonsai had begun turning brown and dying before Vic left, but neither one of them had taken real note of that fact. Concerned that Victor would return home and find the tree completely brown and dead, and that he would probably blame her for its demise, Ellen became creative and developed a plan to deal with the situation. She went to the garage, found a can of green paint and thought, *How perfect!* She then took the totally brown and dead bonsai and began to spray it green—from the top on down to its base.

Ellen honestly thought Vic would not notice that his beloved bonsai had died. She truly did not wish to upset him after his return home from a tough trip. Unfortunately, things did not go as she had hoped.

Victor came in, totally depleted, not in the greatest of moods, and yes, his eyes were immediately drawn to his newly painted bonsai. Without hesitating for even a moment, he exploded, *"What the Hell did you do to my bonsai?"* Obviously, things were not running as smoothly as Ellen would have liked.

However, despite Victor's reaction, he gave Ellen a chance to explain all that had led up to the moment he discovered the tree. Within hours, he had processed his disappointment and let the whole thing go, to the point that he, too, could laugh about the saga of his bonsai tree. Ellen laughed as she told this story, one that had become a source of laughter for them over the years.

Ellen followed this story with a number of others that substantiated how important the bonsai was to Victor and how much she associated him with the bonsai. Since Victor's death, Ellen has, she believes, been gifted with bonsai trees. At Christmas, for example, she said that her financial advisor, Chris, had chosen a bonsai for her, something that she felt was a bit unusual. Not long afterwards, while working with Bob, one of the pilots who was committed to arming the pilots, she received as a gift for a special occasion a bonsai. This individual, like Chris, had no idea of her interest in bonsais.

It hit her then that the gifts of the bonsai trees were Vic's way of letting her know that he was pleased with the people with whom she was working, including her financial advisor and the pilot, and that what she was doing with them was good. The message that she felt coming from Victor, was, "I should be doing what I am doing. I should be working with my financial advisor, Chris, and I should be working to arm the pilots, and this man, Bob, is a good man as well." After learning that the pilots were indeed going to be armed, she received another bonsai from Bob who, according to Ellen, being very spiritual, had come to understand the powerful meaning of the bonsai for Ellen.

An Upside-Down Christmas

Fiona and Ellen seemed to melt into a place of warmth and comfort as they fell into the rhythmic flow of communicating thoughts, feelings and stories surrounding their shared experiences, which they knew belonged to only a few. They were delighted, smiling and laughing as they described how their second Christmas without their husbands was significantly different and better than the year before following the events of September 11th, 2001. I joined in their mirth as they described their determination to make Christmas a symbol of finding joy in the midst of the most "upside-down" time in their lives.

"What better way to get through Christmas during an upside down time in our lives than to have an upside-down Christmas tree!" exclaimed Ellen. This was the sentiment shared by these women. The idea of such a tree felt as absolutely perfect as the idea of being together at a time when they did not feel the Christmas spirit in their hearts. Ellen said that she remembered her sister, Susan, at the party she had given for Victor's birthday, describing her custom of having an upside-down Christmas tree. The thought of this immediately grabbed the imagination of these women. It felt so right. For those of you who may wonder how this is done, this is how they described it to me.

First, put a well-shaped evergreen tree into a planter. Then place a dowel straight up the trunk, attach it, plant it in the planter upside down, put a bow on the top of the tree (which is the bottom of the tree) and then decorate the branches with ornaments.

The tree that these women created that second Christmas was for them the most meaningful symbol of both the holiday and of their present life situation. Ellen and Fiona spoke with great enthusiasm and excitement as they described their Christmas that they shared with one other friend and 9/11 widow, Tara Bane. The idea of sharing Christmas, of being together for a holiday that carried with it painful reminders, was so comforting for each of them. Although they were pained by the awareness of their losses, they felt they had much to celebrate, especially regarding their blessings of family, friendships and accomplishments. And, of course, they wanted to convey the spirit of Christmas to their children.

Fiona smiled warmly as she thought of Christmas Day 2002. She recalled that having just come home from the hospital after two difficult lung surgeries, she had little energy or enthusiasm for anything dealing with Christmas. However, she knew as she spoke with Don on Christmas Eve, after everyone had gone to bed that Christmas had to happen properly for her little one, Michaela, in order for her to be happy. She pushed herself to finish wrapping the stocking stuffers and finally went to bed at 2:00 A.M.

According to Fiona, Michaela came running into her bedroom Christmas morning, awakening her at 8:00 A.M., squealing, "Mommy, Mommy, I was a good girl! Santa came!" Fiona recalls looking at her, noticing that for the first time she was not feeling great pain, that she was feeling really good and that she was genuinely happy.

"Go ahead and open the presents by your bedroom door. Mommy is going to take a shower, and then we'll go downstairs and open presents." Because Fiona was still recovering from her surgery, she needed a good half hour to shower and dress. By the time she was ready to go downstairs, Michaela was nowhere to be found upstairs.

As Fiona walked into the dining room, where the Christmas tree had been set up, she was blown away by the sight of *every* present under the tree belonging to *everyone* having already been torn open. Admittedly, she became upset. However, in just seconds her anger gave way to uncontrollable laughter. She realized that this was what she had been hoping for, an entirely different Christmas.

According to Fiona, "To start with I hadn't wanted Christmas. I wanted it to be completely different. One of the reasons it was so unique was that it was the first time I had to make my child sit down and show me every present since I had not done any of the shopping. Being in the hospital, Tara and Ellen had bought everything and Tara had done all the wrapping. I had no idea what she had received! It was great and the most topsy-turvy, happy Christmas ever!"

*C*lub Membership Qualifications

Fiona and Ellen continued their sharing. It suddenly dawned on Fiona, shortly after my asking Ellen if she wore a watch, that she, too, never wore a watch. "It was like time did not mean anything to me anymore. Period. I found my watch about a week ago and I realized, after putting it on, that I do not even look at it, and I do not even have a clock at my bedside anymore." With this statement suddenly came a memory of a story about her alarm clock, not too different from that told by Ellen earlier in the session.

"After September 11th, I put Michaela in my bed. I did not want her to be alone—and I don't think I wanted to be alone, either. I did not remember that Don's usual custom was to turn off his alarm, and then reset it for the next morning. On the morning of the 12th, the alarm went off and I jumped out of bed just like normal, thinking I was going downstairs to make a cup of coffee. Suddenly, I felt this horrible sense come over me and I knew things were not normal. I ran around the bed and turned off the alarm. I turned it off. I did not reset it. And it did not go off for two or three days.

"However, several days later, the alarm went off again. I ran around the house, asking everyone if anyone had touched the alarm. Why, I do not know because *no one* touched Don's stuff. NO ONE—not even Michaela. That's when I knew that Don was absolutely there."

Both women realized, as they spoke, that the similarities among the families were impressive. "Things are beginning to click as we are sitting here," noted Fiona. For example, they realized that both their husbands played the guitar and were also interested in getting a piano for their families. In fact, Fiona mentioned that Don had wanted to get a piano every time the community college had a piano sale, first for her and then for Michaela. Ellen commented, "Vic did the same thing."

Fiona asked Ellen, "Did Vic take his watch off when he was not working?" Before Ellen answered, Fiona interrupted, "Boy, as soon as Don walked in the house on a Friday night, I would see him take off his watch. There was no time on vacation. When there was no work, there was no watch." Ellen recalled that Vic felt the same way. Vic wore his watch when working but rarely while home or on vacation, unless he needed to get to a function by a certain time.

As for the lights, they both concurred that that their husbands had found a way to communicate their presence via either burning out the lights or by maintaining them! In either situation, the message was a comfortable one.

When Numbers Speak to Us

With the passing of time, both women spoke of their awareness of specific numbers reappearing in their lives—especially the numbers 11 and 13. While Ellen was the first to bring up the "11 stuff," Fiona was immediately reminded of her frequent encounters with the number 13. Actually, she pointed out that the number 13 did not start actively showing up in her life until she had met with her pastor to plan Don's funeral. Doug, her pastor, had said, "Okay, pick a date." Fiona then said that she wanted it to be on a Friday. Doug looked down at his calendar and then up at her and said, "Let's make it Friday the 13th." And Fiona burst into laughter. "Well, that's perfect. What better day!" she said. From that point on, the number 13 kept popping up.

When Ellen made the comment that the number 11 continued to show up, Fiona said that she had really begun to pay attention to the numbers 11 and 13. Fiona also noted that she had heard that 13 is sometimes associated with death. Fortunately, 13 has no longer been appearing in Fiona's life since leaving the hospital, on December 20th, after her surgeries.

Following her hospitalization, the number 11, often in the form of double elevens, has been coming up frequently for Fiona as well as for Ellen. Ellen said that she has become conscious of the circumstances in which the number 11 shows itself, wondering about when and why it pops up. Ellen found the number 11 appearing when she would ask the universe questions about something she was about to do.

"I take eleven as a good sign," said Ellen. For example, when she was going to meet a gentleman and wondering whether she was doing a good thing or not, she looked at the clock and there was the number 11, a sign she took to be a positive answer to her question. When she actually met the man, the number 11 again came up. For Ellen, then, number 11 has become a meaningful communication from the universe and, perhaps, from her Vic.

What Fiona realizes at this point is that the number 13 may have been a warning and a message to "Please pay attention and take care of yourself. This is not a good thing." Since leaving the hospital, the number 13 no longer shows up. She feels that Don was warning her to take care of herself and no longer needs to warn her to do this because she is now taking good care of herself.

A Sense of Urgency

As the days, weeks and months pass following the loss of their husbands on September 11th, 2001, both Ellen and Fiona acknowledge that they seemed to have been living life with a sense of urgency. Ellen explained that though she recognizes that she has lost some of her sense of needing to do everything immediately, she has maintained a sense of urgency regarding anything having to do with arming pilots. The good thing, however, is that she now feels she really does not need to be rushing through life.

Fiona, on the other hand, admitted that she no longer has a sense of physical urgency regarding life. The urgency of having to do things right now left her following her recent close call with death that included her hospitalization and surgeries. However, she has, since 9/11, experienced a sense of spiritual rebirth and an urgency to recover the spiritual aspects of her being that she had buried throughout much of her life.

She spoke of now feeling an urgency, a hunger and a thirst to expand her knowledge by reading books, talking to people and learning in any way she can of her connection to her soul and that which is divine. "Sometimes, I get so frustrated. I cannot get enough of the material. I go and buy several books at a time. I open a book to a page, feeling that every page has something to teach me. I sleep with books. I must have close to ten on my bed. They are in every one of my spaces." Fiona laughed as she shared all of this with Ellen and me, and especially as she noted that she was in need of bookshelves for her new book collection. I laughed along with Fiona because she was expressing my own thoughts and feelings, which I had experienced many times throughout the past fifteen years of my own life.

It was while Fiona spoke of things that she had not told anyone before that Ellen realized that she herself was now able to do the very thing that Vic had encouraged her to do while he was alive, but had difficulty doing. He had urged her to talk more about her feelings, something she is comfortable doing now with her dear friends, all surviving wives of 9/11, because she feels genuinely accepted and loved. With these women and with her therapist, she noted, "I can tell intimate things without feeling anguish or holding back, and I feel I can tell everything. I am allowed to mess up, and you will still love me." This is an extremely powerful awareness for Ellen and a gift she has given herself that serves her and her family.

$\mathcal{A}$ Blend of All Equals One

Having worked with Ellen, Fiona and several other wives whose husbands died in the World Trade Center, I have become unmistakably convinced of the degree of strength each of these women finds in their friendship with one another, and of the stunning growth and development apparent as each woman discovers her own unique identity. The gift of their friendship has provided the roots and the grounding upon which they stand to grow into the fabulously evolved beings that they are.

While we were talking about the unusually close relationship of Fiona, Ellen and some of the other 9/11 wives, Fiona shared the following story. She said that while she was about to be wheeled away for her first lung surgery in December 2002, her surgeon, Dr. Raudat, having observed the tight, supportive friendship of Fiona and her precious friends, had asked where her cohorts were because he felt she needed them with her. When she replied that they were all together, praying for her, he responded, "That's a good thing and something that will truly help you. We all need to be in touch with our spirituality."

Fiona had been impressed with her doctor for realizing the spiritual importance and value of human relationships. She knew she and her friends were as one, and, to her delight, her doctor had a strong sense of this as well. In fact, she felt Dr. Raudat's behavior was a powerful indicator that doctors in general were becoming more open and compassionate.

As I thanked Fiona and Ellen for the opportunity to interview them for this book, and we said goodbye to one another, we all acknowledged how powerful an experience the interview had been for each of us, not unlike the whole 9/11 experience. What had become more evident than ever was the way in which each of their lives had been exquisitely intertwined with one another and with the others who had lost their spouses and children, very much like beautiful silken threads of delicate yet resilient yarn which are woven into creations of magnificent golden tapestries.

While these women continue to heal, they are becoming beacons of light, a light that radiates a glow of warmth, peace, joy and love and that has the power to serve humanity by deeply touching the souls of those who seek well-being. They are examples of alchemy; they are showing us how we can change by moving beyond the unexpected adversities of life. Their lives are demonstrations that we are not necessarily our life experience, our thoughts or our emotions. We all have the potential to be so much more than we can imagine. These women are determined to live in the now, the moment, recognizing that this is where their strength and their power reside. They are our teachers and we are their students. How fortunate we all are!

CHAPTER **11**

More Stories from the Women of 9/11

It is not possible that we should remember that we existed before our body, for our body can bear no trace of such existence, neither can eternity be defined in terms of time or have any relation to time. But notwithstanding, we feel and know that we are eternal.

BARUCH SPINOZA

There is a dark night through which the soul passes in order to attain the Divine Light.

ST. JOHN OF THE CROSS

More Stories from the Women of 9/11

On a cold winter afternoon in February 2003, Clara Chirch-irillo and Tara Bane, wives of men who had died in the World Trade Center on 9/11, met with me in my office. They shared their stories of extraordinary moments in which they had each experienced a connection of some sort: either the presence of their spouses, or some specific communication from them regarding something significant in their lives. Though they had every reason to come with sadness and their pain, both women displayed a remarkable sense of humor as well as a deep, spiritual understanding of the events of 9/11/01.

Hellos and Goodbyes

As I have indicated previously, there are so many ways in which departed loved ones let us know they are with us. Clara began our session by sharing that she knew that her husband, Peter, had been with her during the process of buying a home in Florida. The search had not been easy, but she had no difficulty in recognizing the perfect home for her and her boys. It was a lovely home with a weeping willow on the front lawn, facing the lake. Weeping willow trees had long been favorites of Clara, probably because that tree represents qualities she most associates with Peter. Her love for weeping willows is rooted in seeing them as symbolic of Peter: seeing the tree as "very strong and yet gentle," and when full grown, "majestic and almost bigger than life"—just as Peter was.

However, after telling the realtor she wanted the house and then returning home, Clara was immediately filled with doubts and fears. She wondered if she had done "the right thing." Relief came for her when she went to mass. According to Clara, during the service, all the readings had to do with St. Peter and dealt with the fact that change is good and that we must keep going forward, no matter what. She felt that the pastor had been speaking directly to her. This, she knew, was Peter's way of letting her know that he was supporting her. To top everything off, the papers related to the purchase of the house arrived in the mail on her late husband's birthday.

Clara needed these signs of support because she was entirely overwhelmed by having to do all the paperwork solo. This aspect reminded her once again that Peter was really gone. He had always been the one in their partnership to handle this kind of paperwork, so the signs of his presence were especially meaningful to her.

Tara then recalled the first time after 9/11 that she had a sense of connection with her husband, Michael. On the morning of September 11th, at the exact time the plane had hit Tower One, she was at home, rushing to get to work and to squeeze in some errands beforehand. It was while she was dashing out of the house that she felt a persistent need to call Michael. It was so strong that she rushed back in, thinking, *I have to call him and talk to him.* After dialing his number, she was unable to get through to him but did not think anything of it at the time. Yet in the weeks following September 11th, she revisited those minutes when she felt that urgent need to call and talk with him.

She is convinced that Michael was connecting with her and trying to communicate with her during those moments when she had the need to talk with him. They had been connected, even if only for a moment. Their love for one another had provided the intuitive wisdom for Tara to need to speak with Michael and for him to speak with her.

With these words, Clara was reminded of the last time she saw Peter. She said: "It was on the 11th, at twelve o'clock exactly, that I got to say goodbye to Peter. He came to say goodbye to me. I saw him. I absolutely saw him. I was sitting on my living room couch. The television was on. I don't know what made me look at the clock, but it was twelve o'clock. He came over to me, he hugged me, and he said goodbye. And as I was holding him, I saw my mother from a distance. It was the second time since she died that I had seen her, and she waved to me. She did not say a word. She smiled, and she waved him on. He never said anything to me, and they both left. They were gone! I don't remember him letting go of me or them walking away from me."

When I asked Clara if she could feel his hug, she responded, "Absolutely, without a doubt. That was when everyone in the house thought I had gone ballistic. After he left me alone, whatever I said or did, I don't remember. It worried them and that is when they called the doctor. They thought I needed sedatives. But, from that point on I knew he was gone. I would not allow them to make any more phone calls; I would not let them post anything because I knew he was gone. No one had to tell me after that. I just knew. It was exactly twelve o'clock. I knew. There was no need to look."

"And hugs were significant," she said. "The only time he hugged me was when I really, really needed it, because he was not a hugger." She began to mimic him as she talked of Peter's dislike of showing affection in public. Laughing, she spoke the words that might have been Peter's thoughts: "People can *see*. Oh my God! You know, we can't do *that*!"

When Tara heard this, she could not help but laugh aloud, just as I did. Then she added, "So he waited till you were alone!"

But as Tara said these words, it was as though a light bulb had suddenly gone off in Clara's head. She said that she had not been able to figure out why Peter had not come to her until twelve o'clock. She chose to believe that his death was instantaneous and that he had no idea of what had hit him. Now she understood. Twelve o'clock was the first time Clara had been alone, and Peter must have seized that opportunity to then come to her. She laughed heartily, stating, "Yes, maybe that's it!"

When I asked about the other time she had seen her mom, she said that it had been in a dream at a time when she and Peter were about to move to Pennsylvania. It came immediately after purchasing a home there. In her words, "Again, panic set in that we were making the worst decision of our lives. Here we were leaving Brooklyn to move to a smaller home: from an absolutely detached single house in Brooklyn, to an attached house in Pennsylvania. It was not what I had expected and I panicked. Generally I do not remember my dreams, but I remember waking up that morning, calling Peter and telling him, 'Okay, we can go through with this,' and he responded, "Oh, can we now! Why is that?"

Clara responded to Peter with a description of what she had seen in her dream. She said: "Well, because my mom came to me. She was walking with a shopping cart. She passed our parish church, and all she did was look at me in the doorway and smile, and she kept walking. I knew that meant we could move to Pennsylvania." She shrugged and lifted her eyebrows as she said this. While Peter had not been able to figure out the connection, Clara said that she simply knew the meaning of her mom's coming to her that night had to do with her mom giving her the OK for the move.

As often happens in combined tapings, Tara, upon hearing her friend's story, shared a treasured dream of her own mom. She recalled that at nineteen, her mom, at forty-four, had died suddenly from a heart attack. Tara felt good knowing that she had been with her mom the night before her death.

According to Tara, she had been alone in her room, crying as she grieved for her mom. In the midst of her pain and tears, she experienced her mom's presence. In her words: "I did not see her, but I felt her presence. It was as if a breeze came through the room. I felt this presence brush up against me. I did not see her, but I just knew it was her. I did not tell anyone for years until I took a Death and Dying course while going for my master's degree. All of this stuff was coming up in class and I just shared it. I am not just going crazy," she said as she recounted the experience.

When I asked her how long her mother had stayed, she answered: "It was quick. It was like a gentle glance through the room, but it warmed me. It was what I needed at the time."

Tara admitted that she had always felt that she would see her mom again. She would often pray to her mom, believing her to be her angel, someone who would always be there for her and someone to whom she could offer prayers. When Michael died, she was plagued with doubts as to whether he would be there for her. In fact, she found herself doubting her whole belief system. It was more difficult for her to believe that he would be there for her both in this lifetime and after her death. However, she said that she is now beginning to be comfortable with the belief that he is around her all the time and that he will always be there for her.

These words triggered in Clara a thought regarding the Eric Clapton song, *Will You Know Me?* It was a song that moved her deeply, touching her heart and her memories of Peter. Tara agreed. Both women also stated that they often listen to music that touches their sadness. In fact, in Tara's words: "I don't think I listened to music for a long time, and when I did, I listened to music that made me cry." Both women acknowledged that certain songs affect them differently at times. But both agreed that, even if they know they are going to cry, they do not wish to turn the music off. The song is their connection to their husbands, a connection they treasure.

Sweet and "Not So Sweet" Dreams

Tara said that she had another dream of Michael about six weeks after his death. She admitted that she had been disappointed that he had not come sooner, given that her mom had come to her in a dream almost immediately after her death. Feeling frustrated, she said that she sometimes would ask him, "Why aren't you coming to me?" Then she would add, "Mom came to me right away."

Tara described seeing herself in her dream as being extremely anxious and worried about her future as well as her present situation. There she was, on one end of the couch, and there Michael was, relaxing, on the other end. She saw herself asking Michael, "What am I going to do? How am I going to manage things?" She reported that he replied calmly, "Don't worry about it. Everything will be fine." That exchange was typical of the two of them, she noted. She would be uptight and anxious, and he would be relaxed and confident about how things would turn out.

Clara and I exchanged glances as Tara commented: "I remember right away feeling as though this was not going to be a great dream because I wanted more from him!" She quickly realized that she had gotten just what she needed in this dream—and that she was excited about his coming to her. *It's him! It's him!* had thundered in her head. She knew the dream had been a gift, providing her with a sense of comfort and needed peace.

Not all dreams were happy experiences for her. Since that first dream, she said that Michael periodically has come in and out of her dreams. She admitted, "Sometimes it feels good, and sometimes it does not feel good at all." She stated that since losing Michael, she has also dreamed of her mom. This is often the case. When we lose a loved one, we often dream of other loved ones who have died.

Once again, Clara recalled a special connection with Peter. Actually it was, up to that point, the only time Peter had come to her in a dream. It had been a particularly vivid and clear dream. What made the dream special was that although it occurred after 9/11—and after Peter's death—"It was," she said, "a pre-9/11 dream and it felt pre-9/11. It felt really good." In the dream, she and Peter had been talking and kidding with one another while in bed. She said that they were teasing each other about putting cameras in their room to see who took up the greater part of the bed during the night. They each swore the other took up most of the bed. In her dream, he actually fell off the bed!

Her sons had always taken their dad's side whenever Clara and Peter would talk about who took up the majority of the bed. When she shared the dream with them, she said that her boys responded with laughter, saying, "You see, Mom, even though Dad is not here, you still found a way throw him out of bed!" She recalls that upon awakening the next morning, she felt happy and good, and that as she looked at a picture of Peter that hung on her bedroom wall, she thanked him for the gift of the dream.

Both women stated that in the weeks and months following 9/11, they had disturbing dreams—nightmares—which came to them in both an awakened state and while sleeping. For individuals who have been traumatized, these are typical post-traumatic symptoms. Clara described herself as having daytime nightmares in which she would picture the plane actually hitting the World Trade Center. She said that she worked very hard to stop thinking about that.

These experiences are considered intrusive events that come in both waking and sleep states after a trauma. They are actually a necessary element in processing the trauma, and result in enabling us to heal emotionally, mentally, physically and spiritually. Revisiting the event, as well as replaying it, can come anytime and does so with greater frequency in the weeks and months closest to the actual event.

Tara explained that these kinds of disturbing dreams would come in spurts. Although she did not always remember her dreams, she would often awaken feeling unsettled and agitated, and have a "flick" or a sense of something which enabled her to "just know that it was not a good dream." She also said that she would experience the "awake" dreams or nightmares about which Clara had spoken.

Tara added that although they had diminished in numbers, the most recent awake dream (which is a sort of a replay or revisit) had occurred the week before our meeting, while driving to New York and going through the Holland Tunnel. She stated, "When you drive up from the Jersey side to get to the Holland Tunnel, you are parallel with Manhattan. I remember looking at where the buildings were and just remembering that first week or week and a half when I drove with my family and saw the smoke from the fallen towers. And then the whole thought process of what happened and what could have happened to Michael ran through my mind." Tara was visibly shaken as she described this experience. However, she quickly recovered as Clara began to speak about finding unexpected tranquility at Ground Zero.

Finding Peace of Mind

Clara shared her story of finding peace. She stated with honesty that her husband had never really wanted to work in New York. In fact, she admitted that it angered her to think that his final resting place would be in a place he had not wished to be. Because of this, she had never wanted to visit Ground Zero.

However, on the first anniversary of Ground Zero, she returned to the site where her husband had died. There she made it her goal to stand on the very ground where Tower One had stood. Much to her amazement, she found herself unable to hear anything or anyone else, despite the fact that there were thousands who had gathered that day at this site! She said, "I had never felt such peace since before the 11th. Never."

Hearing this, Tara added quietly and with some hesitation, "I got some peace. I felt them. It was a very powerful feeling, though I don't know if I would describe it as peace."

Clara continued, "You see, I didn't feel it till I was right there. I had to be where Tower One was. All of a sudden, I felt as though I was dreaming because there was nobody else. At that point, I couldn't hear anyone. It was so quiet—so calm—so peaceful. It was just he and I at that moment, which does not make sense, I know." She then recalled that when the security people had come over to her, telling her she had to move, she said she felt like asking Peter, *Why are you still here? I thought you didn't like this place. I have been avoiding it because I thought you didn't like it! The whole idea of you being here just makes no sense to me.* She said all of this with her face contorted in an expression of frustration and confusion, then humor and pleasure.

The bottom line for Clara is that she had made a remarkable connection with Peter, one that she would remember for the rest of her life. She, like so many others, had experienced the presence of her husband and, from her perspective, in the most unexpected place. Clara's sense of her husband's presence was similar to the feelings of peace that Tara had described having in her bedroom, just after her mom died.

Both incidents are great examples of the nonlocal character of consciousness;—that consciousness exists apart from any specific place, time or being. This is nonlocal mind at work, being anywhere and anytime it desires. Given that the quantum physicists tell us that there is no time, and that mind exists nonlocally, one may be comfortable with the concept of loved ones being anywhere, at any time they so choose. Such thinking also helps us to understand how Michael could have communicated with Tara at nine o'clock in the morning, and how Peter could have been present and with Clara at twelve o'clock in the afternoon.

Receiving Loving Reassurance

Repeatedly, those wives of victims of 9/11 with whom I have worked have shared with me their frequent need to ask and receive signs from their loved ones on the other side as to whether they approve or disapprove of their actions on the physical level. Just as Fiona and Ellen had shared stories of their meetings with my intuitive friend, Samantha, Tara had hers to share as well.

Tara recalls that not long after the first anniversary of 9/11, she had experienced a really rough week. She had recently begun cooking school and was having difficulty focusing on her classes. She said that she simply could not focus in the way she once was able to. She also felt tremendous pressure coming from her teachers. In addition, Tara had received a phone call from neighbors that her dogs were howling in her new apartment. She was beside herself, feeling overwhelmed, and not knowing whether or not she had made the right decision in moving to New York City to attend culinary classes.

She remembers getting very down on herself and leaving school, practically in tears, while thinking that she had possibly made a huge mistake with the move. While she was walking, she was trying not to cry. But she kept talking to Michael, tears coming down her face, and telling him, "I don't understand, Michael. I thought I was doing the right thing. You have got to tell me if I am doing the right thing."

She arrived home in a major funk, so hysterical and depressed that, except for hugging her dogs, she did not even feel up to talking to her closest friends, Ellen and Fiona. She just wanted to get out of her bad mood. Throughout the evening, while she attempted to do her homework, she recalls that she continued crying on and off, while talking with Michael and asking him for a sign or signs that she was doing the right thing. She said, "I don't usually ask for signs, but I just need to know."

To Tara's surprise, she slept very well that night. She found herself running a little late for school the following day. Her instructor had grouped individuals into teams, and members of her team were missing that day. Feeling a lack of confidence, she became anxious and panicked; she felt that she was going to "ruin everything" for her partner because it was a joint grade.

Tara was absolutely amazed when the instructor came over to her and, tasting her asparagus soup, declared that the texture, color and taste were excellent and perfect and that he could not have made it any better! This was the sign she had hoped for. In fact, she remembered saying with much positive energy and enthusiasm, "Okay, Mike, I guess that's a sign. I am doing the right thing. This feels a lot better!"

Later that day, Tara said that she had spoken with Fiona, who had been to see my intuitive friend, Samantha, during the afternoon. According to Fiona, while she sat with Samantha, Don did come through with messages for her. However, Tara's husband, Michael, also came through Samantha in order to share with Fiona some of his observations and concerns regarding Tara. He described Tara as having a hard time in New York and that she was feeling depressed. So, when Tara told Fiona that she had had a really bad day the day before, Fiona responded, "Oh, I know! I went to see Samantha today and Michael came to tell me he was very worried about you." This absolutely stunned Tara! *How did she know?* Tara wondered. *Did I call you? I don't remember doing that!*

Tara realized that this, again, was a sign she needed from Michael that he truly was aware of her needs. Between the positive sign she had gotten in school from her instructor, and receiving this news from Fiona, she felt a greater sense of peace and confidence that she was on the right track regarding the changes she was making in her life.

Tara wanted to share a description of the first time she had been with Samantha when Michael had come through. According to Tara, she had recently, before going to see Samantha, started to date a gentleman. However, she had shared nothing personal about this while with Samantha. Samantha told Tara that she was seeing a man present, about 33 or 34. She said that the man was her husband and had died very suddenly. She also described the circumstances as an accident. Suddenly, Samantha stopped, and appearing very confused by what she was seeing, asked Tara, "What happened to him? I see him there and everything is falling around him. At this point, Tara froze and thought, *Okay, she sees him. You can't pull that out of a hat when you know nothing.* Again, confused, Samantha asked, "What happened to him?" With tears in her eyes, Tara then told Samantha that Michael had been in the World Trade Center.

Samantha asked, "Ninety-eight—does that mean anything to you? Did he work on that floor?"

"No, he worked on the hundredth floor," replied Tara.

"No," she said. "He was on the ninety-eighth floor. He was trying to get out and he had walked down two flights when everything happened. And he was thinking about you constantly. He was worried, but even more, he was thinking, *I have to get out.* And he got stuck on the ninety-eighth floor, which makes sense when you think of where the plane hit."

Tara cried while hearing Samantha's description of what she was seeing. Samantha then asked her if they had wanted children and if they had been trying to have children. Tara answered, "Yes," to both questions. Samantha went on to tell Tara, "He's going to get you that boy that you wanted! Don't worry, you will have that boy." Tara laughed at this but admitted that this was particularly meaningful because Michael had always said they were going to have a girl, and she had always said that they were going to have a boy."

Samantha continued to share with Tara what Michael wanted her to know. Among the pieces of information Samantha shared with her was that he wanted her to call Joanna, a good friend of theirs who had been supportive after 9/11. Michael also wanted his wife to know that he was with a good friend of her cousin's who had just died of cancer. Tara was pleased to hear this.

What really threw Tara was Samantha saying to her, "Someone wants to date you?"

In describing how shocked she was to hear this coming from Samantha, Tara said, "I nearly fell off the chair! I thought, *He knows this?* I answered, totally shocked, "Yes."

Samantha responded, "It's okay. Michael is telling me this is a good person—someone who understands your pain. She then asked Tara, "Was he there on 9/11 also?" Tara answered, "No," and Samantha again emphatically stated, "Michael feels this man you are seeing understands your situation."

Tara went on to explain. "Andrew was supposed to be in Windows on the World that morning for a breakfast meeting and, at the last minute, was sent to Germany. He had worked in the vicinity of the World Trade Center for many years and lost many of his friends in the attack on the Towers. His boss' brother-in-law died as well. On some level he was connected to that much more so than someone who had no involvement or connection to 9/11." According to Samantha, apparently Michael thinks Andrew is a good man, and Michael wants her to be happy. Tara was completely thrown off guard by everything Samantha told her.

Tara, however, agrees with Samantha. She believes that Michael sent Andrew to her, as a gift. Why? Because she sees that Andrew seems to be, in some ways, the opposite of Michael. For example, she recognizes that Andrew is very open, not like Michael, and this gets Tara to talk more, something she would not have done with Michael.

Tara laughed as she described her second visit with Samantha. Andrew had grown a beard, something which Michael noted as he described Andrew as having facial hair to Samantha.

Samantha wondered if this was a problem with Tara. (It was not.) Michael once again said, "You need to let him into your life. You will marry again. Do what you want to do regarding children. You do not have to wait to have them."

Tara made a point of emphasizing that she believes Michael specifically sent Andrew to her. Why? It's the coincidences once again. For example, Michael, according to Tara, was not romantic. He sent her flowers just three times in their relationship, and one of those times was their wedding day! Clara, hearing this, laughed hysterically because she experienced the exact same thing with Peter. The only reason both Peter and Michael bought those flowers was because each of their sisters had told them to do it! The bottom line here is that Tara believes Michael knew how much she loves flowers and is finding a way to bring her joy via Andrew.

Several weeks before the interview, Andrew sent Tara flowers for the first time and has several times since. He was stunned to learn that Michael had not done this very often, though he did send Tara a plant a few times. Tara made a point of saying that she did not need flowers from Michael because he showed his love in other ways. Peter was of the same mode of thinking. He sent her real roses on their wedding day, but had then changed to silk, since real flowers die, for their son's birth. She received real, exquisite peachy-pink roses for her recent graduation. Both women could not get over the similarities in the two men. As they laughed about how practical both of their husbands were in their thinking, Clara said, "Yep! They are probably both laughing at us." Tara nodded and smiled in complete agreement.

Tara also noted that as she was going to heat a cup of tea in the microwave oven, Andrew said, "Wait! You can't do that! You have that metal thing on the tea!" Hearing those words, Tara stopped dead. "What did you say?" She was blown away because every time she would reheat her tea, Michael would say, "Oh wait! Don't put that in the microwave! It will explode and cause a fire." They were both referring to the staple on the tea bag. She said that she told Andrew, "I can't believe you just said that!"

Tara went on to describe to Clara, Ellen's visit with Samantha during the time Fiona was in the hospital in December 2002. She described how Michael, one of the deceased 9/11 husbands, came to Ellen, along with her own husband, Vic, and Fiona's husband, Don. It amused Tara that the three husbands appear to be hanging out together. Actually, it has amused all of us—each of the wives, Samantha and myself.

Tara and Clara agreed that as they learn more and more about each other's husbands, they are certain that they would have gotten along beautifully if they had known one another before they died. Consequently, their widows believe that their husbands' spirits truly are together now and, perhaps, they are responsible for their wives being so close.

Divine Guidance and Preparation Brings Laughter and Relief

As Clara Chirchirillo and Tara Bane spoke, they shared stories that clearly reflected their sense that there has been divine guidance and preparation which has assisted them in not only coping with the difficulties of the losses of their husbands, but which have also assisted in moving them into the next phase of their lives. Some might label the events that occurred before 9/11 as precognitive in nature. However, both women had stories that were indicative of their husbands having some higher awareness of what was to come and that preparations needed to be, and were, made.

I have seen this repeatedly. It is as though the Higher Self is guiding the individual to make necessary preparations before his or her departure or death. In the weeks and months before one's death, goodbyes are said, affairs are put in order, discussions take place regarding final wishes, plans are discussed regarding the future, and more time for relationship healing becomes a priority. All of this contributes to a sense of being at peace when a loved one dies. Both Tara and Clara had wonderful stories of this having taken place.

For example, Tara spoke of the relationship between her enrollment in cooking school and Michael. Evidently Michael had been, at one time, in the restaurant business. He had dropped out of high school and worked in a restaurant, first as a dishwasher, and later, after working closely with a chef, as the chef of the restaurant. During the early years of their marriage, Tara had learned to cook with Michael as her teacher. She said that he eventually became her taster and best critic, and urged her to pursue her culinary interests.

In fact, in the summer before 9/11, they had taken many trips driving north, about an hour past New Hope, Pennsylvania. They would talk, dream and fantasize about one day retiring and opening their own little restaurant, with a charming garden in the back. This was the birth of her desire to go to school and make this happen.

Tara also described how, on the Sunday before Tuesday, 9/11, Michael and she sat on their terrace discussing what they wanted as far as last wishes for burial were concerned. Tara recalled saying, "I want to be cremated. What about you? What do you want, Michael?" Michael responded, "I do not really know what I want—to be cremated or buried. I am not sure."

With these words, Tara broke into a smile and then laughter, as only a wife whose husband died in the attack on the World Trade Center has the right to do. "Hence, look what happened! Kind of a little of both," she remarked with amusement.

As Clara listened to her friend, she joined in the laughter, saying, "Peter and I used to talk about that all the time. He would say that he did not want a showing!" Again, laughing, she said, "And he did not get one!" All of us actually laughed at this.

I remember thinking, with great amusement, *What a wonderful gift time is.* How grateful I was that just a little over a year and a half later, these two women, who had experienced complete emotional, physical and mental devastation, were able to see the humor in a situation that had been horrific for the longest time. People need to know that we do heal from the worst of traumas and tragedies. **Healing truly is possible.**

Tara continued. "After discussing burial or cremation, Michael asked, 'If I die, what would you do? Would you stay in the house?' I said, 'I don't know if I could. I don't think I could.' And he said, 'Well, what if we had children? Would you stay in the house?' I said, 'If we had children, I guess I would. But, if it is just me, I don't think so.' He kind of agreed and said, 'Yes, it is a lot of work with just one person.' Then he went on to say, 'Well, you know, if I die there is enough insurance to pay the house off. You can, if you want to, stay in the house and you'll have a little left to take care of other expenses. However, it would be a lot of work for one person."

According to Tara, it was not like him to talk like this. She said, "I was always the one to say I want to be cremated and to think about the what ifs. This conversation took place just a few days before 9/11. The funny thing is after the 11th, everyone was worried about how to pay for their house and whether or not they had life insurance, while I was thinking that I don't know how to mow the lawn and how am I going to do it!" Clara and I were having a good time laughing with Tara at this point.

Yet, we all recognized the *gift* Michael had given her by both taking time to honor Tara's desires and, at the same time, make necessary preparations for the future. Neither one of them could have ever imagined that it was only a matter of days before they would be dealing concretely with those thoughts, words and ideas. The future had become the now. In Tara's words, "I just remember the irony of me worrying about the lawn while others were worrying about much bigger concerns."

I called this intuitive awareness *a gift,* because both Tara and Michael had listened to their intuitive wisdom that then enabled them to be prepared for the worst. This gift allowed Tara to be at peace about major issues. The issues she dealt with, such as cleaning the house without stopping, gave her a sense of control over her environment.

There is, I believe, a Higher Self, which is your intuitive wisdom and which knows what we need. It speaks to us through our emotions. What this inner wisdom requires is that we become mindful of what we are feeling and then make choices which contribute to our well being. There are numerous examples of such wisdom in the literature dealing with hospice doctors, nurses and patients. Many who are nearing death have an awareness of this at the unconscious level, which then influences the cognitive conscious output, providing much-needed information about the time and conditions surrounding death.

Returning to Clara Chirchirillo and Tara Bane, both women admitted that at the time of their husbands' deaths, they each had a need to go crazy cleaning their homes, scrubbing everything they could get their hands on. This, they realized, was something concrete that they could do, something they could control, as opposed to the manner in which their husbands had been taken from them.

As we talked further, the women spoke honestly of their thoughts, feelings and concerns regarding their future, the possibility of another relationship and dating. Each woman admitted that she never thought she would be in the position in which she now found herself: either without a partner or considering the possibility of the dating scene. Yet, each spoke of how wonderful it is to be able to be with another male and feel free and comfortable enough to laugh, be relaxed and have a genuinely good time.

Clearly, it is not easy imagining oneself with another spouse, especially after many years in a relationship with one's husband. After all, both women had been with their husbands for a good part of their lives: in one case, eleven years; in the other, twenty-five. Just as with grief, the pace at which a woman or man moves in terms of readiness to consider dating varies for each individual.

Their bottom-line sense is that their spouses are watching over them, protecting them and, as with Tara, even arranging and connecting them with approved and appropriate partners. This seems to be relatively comforting for both of these remarkable women.

As we drew our interview session to a close, my sense was that this had been, as it had been with Fiona and Ellen, an extremely enlightening and productive session. Both women, in each session, seemed to have had a deeper understanding of the meaning of events that have occurred in their lives since 9/11 and a deeper appreciation for the many ways in which their spouses have maintained the most loving connection with them.

Furthermore, Tara Bane, as well as Clara Chirchirillo, have surprised themselves with regard to their ability to not only persevere and survive, but also to thrive and in such a way that they are noticeably healing and growing emotionally, mentally and spiritually. They also radiate a dynamic energy of newfound exuberance, appreciation for life and joy. We have much to learn from these remarkably strong, wise and intuitive women.

CHAPTER 12

Developing Intuitively— My Journey

We are meant to move toward self-discovery and spiritual maturity, to be ready and able to live a life that matters to us and those around us.

CAROLYN MYSS

Making miracles is the easy part. . . . The difficult part for all of us is to find the meaning in the miracle. I believe the meaning is that there is a lovely sacred chaos to the development of our soul. We make miracles, through our prayers, our creativity, our sacred connection to one another, our faith, and most of all, through our celebration of life's miraculous "way" of teaching us about the evolution of our human spirit.

PAUL PEARSALL

A Visit from Rising Moon

The following story is about one of the most touching and meaningful events I have experienced during my lifetime. It speaks to a number of the themes presented, examined and considered in this collection of extraordinary tales. Even as I write of the events, I become filled with such a sense of awe, even disbelief, that this happened to me, and I also find myself filling with pure delight and joy. In addition to the events that took place, what amazes me, and perhaps will amaze you, is the manner in which events unfold. I believe that what becomes apparent is that life happens to us just as it is meant to happen. If we pay close attention, there is much we can receive from the universe that may enable us to better understand life and our purpose for being here. Let me attempt to illustrate this with my story.

I recall a warm summer day in August when I had finally been able to speak by phone with Dr. Lewis Mehl-Madrona, a Native American physician and author of *Coyote Medicine*.[225] This was not an easy task to do, given his extremely busy schedule. Having tried for close to a week to touch base with him, I was thrilled when he called me that morning from Mount Sinai Hospital in New York City. After we spoke about matters relating to my manuscript and he had graciously offered his support, Lewis mentioned that he was going to be coming to Pennsylvania to do a sweat lodge, something about which he had written extensively in his own book.

Lewis mentioned that I could gather additional information about this by going to Rising Moon on the Internet. Being a true novice, I had difficulty doing this and found that I was going to need further assistance with the Internet address, something that I would have to research further in the coming weeks. However, despite the fact that I could not locate Rising

Moon on the Internet, the name Rising Moon had come to have a significant place of its own lodged in my memory.

Later that same week, on a Friday evening, I attended a class of mine that has become extremely important for me. It had been close to seven months that I had been attending classes, twice a month on Friday evenings, in order to study intuitive development. My decision to further develop my intuition was the natural result of my research, my work and my own personal development.

I recall that at about the same time I had decided to do this, I had come across a statement in *Seat of the Soul* by Gary Zukav[226] which essentially validated my decision. Zukav believes that it is in our best interest as a species, at this period in our development, to take time to develop our intuitive abilities.

Even the events surrounding how I came to the formal study of intuitive development are, I believe, meaningful and noncoincidental. They are, as I view my life, part of a bigger picture. I realize that the universe truly listened to me back in January when I first decided to pursue this area of interest.

In only a matter of days, while dining with my family in a local restaurant, I met a dear friend, Jamie Maniates, and her husband who were dining at the same restaurant with their friends. It just so happened that my friend's husband, Yanni,[227] had recently decided to offer the very class in which I had been interested. Knowing of my research, Jamie later mentioned to Yanni that perhaps I would want to know more about the classes, some of which were given in the form of Intuitive Development Circles. We spoke by phone the following day, and within less than a week I was eagerly participating in my first Intuitive Development Circle. So began the next part of my own spiritual journey.

During the second hour of our class, it is customary for our group, which usually contains the same members, to do a meditation first. Following this meditation, which is done with music, the music is turned off and members of the group begin to share with other members any information we may have intuitively experienced either before, during the meditation or at the time we are sharing the information.

It is in these hours that I have come to realize that it is imperative that I trust my intuition. It is in these hours also that I have discovered that many of those thoughts, feelings and moments that I thought I was just imagining were not my imagination at all, but rather legitimate experiences that I should have honored, but did not.

As I sat quietly during this meditative hour, Yanni, who had just finished sharing his intuitive wisdom regarding several other members in our group, turned to me. "Susan," he said softly, "there is a young Indian woman, more like an Indian girl in her teens, standing to your right. She is dressed in white, has dark hair with pigtails and is wearing turquoise jewelry. I am really not sure what her relationship is to you or what her purpose is for being here. She is there, standing motionless next to you."

When Yanni turned to the group and asked if anyone else had additional information to offer, one member said that she kept getting the words "Rising Moon" and wondered if I might understand what significance this would have, if any.

I remember feelings of astonishment and delight that she had intuited the name, Rising Moon. I immediately knew there was something going on in the way of information being passed along to me, though I did not comprehend what the message was. *There's a connection here,* I thought, *between Lewis Mehl-Madrona, the sweat lodge, Rising Moon and myself.* The fact that Rising Moon should be brought up in my intuitive development group tickled me.

Incidents like this validated my decision to be in this exciting class; it thoroughly energized me. Furthermore, it was moments such as these that reinforced my sense of being guided by a divine wisdom. In fact, I like to think of life as being filled with holy or sacred moments, and that is how this situation felt to me.

I sensed that others within my group had shared my own sense of joy and excitement. They knew, as I did, that I was being guided in some way and in some unknown direction. Our session came to a close not long after this incident took place. Throughout the drive home and for the remainder of the evening, however, I could not stop thinking about the young Indian girl who had come to me that evening and what message she might have wanted to bring me.

Less than a week after meeting my class, I visited with my friend, Samantha. As always, it was a treat for me to be with her. I recall how I excitedly began to recount the amazing incident that had taken place in my intuitive development group. While telling her about the moment that Yanni had described the young Indian girl that he had seen standing to my right, I noticed that Samantha also seemed to be experiencing something unusual.

"Susan," she murmured, "There is someone here now, next to you on your right. I am not sure just yet if it is your mother or . . . " Samantha hesitated for a moment, and then, clearly, looking directly at me, said, "Susan, she is telling me she is your daughter, your Indian daughter, from another time."

As she spoke, I found myself becoming overwhelmed with emotion. I had never experienced anything like this before. Samantha continued, describing the young woman she was seeing before her. "She is young, Susan, probably in her teens. Her hair is dark and in pigtails. She is very pretty. Susan, she says that when she lived, it was just the three of you. That is, your daughter, you and your mother. The three of you lived by yourselves. She says she loved you and her grandmother very, very much and that she is extremely happy to be here with you now. And, she says that this is the first time she has been able to connect or be with you. She feels much love for you."

As Samantha continued speaking, I was filling with feelings of indescribable pleasure and love. This was too much to absorb at once, but it was touching and wonderful. To know that I had had a daughter who loved me enough to travel through time to find a way to communicate her love to me touched my heart at the deepest level. And it was made all the more special by Samantha telling me that my daughter appeared happy to be with me, looking at me, touching me and sharing her thoughts and feelings.

It did not end there. Samantha went on to say that my Indian daughter was showing her where we had lived. According to Samantha, we had lived by the water, up near the Canadian border. The land, the water, everything was described as magnificent.

It was while Samantha was describing the countryside in which my Indian daughter said that we had lived that I had gotten an uncomfortable sense about her death. Intuitively, I felt that she had died of illness and that she had died at a young age. When I asked about these matters, Samantha verified my intuitive hunches. My daughter informed Samantha that she had become extremely ill and had died at a young age, perhaps at about seventeen. I felt a great sense of sadness upon hearing this. I could only imagine my pain at the time my daughter had died. Even as I write this, I cannot help but experience a sense of grief for both my daughter and me as her mother at that time.

Suddenly, I felt the need to ask Samantha about one more thing that had been bothering me from the previous week. "Samantha, what do you suppose the meaning might be of the words Rising Moon? My friend totally stunned me when she went from a puzzled facial expression to a mischievous grin and said to me, "Rising Moon is the name of your daughter."

With those words came an immediate understanding of all the odd, coincidental, puzzling and amusing events of the past week. No more questions, no more wondering, no more confusion. Simply a pure, clear understanding and a sense of connection with the universe that I had never before experienced. My eyes must have opened enormously at this point I do recall gazing at Samantha, stating, "So that's it. Rising Moon is my daughter! Can you believe that? Now everything is making sense!"

I continued to sit there, feeling numb, perhaps, more than anything else. My visit with Samantha was coming to a close. I did not wish it to because it meant the end of my time with Rising Moon. As with all good things, I did not wish to say goodbye to her.

Once again, I do not remember whether I expressed myself nonverbally or verbally. I told Rising Moon how grateful I was that she had come to visit with me, that I loved her very much and that I hoped she would continue to be with me. The moment was bittersweet, having to say goodbye to someone who was such a precious part of my soul and with whom I had just made an exquisite connection.

I do not believe I will ever forget the gift of that particular experience in my life. I left Samantha's full of feelings and thoughts. I found myself reviewing the events of the past week that had led to this incredible day when Rising Moon had actually come to me and made her presence known. *What was the purpose of this?* I wondered. *How and why is it taking place now, at a time when I had no real interest in my past life or lives?*

When working with patients, I always recommend that they ask themselves, "What am I supposed to be learning from this?" and "What is this supposed to be teaching me?" I encourage them to step outside of themselves and look at the situation more impersonally, and with a bigger picture in mind. I took my own lessons to heart.

Given that this experience occurred at a time when I had detached from the need to know of my past life experiences and relationships, I viewed this event as a gift from the universe or

God. I came to see it as a validation of my efforts to develop my intuitive abilities and my spirituality. Nevertheless, I knew I was far, far from where I needed to go in my development.

I felt fortunate that I had been given a connection with a part of my soul's journey. With Rising Moon's visit, I knew that not only had I lived before, but that I had lived as an Indian woman who had a loving relationship with both her daughter and with her own mother, as I have had in this lifetime. And I learned that by giving myself permission to open myself to the wisdom of my soul, I would also be given permission to get a glimpse of the workings of the universe. I felt like an awestruck child, absolutely in awe of the mysterious journeys of the soul and, in this case, my soul.

ℰmerging Intuition

I am finding that as I continue to pursue my interest in intuitive development and to expand my knowledge both experientially and through research, I am gaining the confidence and courage to trust my instincts, my intuition and my gut while working with patients in session. This may not seem like such a big deal to you, but believe me, it is.

While working with a young mother, Anna,* who had just lost her seven-year-old daughter, I began to strongly sense her daughter, whom I shall call Erica.* This took place just after Anna had shown me an impressive collage of photos depicting the many seasons of Erica's young life. I saw a child who appeared full of life and joy. Anna spoke lovingly of Erica, smiling through her tears, as she recalled how her little girl had loved to dress in costume as an angel, star or princess.

Totally unexpectedly, while Anna was describing Erica's bedroom, I caught Erica popping up in several places, always close to her mom. I knew that I was seeing Erica because her cherubic face matched that of the child in the collage. I felt delighted to see Erica, though I was not at all surprised. She also smiled her beaming, winsome smile at me!

At first, I noticed Erica by her mom's knees, nodding her head in agreement with what she was saying. Then, suddenly, I had the strong sense of being shown a locked box in Erica's bedroom, the room that she had shared with her sister, Alisa.* Erica was showing me a box, a pink locked box. "Look at my box," she said to me as she held the box out in her little hands. "Ask Mommy about my box," was my sense of what she was saying to me.

Though I knew what I had seen, or sensed, I nevertheless questioned whether what I saw was my imagination. Quite honestly, I asked myself, "Am I imagining this or not?" I also found reasons to think that by this time Anna had probably already gone through Erica's things and there would be no such box. However, I was being nudged by Erica to ask about it. Though I anticipated a negative response, I knew what I had to do.

Later, as Anna was describing how Erica had loved containers of all shapes and sizes and to keep Anna's written notes to her, I gathered the courage to ask her my question. "By chance, did Erica have a locked box among her many containers?" I remember her reply well. "Funny you should ask me that," she said, smiling and looking somewhat surprised.

She went on to say that yes, Erica had such a box. It matched the box I had seen. It was pink! At this point, I could not help but see Erica giving me an "I-told-you-so" look. She was obviously pleased. I felt a sense of delight as well as validation, not only of what I had intuitively picked up, but, more important, a validation that Erica was right there with us! Because Anna had previously given me indications of having already experienced Erica's presence, I gathered additional courage and shared with her that my reason for asking about the box was because Erica was present and that she had indicated to me that it was important to ask her mother about it.

In my work with my patients, I know I cannot take away their grief. However, there are many individuals who, having lost loved ones, find some comfort in knowing, really knowing, that their loved one is actually there with them, often trying to communicate their presence and their love. As Anna continued to speak about Erica, I observed Erica hugging her mom and attempting to comfort her by running her small, delicate hands through her mom's hair. I knew that Erica would be with her mom and her family as long as they needed her.

One additional note about Erica—ten days or so following her death, Anna said that she went to the laundry room and pulled from the basket a small note, one of many that Erica had written. The note that had left Anna speechless and which

I found so meaningful, said, "Don't cry. I am not hurting." This was, for Anna, a confirmation of Erica's presence. Anna's eyes filled as she spoke of how much it meant to her to receive Erica's gift.

Another special moment that week came while talking with Barbara,* a mother whose daughter, Beth,* had died several years ago at seventeen. As I have said so many times, losing a loved one is always difficult, but the loss of a child is like no other loss. For some parents, it is many years before they are able to accept the reality of the death of their child. Though it had been more than four years since the death of Beth, Barbara finally came to see me at the insistence of her family physician.

Barbara admitted to me that she knew that she was in a state of denial, doing everything possible to not have to deal with her daughter's death. But, as always, her grief would not permit her to escape from her pain. She came ready to pour her heart out, something, according to her physician, she had been refusing to do. For the first time in years, she spoke freely and emotionally about Beth and how much she missed her daughter.

It was during our second session that I experienced Beth's presence. As Barbara was speaking about some of her special memories of Beth's childhood, I found myself looking at none other than Beth, who was standing to the side of her mom. Once again, I knew it was Beth, because Barbara had come into the session with photographs of her daughter and her family. I found her youth and her blond curls to be particularly endearing.

The message I was getting was about a bike. "Ask about the bike, my blue bike," was the gist of the message. Did I think I was imagining it, again? Absolutely! Yet, I strongly sensed, at the same time, that it might have validity. So, I thought, "Here goes!"

While Barbara was sharing a special memory with me, I found myself asking her, "Barbara, forgive me for interrupting, but is there something special or important about a bike that you feel I should know?" She responded by looking at me directly, and quipping, "Funny you should ask me that!" She went on to describe how Beth had had an accident on her special blue bike. The bike seemed to be especially meaningful for Barbara.

Because Barbara had already spoken of having experienced a sense of Beth's presence, I gathered my courage and indicated to her that I had asked her about the bike because it was my sense that Beth, who I felt was present, had wished me to ask the question. Barbara seemed genuinely comforted to know that Beth was with us as we spoke. So was I.

Later that same day, in a session with Sheila,* I had another intuitive experience as she spoke of her mom who died earlier in the year. While the woman I saw did not entirely resemble Sheila's mother, I believed that it was she. When I went on to describe the other woman present, who was petite and frail with her hair pulled back in a bun, Sheila indicated that she believed the woman to be her grandmother. As for Sheila's mom, I noticed her standing close to Sheila, repeatedly expressing her remorse for how she treated Sheila while she was alive. Sheila is in a great deal of pain, working through emotions of hurt and anger. She recognizes that it would be best for her to release her anger and to forgive. Knowing that her mother may be truly sorry for the pain she caused her might serve to help Sheila forgive and move on.

I recall one morning in particular when I was preparing to meet with Fiona Havlish, one of the women of 9/11 whose story is told in Chapter Six. As I was driving to my office, I did what I had gotten myself into the habit of doing each time I was about to meet with a patient whom I was treating for both grief and trauma. I asked the deceased family member if there was something he or she wanted me to know or to pass on to the family members I was about to see or visit.

I recall that just after going through my habitual ritual with the deceased that morning, I was shown a sailboat with a large white sail. This seemed strange to me. However, when I asked Fiona about this in session, she said that Don, her husband who had died on 9/11, had loved sailboats, and that he even had a model sailboat that he kept in their family room. This small piece of information brought my patient comfort and, once again, I felt a sense of gratitude to her husband for coming to me to offer information that I would not have known otherwise.

An Unexpected Morning Visit

The date was February 15th, 2001. Having been up late writing, I was having difficulty awakening. Despite the fact that I could feel the warmth of the sun as it peeked through our window and I could see the minutes ticking away each time I glanced at my alarm clock, I remained warmly snuggled in my comforter. Suddenly, I heard the doorbell ring, or at least I thought I heard it ring. It was the strangest thing.

The bell had rung, but it had not really rung, if that makes any sense. I knew I was not asleep, but I knew also that I was not really awake. I remember feeling annoyed and having a sense of frustration because I knew I had not even a minute to spare. *Oh no!* I thought. *Who could that be?* There was no time to stop and talk to visitors. I already felt excessively pressured by the schedule I knew I had to keep.

Then, instantly, in my mind's eye, the front door opened. Into our foyer stepped my Aunt Ann and Uncle Is, along with a tall young man who, I believe, may have been my cousin. The three were all dressed casually in khaki winter jackets, their hands in their pockets. My aunt and uncle looked relaxed, a bit older, but very much as they had the last time I had seen them. It had been more than a decade since they had died.

I was stunned to see the three of them standing in the foyer, the front door still open behind them with the sunlight framing each of their forms. As soon as I had integrated the idea that they were actually standing in our foyer, I found myself wondering, *Why are they here?* And then, without even a greeting and as though they had heard me, they announced, "We are only staying for a short visit. We will not be here long." And that was it! Finis! The experience was over and I knew I was fully awake.

I was taken aback by this experience. My family members seemed extraordinarily vivid. Whatever had happened, I knew, was meaningful, even if not real. For me, however, it was real! It did not take me long to figure out the significance of their visit. Within the next two weeks, we were to have a family celebration for my dad's 85th birthday. Coming to the celebration were my aunt and uncle's two adult children and their spouses. This was to be a family reunion of sorts. My aunt and uncle, I believed, wanted me to know that they were planning on being with us for the party. *How special,* I thought. *What a wonderful way to let me know that my cousins might be coming, and that their parents would be with us as well.*

During the remainder of the day, just thinking about what had taken place earlier that morning cheered me. I felt tickled, for lack of a better word. What pleased me more was the fact that they came to me that morning, knowing that I was finally at a place in my life where I would be open and wise enough to recognize what they wanted to convey to me. I knew that had this happened maybe four or five years before, I would not have "gotten" their message—at least, not as clearly as I had this time.

I wanted to enjoy this experience from all angles. Beyond the interpretation of the meaning, I studied the means of how they had chosen to communicate with me. So often I had told my patients, whose loved ones had died, that they needed to be especially aware of the kinds of experiences they would have while in the **hypnagogic** state, which lies between the states of being asleep and fully awake. "Write down your images, pictures, everything," I would suggest to my patients, "and then go back and try to make sense of what came to you, but only when you are completely awake."

Think for a moment and recall the times when this type of event took place in your own life; see if you notice any similarities. For example, there are a number of points here that are somewhat extraordinary. For one thing, consider the synchronicity—the timing. I was in the midst of preparing for my father's celebration and talking to my cousins at about the same time this took place, just weeks before the party was to occur. My research had taught me that deceased loved ones love to return to their families to help celebrate special functions and holidays. *So why should this scenario be any different?* I thought to myself.

Consider also that this was a dreamlike experience, because I was not fully awake, though I was more awake than asleep. And, finally, this whole episode had an intuitive ring to it. I believe that because I have opened myself up to various ways my intuition can speak to me, I was more open to receiving their visit. The bottom line is that if you give yourself permission to be open to your own intuitive wisdom, you have a good chance of experiencing similar moments.

Put in different terms, if I am expecting and believing that something could or might take place that would be in my best interest, I am going to attract that to me—"that" being something positive. It is an extension of the power of thought and the law that **like energy attracts like energy** in both the conscious and unconscious states.

$\mathcal{A}$ Story of Hope and Love

Her absolute favorite song, *"You'll Be in My Heart,"* from *Tarzan,* the Disney movie, is the song that often just happens to be playing on the radio or television when her mom, dad, and nana are thinking about her. That was also the song that was playing as Brit drew her last breath and quietly died. According to her mom, Carol, the movie's closing credits were rolling across the screen when Brit, forever affectionately known to her family as "The Drama Queen," decided that would be the cue for her final exit.

But this story that I choose to share with you is not meant to be a sad or morbid tale. Rather, I offer this to you in the same manner that Brit has shared her spirit and soul with her loved ones. This is meant to be a story of hope, inspiration and comfort. It is a story about being happy and living life with joy.

A lover of snakes, spiders and anything that crawled with many legs, as well as every species of the animal kingdom with which she could make a connection (including birds, butterflies, ladybugs, fireflies, dragon flies, deer and rabbits), Brit was not your typical five-year-old. From the time she was old enough to walk and talk, she would make her interests known to those who loved her, especially to her mom and nana, Sunny. She would sit down, look directly at you, and state, "I need to talk to you." She would engage you in conversation; she would shower you with her enthusiasm, exuberance and joy about every aspect of life. With her impish smile, cherubic face and those adorable curls, she was like a cup of hot chocolate with lots of whipped cream on a cold, wintery day, warming your tummy and your heart with her own genuine charm. According to everyone I have met who knew Brit, she simply made you feel good. She was a gift.

As you may imagine, it was extremely difficult for Brit's parents, Carol and Rob, to register the meaning of the diagnosis, neuroblastoma (a childhood cancer), given to them by the doctors at the Children's Hospital of Philadelphia (CHOP) in September 2000. It was because Brit had always been a healthy child that her parents and her pediatrician became alarmed when she began to complain of abdominal pains. Knowing that something was definitely wrong, Brit's pediatrician referred her to CHOP. There she underwent a series of diagnostic tests and a biopsy, all of which confirmed the presence of a large, solid tumor that filled her chest cavity and pushed against her heart and lungs and extended into her stomach.

Admitted to the Pediatric Intensive Care Unit (PICU) just two days later, Brit began her first round of chemotherapy, designed to shrink the tumor so that it could be surgically removed. There would be four more rounds of chemotherapy followed by surgery to remove the tumor, two stem cell transplants and then radiation. This has been the standard protocol for treating a neuroblastoma in children, a cancer which has a national survival rate of 60%.

The family was in shock. While none of this seemed real, they knew what had to be done. In Carol's words, "We were at war." She indicated that she was determined to focus only on the positive aspects of healing and well-being, rather than the diagnosis.

This is what Carol is about: honesty, sincerity, compassion, focus and intuitive wisdom. She saw herself as an advocate for her child, always seeking and demanding not only the best medical care, but also that Brit be treated with the dignity, honor and respect that Brit so richly deserved.

It was because of Carol's approach to the situation that Brit continued to maintain her witty sense of humor. Despite having to endure the impact of the chemotherapy on her little body, Brit managed to smile, laugh and provide comic relief for those who came to visit. Whether you were family, friend, doctor, nurse or physical therapist, she welcomed you with her hidden plastic snakes and insects, delightful laughter and practical jokes, all of which she was known for throughout the hospital. A visit with Brit was very much like receiving a gift.

Brit's response to her illness was typical Brit. As young as she was, Brit brought her strength, determination, and perseverance to the moment. Carol had told Brit the story of the blind man who persevered, despite the elements and other hardships, and succeeded in climbing Mount Everest. Afterward, Brit saw herself as a climber of Mt Everest, always headed for the top of the mountain. In fact, Carol recalls that the day Brit had to be put on a ventilator because she had been having difficulty breathing, the last words she spoke were, "Tell me what I need to do." To this, her parents responded that she needed to keep climbing the mountain and that she was doing a great job.

However, after twenty-five days on the ventilator, everyone recognized that it was not helping, and the decision was made to remove it. Carol and Rob told Brit that they would not be angry with her if she decided that she was tired and wanted to stop climbing. It was then, while viewing the closing moments of *Tarzan*, that Brit, surrounded by her loved ones, chose to die.

Not long after Brit's funeral, which was viewed as a celebration of her life, Carol and I began our therapeutic relationship. As stated earlier in this book, the loss of a child is indescribable. Even when you have been present with your child, witnessing his or her progressive deterioration for many months, accepting the reality of death feels almost impossible. It simply does not feel real. Carol and I worked to process her grief, and especially the pain of not being able to see, hear, cuddle and hold Brit, or do anything to help her feel better.

While she very much missed the physical connection, she felt Brit's presence throughout the day, every day. She read voraciously about the grieving process. She read of others who had lost their children but who, like her, also continued to feel their presence. Carol learned about the near-death experience research and stories of Morse, Moody, Eadie, Kübler-Ross, Sabom and others. She also familiarized herself with the work of Weiss, Altea and Myss.

Carol recognized that unexpected appearances of butterflies, owls, eagles, ladybugs, frogs and rainbows were often ways deceased loved ones enjoy making their presence known to those who miss them. She learned to make the Law of Attraction (**like energy attracts like energy**) work to her advantage; the happier she is and the better she feels, the more wonderful the coincidences and synchronicities in her life. These were all ways she felt Brit was speaking to her and to Rob.

Carol realized that the presence of millions of lightning bugs and fireflies in their backyard (and in none of their neighbors') was more than a simple coincidence. She also realized that it was not an accident that they would also appear on special occasions, such as anniversaries and holidays, when she and Rob would be sitting on their porch. She and Rob both knew that this was her daughter's way of saying, "Hi, Mom and Dad, I am here with you, and I love you."

Yet, like so many others who have lost children, Carol wanted to maintain her connection with her child. This is a natural part of the mourning process. Some call it denial; on one level it is, and on another, it is not. Carol was aware that Brit was no longer present physically. Nevertheless, she wanted to continue to lovingly take care of her daughter, and she wanted to be sure that she was all right. For this, she needed to have a more substantial sense of connection with her. As with many parents who continue to dialogue with their deceased children, Carol needed to know that Brit truly was hearing her. Thus, during the first year following Brit's death, Carol met with several highly respected intuitives, all known for their gift of mediumship.

From what I have gathered, Brit took full advantage of these events as opportunities to converse with her mom. A common theme that ran through these sessions was that Brit came into this lifetime knowing that she would be here for only a short period. Furthermore, she knew her purpose was to bring a magical blend of compassion, joy and love, something she did with ease.

During these sessions, Carol wondered if Brit supported the work she was doing to establish the Butterfly Foundation,[228] which would fund research to fight pediatric cancer. Brit informed her mom that she was fine with it only because it was both important to Carol and because it made her happy. It was not important to Brit. Brit did want her mom to know that she hoped her mom, dad and nana would move on. Brit repeatedly, through different intuitives, came to Carol to tell her that she was fine, happy and well, and that her mom and dad needed to be happy too.

I have previously noted that loved ones who have died often return for the purpose of letting us know that we have grieved enough. Carol and Rob have processed the grief of losing their daughter in very different, very personal and unique ways. This is as it needs to be. There is no right way to say goodbye to your loved one. What makes me smile is that deceased loved ones forget that they are there, on the other side, and that we are here, in our physical bodies, with our egos, thoughts and emotions that accompany any normal human being. Naturally we are going to grieve, and because much of grief is learned or conditioned by our life experience, many of us are going to deeply grieve.

Throughout the grieving process, Carol has truly understood the power of her thoughts and emotions. She recognizes that staying too long in periods of significant pain does not serve her. She wants to heal, to move on and be better. Consequently, Carol has learned the art of minding her emotions and thoughts, which results in her shifting her attention and energy and, ultimately, feeling better.

Somewhere after the first anniversary of Brit's death, Carol shared with me that while with my intuitive friend, Samantha, Brit had come to her. Brit told Carol that she wanted her and her dad to move on with life and to have more children. As most couples do in Carol and Rob's circumstances, they had given consideration to having more children, but had been unable to come to a decision. They were still exploring, working through their thoughts and concerns and not yet ready to make anything happen.

However, Brit had begun to offer her mom and dad the gift of hope. Each time Carol met or spoke with a highly regarded intuitive, Brit would come in to share her observations and finish with a message of another baby in their future. In the later part of the second year following the loss of their daughter, Carol and Rob began to seriously consider having another child.

Unexpectedly, I became a part of this. As a psychologist, I am pledged to maintaining confidentiality. I take this seriously and do not discuss any individual with whom I work with any other person, unless he or she has given me permission. Carol has given me such permission, just as she has for sharing this story with you, because she is aware of both the uniqueness and the significance of the situation.

When I recently visited with my friend, Samantha, Brit made a point of being present. As I recall this particular day, I was talking with Samantha about my own family when suddenly, Samantha announced, "Susan, there is someone here. It is Brit and she is concerned about her mom. She's telling me that she wants her mom to take better care of herself, to take care of her needs and to be sure to rest. She's worried about Carol."

Knowing that Carol and Rob were, by this time, wishing to start a family, Brit's concerns made sense to me. What was especially touching was that Brit shared with me, through Samantha, that she could see that her dad was going to be an especially loving and wonderful father to this new baby. She had also observed how much her parents had grown in their love for one another. Brit went on to describe how her dad's love for her mom had become much deeper, secondary only to his personal growth following Brit's death.

Brit seemed to need to talk, because she continued on for at least another fifteen or twenty minutes, sharing with me information that she wanted me to give to her mom. What came through clearly was how much this sweet, young, yet very wise, old soul, loves her mother.

Brit closed with the most important message of all. She wanted Carol to know that she was keeping her baby (or babies) safe in her arms (Samantha showed me how Brit held two babies close to her heart, criss-crossing her hands over her chest), until it was time for her to give them to Carol. It was unclear to both Samantha and me whether seeing two babies was an indication of Carol having twins or of having one baby and, then, possibly another not long after the first.

However, what was then, and is now clear, is that this is Brit's ongoing gift to her parents; the knowledge that they are meant to have more children and a family, and that it is Brit's intention to keep the babies safe until she can hand them over to Carol. According to Brit, when this has taken place, she will then move on to other work. She believed that her mom would then be truly happy and too busy tending to the baby or babies to miss her. Having expressed this thought, and having offered her mom the gift of hope for a joyful future, Brit departed, as suddenly as she had arrived. Samantha announced to me, "She's gone, Susan."

As I come to the end of the story, I must admit that I, too, had seen Brit in session, seated on the love seat in my office, holding a baby in each arm. I was not at all surprised when Samantha spoke of her confusion over seeing two babies.

Actually, I had sensed Brit many times during my sessions with her mom. During the first year, in the early grieving period, I recall mentioning to Carol that I had seen Brit as a five-or six-year-old sprawled out on the floor near her mom's feet, drawing on a huge pad of paper with her markers or crayons. Carol told me this was something Brit had loved to do. There were also times when I would see Brit seated next to her mom, in the same chair, snuggled deeply into her side. On other occasions, I saw Brit standing on her mom's seat, playing with Carol's hair and, as time progressed, I saw an older Britt in her late teens, seated on the loveseat, listening attentively as her mom would speak with me. I have come to genuinely know that Brit is with her mom and wants the same thing for her mom that Carol wants for herself: to be happy and at peace.

I have learned so much from the children who share sessions with me as their parents grieve their physical, emotional and mental disconnection from them. Probably the greatest lesson of all is that, as we continue to love these children, they continue to be there, loving us in return. They love us by continuing to oversee our well-being and doing whatever they can to ensure our happiness. How wonderful and comforting this thought is!

*T*he Arrival of White Feather

After some fifteen years of research, I have learned that every human being receives guidance from several different sources. While life, without question, is at times glorious, there are many other times when we find life to be, well, in the simplest of terms, tough. It is during these times, when we wish we had all the answers, that we look for and seek additional guidance or wisdom that might be able to see us through our pain and suffering.

Whether we believe that the guidance we receive comes from our own higher wisdom, or that of God, angels or guides, we must be aware that help is there for us. We have to ask for it, but, having asked for it, we must then listen carefully for a response.

So how do we reach those who can help us? It is not difficult. All we have to do is to say the words, "Please, help me" to God, angels, guides, Buddha, Jesus, or Universe or whomever your belief system feels comfortable addressing.

In addition to verbally expressing your wish for help, which may be considered by some to be a form of prayer, you can also envelope your request for assistance in the middle of any prayer you choose. **Prayer works.** The work of Larry Dossey, M.D., has substantiated this. **Meditation works** as well.

In fact, I find that meditation and prayer often are one and the same. I was delighted to find that Dossey, in *Prayer is Good Medicine,* supports this in his own words. He states, "Both prayer and meditation come from the heart, and there are more similarities than differences between them."[228] I use both frequently in my practice and in my personal life.

Meditation provides you with an opportunity to "go inside," to go "deep within you," where there is peace and where the internal guidance you seek can be found. It has been said that when you meditate, you listen to the Divine. When you pray, you speak to the Divine. This has been my experience.

What takes place in meditation is that the experience enables you to connect with your intuitive wisdom, a most remarkable and rewarding experience. I encourage many of my patients to become familiar with the basics of meditation. Even if they do not meditate daily, they learn to live life with a meditative mind.

I also suggest that if guidance is needed, the request is made for this just before going into the meditation. If you ask for it, the guidance will come. Please, do not be disheartened if your answers do not come immediately. In time, you will have a sense of the direction in which you need to move.

With regard to prayer, having learned of the scientific studies that have validated that prayer works, I pray daily for my loved ones and for my patients. Whenever I begin a session in which my patient is experiencing emotional, mental and/or physical pain, I silently offer a prayer to God, my guides, my angels and to departed loved ones. Essentially, I ask for assistance in helping to alleviate some of the pain of those present and, at the same time, to bring them a sense of comfort and healing. I also respect and work with the energy of those present and that of the universe.

Over the years I have read about and heard many who speak of their guides. While I had never actually experienced the presence of a personal guide, I had, as the result of my research and interviews, concluded that we each have at least one guide and, I believe, probably more. So many of those whose names can be found in the bibliography of this book have come to a similar conclusion. Truthfully, I often wondered who my guide might be. Given the type of work I do (dealing with many who have lost loved ones), I have thought, at times, how helpful it would be to have a guide intuitively assist me with bringing comfort and a sense of healing to my patients.

I clearly recall that it was the day after Thanksgiving 2000 that I had my first meeting with, or I should say glimpse of, White Feather. I had gone to the office for an emergency session with a young woman who had been severely traumatized about ten days before our meeting. It was to be the first of four sessions that I was to have with her before she returned to school.

I knew that I had my work cut out for me and that I needed to help her on several different levels. She was in great pain, emotionally and psychologically, and was anticipating even greater pain when she returned to school. In addition to alleviating some of her pain and helping her feel safe, I wanted to help her deal with the terrible reality she was to face when she went back to her dorm. As always, I silently prayed for the blessings of guidance and wisdom to do whatever was needed to assist her.

No more than a few moments after we had begun the session, and after having prayed, I recall that while sitting in my usual chair and listening to my patient, suddenly, he flashed before me. It was not my imagination; he was clearly there and then he was not. *What was that!* I wondered to myself. I was confused for a moment and I was in awe. Again, I tried to make sense of what I had just seen and heard.

What had appeared before me was an Indian gentleman who appeared to be an elder. He (although I was confused initially as to whether I had seen a male or a female), had long white hair, a face that was aged with lines of wisdom and hardship, and was dressed in a white or beige-white leather Indian garment. It was his large, strong build and his face that convinced me he was a male. He conveyed to me, with great compassion and gentleness, that what I was doing with my patient was just fine and that I was doing what needed to be done to help her.

It was not until after my patient had left my office that I was able to review and attempt to make sense of what had transpired. As I drove home that day, his face flashed before me many times. I realized that I had heard him communicate to me the message that he supported what I was doing in session. These were words of encouragement that I very much appreciated, though I intuitively felt I was doing what was needed.

When I questioned what his name might be, what kept coming to me was the name "White Feather." I remember how grateful I felt to him for making his presence known to me. I recall how delighted I was by the whole episode!

Following this experience, there were several other moments in the month that followed when White Feather flashed before me, but they were extremely brief. Yes, these were times when I wondered if I was imagining White Feather. It was during these moments that I felt rather foolish, as well as frustrated.

My intuitive development circle met in December. Although I had not planned things as they eventually turned out, I learned that White Feather was more than just a figment of my imagination. What a relief this was for me!

We were at the end of our second hour, and about to close, when Yanni, our teacher, asked if there was anyone who had something that needed to be presented to the group. Suddenly, without having thought this through or planned on presenting it to the group, I asked those present to help me. I described what had taken place in my session with my patient and spoke of my sense of White Feather being with me. Essentially, I wanted to know if I was imagining everything.

Not at all to my surprise, at least three of my peers shared what they were experiencing while I spoke. They all verified that White Feather was, indeed, real and there. They were able to see him standing by my side. I clearly recall one of the members of the group describing him as a presence close to me and indicating that he was handing me something. The symbolic significance of this was, I was told, that he was sharing his wisdom with me. I was told that he wished me to know that he would be giving me physical signs of his presence.

My heart filled with an overwhelming sense of gratitude. I felt grateful to White Feather for considering me worthy enough to assist me, and to my group for enabling me to connect with White Feather. At the same time, I recall a sense of heaviness in my heart as I thought, *Oh no! I am so inept at noticing signs, I will probably never figure out when he is or is not with me.* However, it was only moments before White Feather gave me his first sign.

After completing our evening ritual of joining hands and singing a moving song that we customarily sing as we close, Yanni began to end our session. It was then that he was presented with two gifts. After receiving a holiday gift from the entire group, he was given a personal gift from one of our members. The gift was a distinctly graceful, large, beige-white feather. I should have, at that very moment, read that as a sign, but I admit I am rather thick. While there was something that touched me about the feather, it was not until the following day that I was struck by the fact that the feather was meant to have been my first sign from White Feather. I recall smiling with a sense of pleasure and delight at the time I became aware of this.

The realization came as I sat with a patient whom I shall call Lee.* Lee has had a number of extraordinary experiences involving a connection with her father who died several years ago. Though she initially came to me to deal with bereavement issues, it quickly became apparent to both of us that she has lived a life filled with special spiritual moments that she had chosen to bury.

As a very bright and intuitive woman, she began to give validation to her life experiences by remembering and talking about them. This came about as the result of her father finding his own interesting way to communicate with her. Lee's story appears in another chapter, but I will refer to just one episode with which I personally had a connection.

I recall that shortly after we began our session, Lee said she had something special to share with me. Her story had to do with her dad coming to her, as he had done on numerous occasions. As the reader may already have guessed, it was while she was describing the unexpected presence of a FEATHER, her dad's usual means of saying hello, floating down to her while she had been thinking of him, that once again I had a moment of incredible awareness. This was White Feather letting me know, through both Lee and the events of the evening before, that he was there with me.

I remember that as Lee spoke, it simply "hit" me. I put my hands to my mouth and exclaimed to myself, *Oh, my God! That's it! That's a sign! And last night also was a sign!* Though annoyed with myself for not picking up on the incident of the evening before, I felt more joy than annoyance that White Feather was present and had found signs that I could easily "read." How interesting it is that a feather can communicate so much! Having herself become extensively involved in research related to matters of the soul, I believe that Lee shared with me a similar sense of awe and profound respect for the workings of the universe.

The work and the research I have done have added such rich and vibrant colors, as well as a sense of endurance, to the threads that make up my own fabric of life. The unexpected spiritual encounters with guides and parts of my soul have contributed to the sanctity of the moments I share with my loved ones, friends and patients. The majority of these experiences were not a part of my life until I made the conscious decision to listen to my own intuitive wisdom. It has been amazingly rewarding ever since!

We are here to grow, to learn, to love and to forgive. We are here to connect with our soul. When we allow ourselves to be more open to our own soul's wisdom, our lives take on a sense of depth that we could never have dreamed possible. I encourage you to begin to listen to your own wisdom. It waits deep within you, desiring only to guide you.

The Path of Developing Intuition

Developing the gift of intuition is a process and, like everything else, if one wishes to develop something, one must practice. Thus, I have made it my intention to be open to all physical and nonphysical beings whose hearts are pure and loving, but who are experiencing pain. Those who grieve or who are dealing with any significant loss are hurting emotionally, mentally, and often, physically. Though death is a natural part of life, the pain one feels is often exacerbated by the death occurring with little or no warning, making final goodbyes an impossibility, and/or the death leaving in its path a variety of unresolved issues between individuals.

I frequently convey, through prayer, my desire to be open to assist those who are in need of healing. Consequently, I occasionally intuit or receive a sense of connection and a message or presence from a loved one of a friend or patient who has recently died. If I intuitively receive messages of affection, caring and love, I find it most therapeutic to share this with those who are grieving. This may occur while I am in session at the office or while I am going about my personal business. There are no words that adequately convey the power and delight of discovering a sense of connection with a deceased loved one.

I must admit that I am often not completely sure if what I have gotten is legitimate or not. In such situations, I like to ask for some sort of sign or indication that the information given to me is valid. The interesting thing I wish to note here is that I usually do receive some form of validation.

For example, I recently experienced a connection with a friend of ours who had just died that morning. My sense was that he was with both his parents and that he was at peace, though I felt that he was concerned about his wife. When I asked for some names, what I received was something like Mae or Mar. I thought he was trying to convey his mother's name to me, though I knew her name was not Mary, so I felt some confusion. What I also intuited were the names of Is, Isadore and Isaiah. This made no sense to me.

Wondering if I was imagining the experience, I asked our friend if he might give me a sign, something that would legitimatize the information I had received and assure me that the information did, indeed, come from him and not my imagination. With this, I just let the whole thing go.

Within an hour or two I had arrived at our friends' home where the whole family had gathered to support their mom and one another, as well as to make the necessary preparations for the funeral and the shiva. While helping the family to set up for the events of the following day, I noticed our friend's son go into his dad's office and re-enter the kitchen, where I was busy cleaning the silver, with a book in his hand.

Curious, I asked him the name of the book that he seemed to be holding so dearly. "Isaiah," he said. I was stunned. That was my first sign and there were more. During the funeral the following day, one of the selections that the rabbi had chosen to read was also Isaiah. With this, I silently thanked our friend for verifying our exchange the previous day.

Later that evening, after the funeral, I had a moment to catch up with our friend's other son. I was curious about the names of his grandparents—his father's parents, that is. When he told me that his father's father was Meyer, I understood the significance of the Mar or Mae that I had received. What I had done was to assume that the name belonged to his grandmother when it actually had been part of his grandfather's name. I simply had not gotten all of the necessary information. I smiled to myself when told the correct name and, once again, thanked his dad for giving me one more piece to validate our meeting.

Our friend's son responded to my description of the events concerning his dad and Isaiah with a knowing look of acknowledgement. He understood that his dad had in some way communicated with me.

*V*alentines Are Forever

It was a clear, not too cold evening in February, and I found myself thoroughly enjoying our ride into the country. I could not stop admiring the beauty and charm of the countryside that appeared to be set against the backdrop of the setting sun. What a treat! My husband and I were on our way to meet a dear friend, Lisa,* and take her to dinner.

Both Lisa and her husband, Mike,* had been good friends of ours for many years.

Unfortunately, Mike had died suddenly several months before, leaving Lisa and their children totally devastated. This was the first time we were able to be with our friend since Mike had died.

With the arrival of evening, we were enveloped by the dark as we traveled along narrow country roads. I recall that as some of my favorite Enya music played in the background, my mind wandered to Mike. Having studied intuitive development for several years, I wondered whether or not Mike might want me to know something he wished me to share with Lisa.

Not long after he died, Mike had shared something that I thought was probably my imagination but proved to be factual when I shared it with Lisa. In addition to expressing some of his feelings, he had shown me a picture of himself eating ice cream. Of course, I thought this was my imagination creating something out of nothing. However, when I spoke to Lisa, it brought her great pleasure. She laughed and told me that eating ice cream was one of Mike's greatest pleasures. Mike loved ice cream and it really represented a significant source of joy for him. This small piece of information that I had not known verified his presence on some level. And that was good for Lisa.

Here in the car, on the way to see Lisa, I invited Mike to share with me something special for his wife. I saw a heart, a large pinkish-red heart. It seemed to have a line down the middle, as though it had been broken. This pinkish-red heart also appeared to have a brilliant quality, similar to that of diamonds. Finally, it seemed to be hanging from something, perhaps a string or chain. I felt that this was a sort of Valentine gift in which he was expressing his eternal love for his beloved wife. I could not get the heart out of my own mind and heart.

After picking up Lisa at her home, we drove to a nearby restaurant where a table was being prepared for us. We stood in the crowded bar area and, while waiting to be seated, I turned to Lisa and shared with her what I had received from Mike. She looked at me, eyes wide, reached into the collar of her turtle-neck and pulled out an exquisite diamond necklace in the shape of the heart!

"Susan," she said, "he was referring to this." She extended the gorgeous heart to me. "This is what he was showing you. Mike gave this to me over a year ago. Within the past few weeks, I do not know why, but I had an enormous desire to take it out of its case and wear it. I have been wearing it all the time. In fact, I rarely take it off. It just feels so good to have it close to me—and I know how much Mike wanted me to have this." Lisa then gave me a huge hug. Once again, Lisa knew that Mike was finding ways to express his eternal love for her and this touched her deeply.

*T*reasured Gifts from Feathered Friends

It was a magnificent Saturday morning in early May, a perfect day for a retreat. I was eagerly looking forward to having a day to do nothing more than meditate, go within and connect with parts of myself that seemed to have moved eons and eons away. Just getting out of the house was hard to manage. The morning had been uncomfortably crazy and I ended up leaving home later than usual. No surprise for me.

By the time I was on my way, not sure of the directions, I found that with the help of some deep breaths I was able to relax and regain a sense of composure. I recall taking a few moments in the car to pray, speak to the universe, to God and any angels, guides or loving spirits who chose to hear me of my intentions that day to honor my highest good and to ask for assistance from any and all who might be able to help me fulfill my intentions. I also asked those who had come to me in the past to come and be with me again in order to bring clarity, wisdom and guidance to either myself or to others in the group.

It was an extraordinary day. I use the word extraordinary because I seemed to go deeply into our guided meditations almost immediately. It was amazing to feel the shift occurring from my physical being to a place of great calm and serenity. I truly had a sense of healing my entire being. Each meditation added to my own sense of clarity regarding issues I had been struggling with, such as the writing of this very book. Suddenly, instead of seeing clutter and disorganization regarding the state of everything that dealt with my creative endeavor, I was being shown just how valuable my material was, how precious and golden. Somehow, I knew I would be given the assistance I needed to make it all happen.

Just before lunch, our teacher suggested that while strolling around the grounds of the retreat, we look for some sort of an object that would serve as a touchstone for us, something that would have sacred and special meaning. Following lunch, I stepped out onto the porch and viewed the most remarkable scene. Some of the oldest, grandest oak trees I have ever seen, the kind you see yourself climbing and snuggling in, adorned the lawn. At the bottom of a gentle slope stretching before me was a lake, rather small, but with much charm and definitely very inviting. For anyone interested in contemplation, there was a bench perfectly placed under a huge oak tree off to the side of the lake, and a cement path, about a foot or so wide, around part of the lake which was closest to the house.

I was immediately drawn to the bench. *A perfect place,* I thought, *to do some reflecting.* As I began descending this sweet hill, I noticed two large birds at the other side of the property, behind the lake. *Are they swans?* I wondered. It became clear as I approached the bench that the birds were actually large white geese, and very noisy geese at that.

Sitting down, I noticed that the geese were interested in me as well. There was something different in my perspective on these two. They reminded me of a couple, a darling, elderly couple. They approached me, waddling with determination, honking loudly, as if in conversation with one another. Their necks were in an extremely stretched position that raised their little heads so that they actually looked like little people.

There I was, sitting by the water, enjoying the warmth of the mid-day sun, feeling blessed to be in that idyllic setting, and here were these two very large, white geese coming right up to my side, honking excitedly, as if I were the new kid on the block. By this time, I had decided to name them Max and Mabel.

I was especially drawn to their eyes. Their eyes reminded me of the sharp eyes of a regal white eagle. As the reader may recall, the guide who has blessed me with his presence for the past few years and who had come to me in my meditations is White Eagle, whom I have often called White Feather. I have come to associate with White Eagle and White Feather the eyes of a white eagle and its white feathers. I intuitively felt that there was something more going on here than just two white geese visiting me. I have learned from White Eagle that I am given signs from him to let me know that he is indeed with me. *Could these geese be a sign?* I wondered.

In any case, feeling a great sense of connection with animal life, I began to chat with them—mind to mind. No words were spoken, but I began conversing with them, letting them know that I was pleased that they had come to join me and that I was glad that we were having this opportunity to get to know one another. Max and Mabel became quiet immediately, tilting their heads one way and then another, as if they were trying to take in all that I was saying.

I felt we were hearing one another and that they knew that I genuinely cared about them, and I did! They were so sweet. As they quieted, they nuzzled their beaks into my sweater, coming right up to my face and never, never biting or hurting me. They were gentle and adorable. This went on for a good five to ten minutes or more.

While engaged in animated conversation with my new friends, several members of our meditation group had come down to the lake and were seated about twenty feet away, by the side of the lake, watching all of this take place. As I walked over towards them, my new little friends followed. I needed to step down onto a cement barrier and step up again to get to the others who were amused by the whole scene. This seemed to be a reason for the geese to stop and ponder whether or not they wanted to join us. My friends from our group were kidding me as they welcomed Max and Mabel, who finally decided to join us. They came and nuzzled next to us. We sat by the water, all of us grateful for the opportunity to be there, enjoying the sun and its gifts, on this special day. As we sat and talked, one of the geese, Mabel, the smaller of the two, wiggled her tush and out came a long, white feather that fell into the water. This, I knew, was a gift for me, perhaps from White Eagle, and was to be my touchstone. I quickly picked up the feather and rinsed it in the water, planning to give it a thorough washing when we returned to the house.

I recall that our teacher, Yanni, had come down the hill to join us for a few minutes, but this did not please the geese. They waddled over to him, sniffed the cuffs of his trousers and began to nip and bite! In a flash, Yanni was gone! Shortly after this, I quietly bid goodbye to my new friends and returned to our retreat center for the afternoon meditations.

When we gathered for the afternoon activities, my friends from the group, who had witnessed everything, felt that it had been a special time that needed to be shared with the others. I retold the events and explained my connection with White Eagle, and how he had, in the past, told me that he would provide me with a sign of his presence. He had done just that with the large, white feather. I, too, was aware of how special the earlier events of the day had been.

I do recall being asked about my communication with animals and whether or not I had done that before. I had not thought much about it until then. When I answered that the way I responded to the geese was the manner in which I normally respond to animals of all kinds, I was told that this was the "shamanic way" since it was somewhat out of the box, traditionally-speaking. This comment caught me by surprise. However, after giving it some thought, I realized that this was the case and that it felt good to be interacting with animal life in this way.

When I took the time to look back on my intuitive training, it had included studying with a gifted animal communicator in addition to spending several years studying intuitive development. Furthermore, several months after my encounter with Max and Mabel, I found myself in a seminar dealing with animal communication. The instructor, Sharon Orlando,[229] was a highly-qualified and respected woman who had trained with Penelope Smith,[230] who is renowned for her work as an animal communicator and teacher of animal communication. I found that much of what I had learned in developing my intuitive abilities was completely appropriate for connecting with animals. I have a long way to go in this area, but I see growth in intuitive communication with both human and animal life.

An Extraordinary Mother's Day Healing

Mother's Day has always been a special day in our family, both while my mom was alive and after she died. It was a hard decision to decide whether or not to attend an advanced healing seminar in upstate New York, which took place over a four-day period that included Mother's Day. The irony of the situation was that it took our daughter Rebecca's coming home for the weekend for me to feel comfortable about going off to New York for the seminar. Knowing that Rebecca would be home, watching over everyone, provided me with the gift of knowing that I could actually go away and not have to worry about my family and home.

Given that the week leading up to the seminar had been stressful and that I was not accustomed to driving four hours on my own, I was exhausted by the time I arrived at the retreat center. Fortunately, the day had been warm and sunny, making the drive agreeable.

I arrived in mid afternoon, just in time for the afternoon break. The building in which I would be spending the next three days was a large, old, stone edifice, with delicate white lace curtains decorating each of the windows. It was surrounded by azaleas blazing with shades of pink, exquisite white and pink rhododendrons and magnificent forsythia in bloom. Huge pots of geraniums that adorned both the kitchen and the main entrances welcomed all visitors. *What a charming place to have a retreat,* I thought, as I drove into the parking lot adjacent to the center.

I entered quietly, noting that the members of the group were seated in the large living room of the home, deep in the throes of a healing meditation. Though it felt great to have finally arrived, I was burned out. Putting my bags down, I slipped into the room and fell into a large, inviting and comfortable chair that had been saved for me. How good it felt to just be there and to know that I had nothing more to do than sit and lose myself in meditation.

Not until Sunday morning did I regain my strength and sense of well-being. At breakfast, while pouring a cup of coffee, Joyce, our teacher, asked me if I wished to be the healee that morning and I happily accepted. I felt I was energetically strong enough to agree to be the subject of a healing experience.

Undergoing a healing was a gift that each of us experienced during the four-day period. I really wished to make the most of my healing. After all, how often does one have the opportunity to have a group of healers intend healing for him or her?

Though I had looked forward to the healing encounter, I had no idea that it was going to be one of the most powerful and meaningful events of my life. There were synchronicities that contributed to its being so powerful. For one thing, about an hour before my healing took place, a seminar participant, Pat, who appeared to be a friend to a number of others in our small group, arrived. I could see her as she entered the room and was immediately struck with a strong sense of knowing her and of being drawn to her. She was tall, looked about my age—in her late fifties—carried herself with stately grace, confidence and elegance, and was warmly received by everyone in my group who knew her.

Something about this woman touched my soul. Her smile felt familiar, as did her very presence. Though we said hello to one another, we did not actually engage in conversation until after my healing meditation had taken place.

Not long before Pat arrived, I recall that our teacher decided to make a fire in the fireplace since the weather had changed and day was quite rainy and damp. I had not really thought too much about this until the latter part of my healing experience, when I suddenly realized how significant the fire was to my own healing.

I, as the healee, was given the choice of sitting or lying down for the adventure. I chose to lie down on the floor. The fire was energetically burning away, speaking to us with its language of snapping and crackling sounds and offering those of us there its comforting warmth and heat. I recall that as I gathered pillows and a blanket, Pat, who was seated just a foot or so from where I was going to be lying, quickly stood up and offered to help make me as comfortable as possible. She placed a pillow under my legs and a warm afghan over my body, much as my mother would have done. This motherly gesture touched me deeply.

I remember that as we began the healing, I was feeling blessed and fortunate to be there, in the center of this dedicated group of individuals whose intentions were to focus their loving and healing energy on me while a blazing fire filled the room with its delicious heat. In this state of coziness, I opened myself to receive their loving, healing intentions as they began their initial centering work. I also asked that those who were working to heal me be blessed with peace and whatever else they needed to assist them in their work.

Then I noticed that my feet and legs were beginning to feel numb. *What is happening?* I thought. *I cannot feel my feet nor recall whether or not I had crossed them initially.* At the same time, I realized I was beginning to feel lighter and as though I was expanding. I was aware that my arms were slowly rising, as they often do when I meditate during healing work. I could actually feel a sense of loving energy coming into my being.

Suddenly I was aware that familiar Native American ancestors who had made themselves known to me in the recent past were present: specifically Rising Moon, my Indian daughter who had come to me on previous occasions (some of which have been corroborated by others) and White Eagle, my Native American Indian guide (who has also been corroborated by others, including Elisabeth Kübler-Ross)[231] were present.

I could see Rising Moon gently kneeling by my right side, whispering in my ear that she was nearby. She reassured me that they were there to assist everyone and me with the healing and told me also that she loved me. I saw White Eagle standing to my right and had a sense that my other guide, whose name I do not yet know but whom I call Black Feather, was also present. I felt that they were assisting in some way with the healing process. I saw many others, all seated in a circle around me, before the fire. I could hear the wind howling and the rain beating against the windows, and yet I felt protected, safe and loved.

I was not at all surprised by White Eagle's appearance. You may recall from a previous story entitled *The Arrival of White Feather* that White Eagle, who, at the time, I called White Feather, appeared to me quite unexpectedly while I was doing an emergency session several years ago. Due to the relevance of the story, part of White Feather's story is included here once again.

My young patient had been traumatized by the unexpected death of several of her closest friends in a car accident. One of the girls killed included her college roommate. Whenever I begin a session with a fragile patient, I always silently pray for guidance and assistance so that I will do only what is in the highest good of the individual. I had been doing this for years and, in fact, continue to do it with all my patients.

White Eagle appeared to me while I was actively engaged in listening to my patient. Suddenly, I noticed off to my right this incredibly old and wise being. The face first struck me. It was so old, filled with many, many lines, but lines of wisdom, and, intuitively, I knew, lines of compassion. There was so much gentleness and compassion in the face that I was confused as to whether it was the face of a man or woman. The beautiful long white hair also added to my confusion. He, or she, wore a light beige buckskin top, pants and moccasins. Gradually, I sensed that the body was that of a male, stocky with boxlike shoulders.

I was trying to listen attentively to my patient, but attempting to deal with the added reality of my Indian visitor. Though I did not know his name, I felt strongly that he had come to assist me in some way. As crazy as it may sound, I conversed with him, mind to mind. What I received, intuitively, was that I was on the right track and that I was doing just fine in my work. It was the gift of reassurance that he came to give me. I was moved by this, but quickly refocused my attention on my patient.

In the days and weeks following this event, White Feather came to me several times. Unsure whether or not I had imagined the whole thing, though I intuitively knew I had not, I brought the whole encounter to my intuitive development circle about two weeks later. "Am I crazy, or did this really take place?" I asked my group and my teacher, just before our evening was to come to a conclusion.

The room was barely lit; just a small light burned in one corner. With our eyes still closed, two women in the group, one just across from me and one about four or five people to my right answered that they were aware of his presence. The woman seated across from me had been studying with a shaman at the time. She told me that he was off to my side and that he was telling her that he was going to remain with me, assisting me in my work. Furthermore, he said that he would be giving me signs to assure me of his presence. I was deeply moved by the responses I received to my question and by the fact that White Feather had chosen to grace me with his guidance.

Our meeting was about to end. Since it was just before the holidays, one of the group members addressed our teacher, telling him that she had a special gift for him from the group. There really are few words to describe my reaction to what followed. She took from her bag a large, handsome whitish-beige feather, one of the largest I had ever seen. I could not believe what had just transpired. In fact, I was completely stunned and awestruck by the incident. I also felt immense gratitude to my fellow group members and to White Feather for validating my experience.

Returning to my healing experience, I was still lying on the floor on soft pillows and nestled in an old, cozy, handmade afghan. I felt grateful for the appearance of White Feather and my other Indian relatives, especially my Indian daughter, Rising Moon, who first had come to me over a series of weeks, several years earlier, and whose story is also told in this book. As I lay there, an almost indescribable sense of well-being came over me. Then, without any warning, I underwent the most incredible vision. It came out of nowhere and took me completely by surprise.

Given that I was not physically ill, I had specific goals or intentions that I had hoped would come from the healing process. Specifically, I had been feeling "stuck," energetically-speaking. In the months, weeks and days leading up to this healing, I had felt as though I were blocked and that it was difficult for energy to flow comfortably through my energy centers, my chakras. My heartfelt hope was that the healing would lead to a clearing of my centers, allowing me to serve as a channel for my healing work. I knew that this would provide me also with something I very much needed: a heightened sense of peacefulness and inner serenity.

Bearing in mind my intentions for the healing, the vision I received certainly made sense. Out of nowhere, I saw each of my chakas, beginning with my crown chakra, bursting open, spitting out fumes of powerful energy and all colored appropriately to correspond with the location of the chakra. That is, what I saw was each cone-shaped chakra facing outwards, spinning quickly and pushing out energy colored to match the chakra. Thus, the crown chakra threw out a clear white energy; the third eye, indigo; the throat, blue; the heart, green; the solar plexus, yellow; the sacral, orange; and the root chakra, red.

In that moment I knew that, thanks to my fellow group members and my Indian ancestors and guides, I had been blessed with the gift of the clearing of my energy centers. The meaning of this vision was so powerful that I found it difficult to hold back my emotions. As I lay there, tears came. These were not tears of sadness. Rather, they were tears of gratitude, love and appreciation.

As I quieted myself, I thought that the healing was coming to a close. However, there was still more to come. I began noticing that the numbness that had been initially in my feet and legs was now spreading. I could not believe what was happening. It seemed to me that the feeling of numbness was moving relatively quickly up into my torso, my arms and my hands. Once again, I felt such a sense of surprise! The meditation was drawing to a close and I was aware of my inability to move my legs. I recall slowly sitting up, while on the floor, and attempting to unlock my legs, which I had crossed at the beginning of the healing.

I can't unlock my legs! I thought. In the same instant that I registered this thought, I realized that this was a communication of sorts from my nonphysical friends and family and that the healing had actually taken place—and that I would be able to move my legs and be all right within moments. The experience had taken a toll on me emotionally. I found myself needing to cry in order to release my feelings of gratitude and love. I had never before encountered anything with such power and impact. I sat there and wondered if anyone else had gotten any part of what I had received.

As is our custom after someone undergoes a healing, he or she is asked to provide feedback regarding the experience. Sitting on the floor, leaning against the leg of my chair, right by the fire, I turned to everyone and attempted to describe not only the events of the healing, but also the significance of those Native Americans who were present. They appeared to be genuinely interested in the events, which pleased and touched me.

I also shared with them a sudden realization I had just before the healing was completed. While lying there and listening to the sounds of the fire as it burned, I had an instant awareness that the fire had not been a coincidence. The fire had been necessary for my Indian ancestors, family and guides to do their work. Whenever I have experienced them in large numbers, I have seen them before or around a fire. *Of course,* I thought, *there had to be a fire.*

As is also our custom, our teacher asks each of the healers if he or she has anything to offer that might be constructive for all concerned. When Joyce asked Pat, the woman with whom I had felt an enormous sense of connection, her response was absolutely on target. She remarked that all she had for the majority of the healing was a dark, peaceful feeling. However, she said, just before the healing was concluded, she had received a "beautiful clear channel," and as she said this, she described it by running her hand over an imaginary clear, flat channel in front of her. She stated that she had not thought much of this until she heard me describe my experience of my chakras bursting forth with energy. Then she knew that she had received what I had received. We had indeed been on the same wavelength—intuitively, that is.

With the conclusion of the morning healing, Pat approached me, and, when I had told her that I had immediately felt drawn to her, she admitted that she had felt the same.

Then, looking me straight in the eyes, she said, "Susan, you are not only beautiful on the outside but also . . ."

Not feeling comfortable with what she was saying to me, I said, "No, I am not."

To which she responded, "Yes, you are."

Once again, I answered, "No. I am not, but that is something my mother would often say to me."

Again, looking me straight in the eyes, she gently, but firmly, said, "Well, since this is Mother's Day, perhaps you will allow yourself to accept what I am saying as though your mother were saying it to you."

In that moment, something clicked, intuitively, that I still couldn't adequately describe in words. But I know that I felt a connection with my mother through Pat. We hugged one another affectionately at this point.

Pat went on to tell me that she and her husband lived just an hour away in Connecticut and that part of their property includes land that was once part of a Native American Indian reservation. Furthermore, adjacent to their property is a Native American Institute, something that she thought I would find unusually interesting and informative.

"I invite you and your husband to come and visit with us. I know you will enjoy it and it will give us a chance to get together again."

She repeated her invitation several times before we hugged once more and said goodbye. Although we had the pleasure of talking over lunch, Pat was on her way not long after that. Pat had come for essentially one meditation and one healing: mine. Then she was off. We promised that we would reconnect and we shall. However, the feeling of having had an unexpected connection with my mother that Mother's Day will be with me forever.

There are moments in life that cannot be explained. In these moments we have a sense of something extraordinary taking place. Some call such experiences coincidences, and some call them something else. These are the moments when we feel a connection with our soul, and in these moments we give thanks for recognition of the possibilities of our being so much more than we are physically.

Conclusion

We have forgotten how to die, as it is no longer a part of our ordinary lives. At the same time, we have forgotten how to live . . . we have forgotten that our ordinary lives are spiritually important.

BETTY EADIE

The extraordinary touches us on so many levels, forcing us to stop and ask questions regarding the nature of life and death and life after death, as well as the meaning and purpose of life. It also gently nudges us to get to know who we are at the level of the soul, a level that feels familiar and good when we allow ourselves to go there.

The next time a mystifying, unusual, coincidental event touches you, be sure to take time to notice it and then realize that you have a choice. The choice will be to either allow it to occur without listening to it and without growing from it, or to choose to honor the experience by giving it your attention and by listening to what it is saying to you at the level of your heart. The choice is always yours. This is your journey, and yours alone. We all get to the same place, eventually. It is just that we take different paths.

I sincerely hope that this book has not only comforted you if you have lost loved ones, but enlightened you as well. We seek answers to our questions, never realizing that the answers lie within. As a student of intuitive wisdom, I have learned, firsthand, that we already know what we need to know, and that we already have all the answers to our questions. We tend to look outside of ourselves when the wisdom of our soul, and our Higher Self, can be found within.

We were born with a knowing, a knowing of our greatness, and that joy and love are what we are. We were born knowing that we are never alone. We knew at the time of our birth that whenever we would need help, we would only have to ask, and it would be available to us. We were born with a sense of destiny, purpose and excitement about becoming all that we knew we could be.

My research and my work have taught me that we were born knowing that this lifetime would have many challenges, all necessary for us to heal our soul. We knew that our life would be our classroom, that we would be the students, and that the Universe would be our teacher. We knew that we would always have all that we needed to handle whatever would fall onto our path.

The end result of my working with all my patients, and especially those who are ill, close to dying and those who have lost loved ones, has taught me that we are absolutely never alone. Despite the physical loss of an individual, their energy, spirit and soul continue to be, for that is what we all are—pure energy. We are eternal beings. Of this I am sure. I am certain, based on years of research and clinical work that the gift with which we came into physical form, our intuitive wisdom, allows us to not only connect with nonphysical energy, but, more important, allows us to connect with our own soul and with Source. This, I believe, permits us—no, rather demands of us—that we be all that we know we can be.

Here's to a joyful, loving, wonderful experience in this lifetime and throughout eternity!

Chapter Notes

PART ONE:

The Nature of the Extraordinary

Chapter 2: Extraordinary Connections and Communications

1. Melvin Morse with Paul Perry, *Parting Visions* (New York: Villard Books, 1994), p. 15.
2. Ibid., p. 16.
3. Larry Dossey, *Reinventing Medicine: Beyond Mind-Body to a New Era of Healing* (San Francisco: Harper, 1999),pp. 24–25.
4. Raymond A. Moody and Paul Perry, *Reunions: Visionary Encounters with Departed Loved Ones* (New York: Villard Books, 1993), pp. 103–148.
5. Jess Stearn, *The Sleeping Prophet* (New York: Bantam Books, 1968).
6. Joseph Campbell (Ed.), *A Portable Jung* (New York: Penguin Books, 1971), p. 68.
7. Ibid., p. 75.
8. Judith Orloff, *Second Sight* (New York: Warner Books, 1996), p. 209.
9. Ibid., pp. 209–210.
10. Ibid., p. 233.
11. Campbell, *A Portable Jung.*
12. Rupert Sheldrake, *Dogs That Know When Their Owners Are Coming Home* (New York: Three Rivers Press, 1999).
13. Wayne Dyer, *Your Sacred Self: Making the Decision to Be Free* (New York: HarperCollins, 1995), p. 78.
14. Ibid.
15. Dossey, *Reinventing Medicine*, p. 207.
16. Ibid., pp. 214–216.
17. Elisabeth Kübler-Ross, *Death Is of Vital Importance* (Barrytown, New York: Station Hill Press, 1995), pp. 114–116.
18. Ibid., p. 116.
19. Ibid.

20. Sophie Burnham, *A Book of Angels* (New York: Ballantine Books, 1990), p. 72.

21. Sheldrake, *Dogs That Know When Their Owners Are Coming Home.*

22. Penelope Smith, *Interspecies Telepathic Communication* tape series (Point Reyes, CA: Pegasus Publications). Penelope Smith, *Animal Talk: Interspecies Telepathic Communication* (Hillsboro, Oregon: Beyond Words Publishing, Inc., 1999). Penelope Smith, *When Animals Speak: Advanced Interspecies Communication* (Hillsboro, Oregon: Beyond Words Publishing, 2001).

23. Sheldrake, *Dogs That Know When Their Owners Are Coming Home,* pp. 235–236.

24. Ibid., pp. 237–238.

25. Mona Lisa Schulz, *Awakening Intuition* (New York: Three Rivers Press, 1998), pp. 36–38.

26. Carolyn Myss, *Anatomy of an Illness: The Seven Stages of Power and Healing* (New York: Random House, 1997).

27. Gary Zukav, *Seat of the Soul* (New York: Simon & Schuster, 1989).

28. Schulz, *Awakening Intuition,* pp. 31–32.

29. Russell Targ and Jane Katra, *Miracles of Mind: Exploring Nonlocal Mind and Spiritual Healing* (Novato, California: New World Library, 1999), p. 107.

30. Schulz, *Awakening Intuition,* p. 106.

31. Ruth Montgomery, *The World to Come* (New York: Three Rivers Press, 1999), pp. 29–37.

32. James Van Praagh, *Heaven and Hell: Making the Psychic Connection* (New York, Simon & Schuster Source, 2001), p. 68.

33. Ibid., p. 70.

34. Dossey, *Reinventing Medicine,* p. 123.

35. Judith Orloff, *Second Sight* (New York: Warner Books, 1996), p. 230.

36. Sheldrake, *Dogs That Know When Their Owners Are Coming Home,* p. 277.

37. Dean Radin, *The Conscious Universe: The Scientific Truth of Psychic Phenomena* (San Francisco: Harper *Edge,* 1997) p. 112.

38. Ibid., pp. 112–113.

39. Raymond Moody, *Life After Life* (New York: Bantam Books, 1975), p. 5.

40. Ibid.

41. Ibid., p. 184.

42. Elisabeth Kübler-Ross, *On Life After Death* (Berkley, California: Celestial Arts, 1991).

43. Michael B. Sabom, *Recollections of Death: A Medical Investigation* (New York: Harper & Row, 1982).

44. Kenneth Ring, *Heading Toward Omega: In Search of the Meaning of the Near-Death Experience* (New York: William Morrow, 1985).

45. Melvin Morse with Paul Perry, *Closer to the Light: Learning from the Near-Death Experiences of Children* (New York: Ivy Books, 1990).

46. Betty J. Eadie, *Embraced by the Light* (New York: Bantam Books, 1994).

47. Dannion Brinkley with Paul Perry, *Saved by the Light* (New York: Harper Paperbacks, 1994).

48. Jan Price, *The Other Side of Death* (New York: Fawcette Columbine, 1996).

49. Pam Kircher, *Love Is the Link: A Hospice Doctor Shares Her Experience of Near-Death and Dying* (Burdette, N.Y., Larson Publications, 1995).

50. Melvin Morse with Paul Perry, *Transformed by the Light: The Powerful Effect of Near-Death Experiences on People's Lives* (New York: Villard Books, 1992), pp. 166–167.

51. Ibid., p. 201.

52. Ibid., p. 135.

53. Ibid., p. 200.

54. Ibid., p. 202.

55. Moody, *Life After Life*, p. 6.

56. Morse, *Transformed by the Light*, pp. 189–190.

57. Joan Borysenko, *Fire in the Soul: A New Psychology of Spiritual Optimism* (New York: Warner Books, 1993), p. 147.

58. Joan Borysenko, *A Woman's Body: The Biology, Psychology, and Spirituality of the Feminine Life Cycle* (New York: Riverhead Books, 1997), p. 250.

59. Borysenko, *Fire in the Soul*, p. 147.

60. Ibid.

61. Borysenko, *A Woman's Body*, p. 250.

62. Ibid.

63. Borysenko, p. 148.

64. Neile Donald Walsch, *Conversations with God: an uncommon dialogue. Book 2* (Charlottesville, Virginia: Hampton Roads Publishing Company, Inc., 1997). Neile Donald Walsch, *Conversations with God: an uncommon dialogue. Book I.* (NewYork: G.P. Putnam's Sons, 1996). Neil Donald Walsch, *The Little Soul and the Sun: A Children's Parable Adapted from Conversations with God.* (Charlottesville, Virginia: Hampton Roads Publishing Company, Inc. 1998.)

65. Carolyn Myss, *Sacred Contracts: Awakening Your Divine Potential* (New York: Three Rivers Press, 2002).

66. Larry Dossey, *Recovering the Soul: A Scientific and Spiritual Approach* (New York: Bantam Books, 1994).

67. Myss, *Anatomy of an Illness*.

68. Orloff, *Second Sight*.

69. Schulz, *Awakening Intuition*.

70. Rosemary Altea, *You Have the Power: Stories and Exercises to Inspire and Unleash the Force Within* (New York: Eagle Brook, William Morrow & Co., Inc., 2000)

71. Judith Orloff, *Judith Orloff's Guide to Intuitive Healing: Five Steps to Physical, Emotional and Sexual Wellness* (New York: Times Books, Random House, 2000).

Chapter 3: Extraordinary Communication Players

72. Bill and Judy Guggenheim, *Hello from Heaven* (New York: Bantam Books, Inc., 1995), p. 12.

73. Ibid., p. 20.

74. James Van Praagh, *Heaven and Earth: Making the Psychic Connection* (New York: Simon & Schuster Source, 2001).

75. Rosemary Altea, *The Eagle and the Rose* (New York: Warner Books, 1995).

76. John Edward, *Crossing Over* (San Diego, California: Jodere Group, Inc., 2001).

77. Sylvia Browne, *Conversations with the Other Side*. (Carlsbad, California: Hay House, 2002).

78. Elisabeth Kübler Ross, *The Wheel of Life*: *A Memoir of Living and Dying* (New York: Simon & Schuster, 1997).

79. Altea, *The Eagle and the Rose*.

80. Gary Zukav, *Seat of the Soul* (New York: Simon & Schuster, 1989), p. 99.

81. Van Praagh, *Heaven and Earth*, p. 88.

82. Ibid., pp. 89–90.

83. Ibid., p. 90.

84. Zukav, *Seat of the Soul*, p. 101.

85. Ibid., p. 102.

86. Melvin Morse with Paul Perry, *Transformed by the Light: The Powerful Effect of Near-Death Experiences on People's Lives* (New York: Villard Books, 1992), pp. 166–167.

87. Melvin Morse with Paul Perry, *Where God Lives: The Science of the Paranormal and How Our Brains Are Linked to the Universe* (New York: Harper Collins Publishers, 2000), pp. 6–7.

88. Ibid., p. 8.

89. Ibid.

90. Nancy Gibbs, "Angels Among Us" *Time Magazine*: (December 27, 1993), pp. 56–65.

91. Burnham, *A Book of Angels: Reflections on Angels Past and Present and True Stories of How They Touch Our Lives* (New York: Ballantine Books, 1990), p. 19.

92. Ibid., p. 17.

93. Ibid., pp. 18–19.

94. Zukav, *Seat of the Soul,* pp. 182–183.

95. Rex Hauk (Ed.), *Angels, The Mysterious Messengers* (New York: Ballantine Books, 1994), p. 59.

96. Ibid., p. 196.

97. Ibid., p. 223.

98. Burnham, *A Book of Angels,* pp. 22–26.

99. Ibid., p. 24

100. Ibid.

101. Ibid., p. 26.

102. Morse, *Parting Visions* (New York: Villard Books, 1994), p. 91.

103. Hauk (Ed.), *Angels, The Mysterious Messengers,* p. 223

104. Morse, *Parting Visions,* p. 22.

105. Ibid., p. 21.

106. Zukav, *Seat of the Soul,* pp. 184–185.

107. Burnham, *A Book of Angels,* p. 17.

108. Ibid.

109. Eadie, *Embraced by the Light* (New York: Ballantine Books), pp. 126–128.

110. Brian Weiss, *Many Lives, Many Masters* (New York: Simon & Schuster, 1988), pp. 25–31

111. Ibid., p. 46.

112. Ibid., p. 54.

113. Ibid., p. 56.

114. Ibid. p 56.

115. Ibid. p. 56.

116. Brian Weiss, *Messages From the Masters: Tapping into the Power of Love* (New York: Warner Books, 2000).

117. Weiss, *Many Lives, Many Masters,* p. 140.

118. Ibid., p. 123.

119. Ibid., p. 120.

120. Ibid., p. 140.

121. Ibid., p. 124.

122. Ibid., p. 161.

123. Ibid., pp. 159–160.

124. Ibid., p. 195.

125. Yanni Maniates, Master teacher and educator of meditation and intuitive development, is founder and director of The Life Mastery Institute., Morrisville, PA. Phone: 215–295–5444. WebAddress: www.LearnMastery.com; email: yanni.maniates@verizon.net

Chapter 4: More About the Extraordinary

126. Gary Zukav, *Seat of the Soul* (New York: Simon & Schuster, 1989), p. 241.

127. Lawrence LeShan, *The Medium, the Mystic and the Physicist: Toward a General Theory of the Paranormal* (New York: The Viking Press, Inc., 1975), pp. 3–5.

128. Russell Targ and Jane Katra, *Miracles of Mind: Exploring Nonlocal Mind and Spiritual Healing* (Novato, California: New World Library, 1999), p. 3.

129. Targ and Katra, *Miracles of Mind.*

130. LeShan, *The Medium, the Mystic, and the Physicist,* p. 3.

131. Ibid., p. 16.

132. Ibid., p. 34.

133. Ibid., p. 37.

134. Ibid., p. 38.

135. Ibid., p. 39.

136. Ibid., p. 61.

137. Ibid., p. 73.

138. Gary Zukav, *Seat of the Soul* (New York: Simon & Schuster, 1989).

139. Herbert Benson, *The Relaxation Response* (New York: William Morrow, 1975).

140. Andrew Weil, *Breathing: The Master Key to Self-Healing*—The Self Healing Series (Boulder, Colorado: Sounds True Audio, 1999).

141. Doris Kunz, *Therapeutic Touch* (New York: Prentice-Hall, 1979); Doris Kunz, *Accepting your Power to Heal* (Santa Fe, NM: Bear & Company, 1993).

142. Larry Dossey, *Recovering the Soul: A Scientific and Spiritual Search* (New York: Bantam Books), p. 55.

143. Ibid.

144. Ibid.

145. Ibid., p. 56.

146. Ibid., pp. 56–58.

147. Dean Radin, *The Conscious Universe: The Scientific Truth of Psychic Phenomena* (San Francisco: HarperEdge, 1997), pp. 150–151.

148. Dossey, *Recovering the Soul*, p. 47.

149. Larry Dossey, *Healing Words: The Power of Medicine and the Practice of Medicine* (San Francisco: HarperCollins, 1993).

150. Larry Dossey, *Prayer Is Good Medicine* (San Francisco: HarperCollins Publishers, Inc., 1996).

151. Ibid., p. 4.

152. LeShan, *The Medium, the Mystic, and the Physicist.*

153. The Institute of Noetic Sciences is an organization founded by Edgar Mitchell (the Apollo 14 astronaut who is known for his walk on the moon) for the purpose of studying consciousness. According to the editors of IONS, "Noetic comes from the Greek word nous, which means mind or ways of knowing. Noetic sciences further the explorations of conventional science by rigorous inquiry into aspects of reality—such as mind, consciousness, spirit—that include yet go beyond physical phenomena." For membership information visit IONS' website: www.noetic.org, e-mail membership@Noetic.org or phone 877–769–4667.

154. Dossey, *Reinventing Medicine*, p. 40.

155. Ibid., pp. 41–42.

156. Ibid.

157. Ibid., pp. 43–44.

158. Elisabeth Targ, "Distant Healing," *IONS Review*, August-November, 1999, Number 49, p. 24.

159. Ibid.

160. Ibid., p. 26.

161. Ibid.

162. Ibid.

163. Ibid.

164. Ibid.

165. Ibid., p. 28.

166. Ibid.

167. Larry Dossey, *Reinventing Medicine: Beyond Mind-Body to a New Era of Healing* (San Francisco: HarperCollins, 1999), p. 37.

168. Ibid., p. 47.

169. Dossey, *Prayer Is Good Medicine*, p. 91.

170. Foundation for Inner Peace, *A Course in Miracles* (New York: Viking Penguin, 1996), Preface.

171. Ibid.

172. Ibid.

173. Yitta Halberstam and Judith Leventhal, *Small Miracles for The Jewish Heart* (Avon, MA: Adams Media Corporation, 2002), p. vi.

174. Ibid., pp. vi-vii.

175. Targ and Katra, *Miracles of Mind*, pp. 113–131.

176. Foundation for Inner Peace, *A Course in Miracles*, p. 1.

177. Ibid., p. 4.

178. Targ and Katra, *Miracles of Mind*, pp. 113–131.

179. Ibid., p. 190.

180. Ibid., p. 121.

181. Ibid., p. 120.

182. Ibid., p. 121.

183. Caryle Hirshberg and Marc Ian Barasch, *Remarkable Recovery: What Extraordinary Healings Tell Us About Getting Well and Staying Well* (New York: Riverhead Books, 1995.)

184. Ibid., p. xiv.

185. Ibid., pp. xiii-xiv.

186. Ibid., pp. 19–20.

187. Ibid., pp. 19–20.

188. Paul Raud, *Making Miracles; An Exploration into the Dynamics of Self-Healing* (New York: Warner Books, 1990).

189. Paul Pearsall, *Miracle in Maui: Let Miracles Happen in Your Life* (Makawao, Hawaii: Inner Ocean Publishing Co., 2001); Paul Pearsall, *Making Miracles: A Scientist's Journey to Death and Back Reveals the Powerful Hidden Order Behind Chaos, Crises and Coincidences* (New York: Prentice Hall Press, 1991).

190. Larry Dossey, *Reinventing Medicine*.

191. Foundations for Inner Peace, *A Course in Miracles*, p. 1.

192. Ibid.

193. Ibid., p. 3.

194. Ibid., p. 1.

195. Targ and Katra, *Making Miracles*, p. 186.

196. Ibid., p. 223.

197. Dossey, *Reinventing Medicine*, p. 225.

198. Targ and Katra, *Making Miracles,* pp. 3–4 & 194–196.

199. Integrated Energy Therapy (IET) is a holistic therapy system developed by Stevan J. Thayer which blends spiritual counseling and touch-based energy therapy. Stevan Thayer, an ordained Interfaith Minister and a Reiki Master, is also creator of a holistic health center, The Center Of Being, Inc., and conducts Healingwith the Energy of Angels workshops. For Information regarding IET training, seminars and educational materials, Steven Thayer may be contacted at www.centerofbeing,com. He can also be reached at The Center of Being, Inc., PO Box 883, Woodstock, NY 12498-0883. Phone—845–657–7220.

200. Dr Joyce Goodrich is President and Coordinator of the Consciousness Research and Training Project, 315 East 68th St., Box 9G, New York, New York, 10021. A psychologist and educator, Joyce conducts seminars in which she teaches the approach to healing developed by Dr. Lawrence LeShan, psychologist, author and theoretician in consciousness studies, parapsychology and other areas of science. Phone 212–879–9771. E–mail: crtp@mindspring.com.

201. Louise I. Morin, DVD, specializes in alternative or integrative medicine for animals. She can be reached at VCA Delaware Valley Animal Hospital, Fairless Hills, PA, 19030. Phone: 215–946–1111.

202. Tahitian Noni juice information and products can be ordered from Penny Gray, 430 S. Olds Blvd., Fairless Hills, PA, 19030. Phone: 215–943–8860.

203. Transfer Factor information and products can be ordered from Steve & Peg Kostorowski, 14955 West Crenshaw Dr., Goodyear, AZ, 85338. Phone: 623–535–7000. E-mail: healthy@my4life.com; Web Address: www.my4life.com/healthy.

204. Judith Orloff, *Second Sight* (New York: Warner Books, 1996), p. 25.

205. Melvin Morse, *Where God Lives: The Science of the Paranormal and How Our Brains Are Linked to the Universe* (New York: Harper Collins Publishers, 2000), p. 102.

206. Ibid.

207. Ibid., p. 101.

208. Rupert Sheldrake, *Dogs That Know When Their Owners Are Coming Home: And Other Unexplained Powers of Animals* (New York: Three Rivers Press, 1999), pp. 301– 317.

209. Orloff, *Second Sight,* p. 256.

210. Ibid., p. 259.

211. Ibid., p. 260.

212. Maril Crabtree, *Sacred Feathers: The Power of One Feather to Change Your Life* (Avon, MA: Adams Media Corporation, 2002).

213. Elisabeth Kübler-Ross, *Death Is of Vital Importance: On Life, Death, and Life After Death* (Barrytown, New York: Station Hill Press, 1995), p. 1.

214. Ibid., pp. 6–7.

215. Ibid., pp. 95–98.

216. Viktor Frankl, *Man's Search for Meaning* (New York: Pocket Books, 1959).

217. Melvin Morse with Paul Perry, *Parting Visions* (New York: Villard Books, 1994), p. 179.

218. Ibid.

219. Ibid., pp. 180–181.

220. Viktor Frankl, *Man's Search for Meaning* (New York: Pocket Books, 1959).

221. Ibid., p. 170.

Part Two

The Stories

Chapter 6: Intuitive and Precognitive Wisdom

222. Maggie Callanan and Patricia Kelley, *Final Gifts: Understanding the Special Awareness, Needs, and Communications of the Dying* (New York: Bantam Books, 1992), pp. 77–78, 199–135.

223. Pamela Kircher, *Love Is the Link* (Burdette, New York: Larson Publications, 1995), p. 140.

Chapter 8: Extraordinary Encounters and Connections

224. Gary Zukav, *Seat of the Soul* (New York: Simon & Schuster, 1989). pp. 178–179.

Chapter 12: Developing Intuitively—My Journey

225. Lewis Mehl-Madrona, *Coyote Medicine: Lessons from Native American Healing* (New York: Simon & Schuster, 1998).

226. Gary Zukav, *Seat of the Soul* (New York: Simon & Schuster, 1989).

227. Yanni Maniates, Master teacher and educator of meditation and intuitive development is founder and director of the Life Mastery Institute. Phone: 215-295-5444. E-mail:Yanni.Maniates@verizon.net. Web Site: http://www.LearnMastery.com.

228. The Butterfly Foundation—The Brittany Pasqual Oncology Research Foundation was created in 2002 in memory of four-year-old Brittany Pasqual who succumbed to a rare pediatric cancer called neuroblastoma. The Butterfly Foundation works to find a cure for pediatric cancer and support families whose children are diagnosed with cancer. Specifically, the Butterfly Foundation is dedicated to: 1. The investigation and discovery of the causes of pediatric cancer; 2. The development of effective strategies for the prevention of pediatric cancer; 3. The education and empowerment of those who are dealing with pediatric cancer. Those who desire further information regarding contributions to—or the work of—The Butterfly Foundation, may contact Carol S. Pasqual, at 215–504–5441. Also, visit www.thebutterflyfoundation.org.

229. Larry Dossey, *Prayer Is Good Medicine* (San Francisco: HarperCollins Publishers, Inc., 1996), p. 91.

230. For information regarding animal communication consultation and seminars taught by Sharon Orlando, contact Sharon at 10 Sheffield Station Rd., Flemington, NJ 08822. Phone: 908–284–9160.

231. For books, audiotapes, CDs, videos and information regarding animal and communication training seminars and workshops taught by Penelope Smith, visit www.animaltalk.net. E-mail: Penelope@animaltalk.net Phone: 415–663–1247. Address: Anima Mundi Incorporated, P.O. Box 1060, Point Reyes, CA 94956. Those wishing information regarding animal communication and consultation may also contact Marlene Sandler who also trained with Penelope Smith. Marlene can be reached at Animal Communications, Marlene Sandler, M.Ed., P.O. Box 476, Warrington, PA 18976. Phone: 215–491–0707 / Fax: 215–491–0202.

232. Dr. Elisabeth Kübler-Ross is a renowned psychiatrist and researcher of near-death experiences, the process of dying, and life-after-life. She is also author of more than a dozen books. During an interview with Dr. Ross in 2001, Dr. Ross recommended that I read the wisdom of White Eagle which appears in thefollowing books: *Spiritual Enfoldment 1,2, and 3; Quiet Mind*; and *Walking with the Angels*. All are published by The White Eagle Publishing Trust in Great Britain by Cambridge University Press.

Bibliography and Recommended Material

Abraham-Hicks Publications, Workshops, Cassette Tapes & CDs. San Antonio, Texas: (830–755–2299 or www.abraham-hicks.com).

Achterberg, Jeanne, Barbara Dossey and Leslie Kolkmeirer. *Rituals of Healing: Using Imagery for Health and Wellness.* New York: Bantam Books, 1994.

Achterberg, Jeanne. *Imagery in Healing: Shamanism and Modern Medicine.* Boston: Shambhala, 1985.

Achterberg, Jeanne and G. Frank Lawless. *Imagery and Disease.* Champaign, Illinois: Institute for Personality and Ability Testing, Inc., 1978 and 1984.

Altea, Rosemary. *You Have the Power: Stories and Exercises to Inspire and Unleash the Force Within.* New York: Eagle Brook, William Morrow & Inc., 2000.

———. *Proud Spirit: Lessons, Insights & Healing from "The Voice of the Spirit World," Rosemary Altea.* New York: William Morrow and Co., Inc.

———. *The Eagle and The Rose.* New York: Warner Books, 1995.

Andrews, Ted. *Animal-Speak: The Spiritual & Magical Powers of Creatures Great & Small.* St. Paul, Minnesota: Llewellyn Publishers, 2001

Bach, Richard. *Jonathan Livingston Seagull: a story.* New York: The Macmillan Co., 1970.

Bekoff, Marc (Ed.). *The Smile of a Dolphin: Remarkable Accounts of Animal Emotions.* New York: Discovery Books/Random House, 2000.

Benson, Herbert. *Timeless Healing: The Power and Biology of Belief.* New York: Simon and Schuster, 1997.

———. *The Relaxation Response.* New York: William Morrow, 1975.

Berman, Phillip L. *The Journey Home: What Near-Death Experiences and Mysticism Teach Us About The Gift of Life.* New York: Pocket Books, 1996.

Bloom, Pamela, (Ed.). *Buddhist Acts of Compassion.* Berkeley, California: Conari Press, 2000.

Borysenko, Joan. *A Woman's Book of Life: The Biology, Psychology, and Spirituality of the Feminine Life Cycle.* New York: Riverhead Books, 1997.

———. *Fire in the Soul: A New Psychology of Spiritual Optimism.* New York: Warner Books, 1993.

Bowman, Carol. *Return from Heaven: Beloved Relatives Reincarnated within Your Family.* New York: HarperCollins, 2003.

———. *Children's Past Lives: How Past Life Memories Affect Your Child.* New York: Bantam Books, 1997.

Brennan, Barbara Ann. *Hands of Light: A Guide to Healing Through the Human Energy Field.* New York: Bantam Books, 1987.

Brinkley, Dannion with Paul Perry. *At Peace in the Light.* New York: HarperCollins, 1995.

———. *Saved by the Light.* New York: Harper Paperbacks, 1994.

Browne, Sylvia. *Conversations with the Other Side.* Carlsbad, California: Hay House, 2002.

Burnham, Sophy. *A Book of Angels: Reflections on Angels Past and Present and True Stories of How They Touch Our Lives.* New York: Ballantine Books, 1990.

Callanan, Maggie and Patricia Kelley. *Final Gifts: Understanding the Special Awareness, Needs and Communication of the Dying.* New York: Bantam Books, 1992.

Campbell, Joseph (Ed.). *The Portable Jung.* New York: Penguin Books, 1976.

Childs-Ortiz, Ph.D, Annette. *Will You Dance?* Incline Village, NV: The Wandering Feather Press, 2002. (A small, beautiful book filled with great wisdom that will touch the heart.)

Chopra, Deepok. *The Seven Spiritual Laws of Success: A Practical Guide to the Fulfillment of Your Dreams.* San Rafael, California: Amber-Allen Publishing Co., 1993.

———. *Quantum Healing: Exploring the Frontiers of Mind/Body Medicine.* New York: Bantam Books, 1990.

Coelho, Paul. *The Alchemist.* New York: HarperCollins, 1994.

Cooper, David A. *The Mystical Kabbalah.* Boulder, CO: Sounds True Audio, 1994. (A gentle, comfortable and entertaining introduction to the wisdom of Kabbalah.)

Cowan, Tom. *Shamanism: As a Spiritual Practice for Daily Life.* Freedom, CA: The Crossing Press, 1996.

Crabtree, Mariel. *Sacred Feathers: The Power of One Feather to Change Your Life.* Avon, Massachusetts: Adams Media Corporation, 2002.

Dossey, Larry. *Reinventing Medicine: Beyond Mind-Body to a New Era of Healing.* San Francisco: HarperCollins, 1999.

———. *Prayer Is Good Medicine.* San Francisco: HarperCollins, 1993.

———. *Healing Words: The Power of Prayer and the Power of Medicine.* San Francisco: HarperCollins, 1993).

———. *Recovering the Soul: A Scientific and Spiritual Search.* New York: Bantam Books, 1989.

Dyer, Wayne W. *The Power of Intention: Learning to Co-create Your World Your Way.* Carlsbad, CA: Hay House, 2004.

———. *There's A Spiritual Solution to Every Problem.* New York: Harper-Collins, 2001.

———. *Your Sacred Self: Making the Decision to Be Free.* New York: HarperCollins, 1995.

Eadie, Betty. *Embraced by the Light.* New York: Bantam Books, 1994.

Edward, John. *Crossing Over.* San Diego, California: Jodere Group, Inc., 2001.

Emoto, Masaru. *Messages from Water.* El Segundo, CA: Hado Publishing, 1999.

Epstein, Fred and Joshua Horwitz. *If I Get to Five: What Children Can Teach Us about Courage and Character.* New York: Henry Holt & Co., 2003.

Frankl, Viktor. *Man's Search for Meaning.* New York: Pocket Books, 1959.

Foundation for Inner Peace. *A Course in Miracles.* New York: Viking Penguin, 1996.

Gallup, George. *Adventures in Immortality: A look beyond the threshold of death.* New York: McGraw Hill Book Company, 1982.

Gass, Robert and On Wings of Song. *Songs of Healing.* Carlisle, MA: Spring Hill Music, 1992. (Music that touches the heart.)

Gibbs, Nancy. "Angels Among Us." *Time Magazine.* (December 27,1993), 56–65.

Gibran, Kahlil. *The Prophet.* New York: Knopf, 1969.

Goldman, Jonathan. *Chakra Chants.* Boulder, Colorado: Etherean Music for Spirit Music, 1998. (Extraordinary music that heals by shifting frequency and balancing the chakras.)

Griscom, Christine with Wulfing Von Rohr. *There Is No Time.* New York: Simon & Schuster, 1986.

Guggenheim, Bill and Judy Guggenheim. *Hello from Heaven.* New York: Bantam Books, 1995.

Halberstam, Yitta and Judith Leventhal. *Small Miracles for the Jewish Heart.* Avon: Massachusetts: Adams Media Corporation, 2002.

Halpern, Steven. *Chakra Suite: Music for Sound Healing & Meditation*. San Anselmo, CA: Steven Halpern's Inner Peace Music, 2001. (Exquisite, healing music to accompany relaxation, meditation, and yoga).

Harner, Michael. *The Way of the Shaman*. San Francisco: HarperCollins, 1990.

Hawkins, David R. *Power vs. Force: The Hidden Determinants of Human Behavior*. Carlsbad, CA: Hay House, Inc. 1995. (A magnificent guide to discovering your authenic power.)

Hirshberg, Caryle and Marc Ian Barasch. *Remarkable Recovery: What Extraordinary Healings Tell Us About Getting Well and Staying Well*. New York: Riverhead Books, 1995.

Hauk, Rex. (Ed.) *Angels, The Mysterious Messengers*. New York: Ballantine Books, 1984.

Hiby, Lydia with Bonnie S. Weintraub. *Conversations with Animals: Cherished Messages and Memories as Told by an Animal Communicator*. Troutdale, OR: New Sage Press, 1998.

Hicks, Jerry and Esther Hicks. *The Science of Deliberate Creation Tapes*: Boston, MA, 10/5/02. San Antonio, Texas, 2002. (830–755-2299 or www.abraham-hicks.com)

———. *Ask and It Is Given*. Carlsbad, CA: Hay House, Inc. 2004.

———. *A New Beginning I*. San Antonio, Texas: Abraham-Hicks Publications, 1988.

———. *A New Beginning II*. San Antonio, Texas: Abraham-Hicks Publications, 1991.

Ions Noetic Sciences Review. Sausalito, California: The Institute of Noetic Sciences,1999. (www.noetic.org.)

Jampolsky, Gerald G. *Love Is Letting Go of Fear*. Berkeley, California: Celestial Arts, 1979.

Jarry, Francine & Abraham-Hicks. *A New Adventure*. San Antonio, Texas: Abraham-Hicks Music: 2003. (Joyful, uplifting music and affirmations for the soul.)

Kabat-Zinn, Jon. *Wherever You Go There You Are: Mindfulness Meditation in Everyday Life*. New York: Hyperion, 1994.

Kaur, Singh, Kim Robertson, & Mosaic. *Crimson Collection: Volumes 6 &7*. Phoenix, Arizona: Invincible Productions, 1991. (Harp and vocal selections to touch the soul.)

Kaur, Singh, and Kim Robertson. *Crimson Collection: Volumes 1 & 2*. Phoenix, Arizona: Invincible Productions, 1991. (More beautiful music to soothe the soul.)

Kircher, *Pamela M. Love Is the Link: A Hospice Doctor Shares Her Experience of Near-Death and Dying*. Burdette, New York: Larson Publications, 1995.

Kirven, Robert H. *Angels in Action: What Swedenborg Saw and Heard.* West Chester, Pennsylvania: The Swedenborg Foundation, 1994.

Kübler-Ross, Elisabeth. *The Wheel of Life: A Memoir of Living and Dying.* New York: Simon & Schuster, 1997.

———. *Death Is of Vital Importance: On Life, Death and Life After Life.* Barrytown, New York: Station Hill Press, 1995.

———. *On Life After Death.* Berkley, California: Celestial Arts, 1991.

———. *On Children and Death.* New York: Macmillan Publishing, 1983.

LeShan, Lawrence. *The Medium, the Mystic and the Physicist: Toward a General Theory of the Paranormal.* New York: Viking Press, 1974.

Lundahl, Craig R. and Harold A. Widdison. *The Eternal Journey: How Near-Death Experiences Illuminate our Earthly Lives.* New York: Warner Books, 1997.

Matt, Daniel C. *The Essential Kabbalah: The Heart of Jewish Mysticism.* San Francisco: HarperCollins, 1995.

Mehl-Madrona, Lewis. *Coyote Medicine: Lessons from Native American Healing.* New York: Simon & Schuster, 1998.

———. *Coyote Healing: Miracles in Native Medicine.* Rochester, Vermont: Bear & Company, 2003.

Mitchell, Stephen (Translator). *Bhagavad Gita.* New York: Three Rivers Press, 2000.

Montgomery, Ruth. *The World to Come.* New York: Three Rivers Press, 1999.

Moody, Raymond. *Reunions: Visionary Encounters with Departed Loved Ones.* New York: Villard Books, 1993.

———. *Life After Life.* New York: Bantam, 1976.

———. *Reflections on Life After Life.* New York: Bantam Books, 1977.

Morgan, Marlo. *Mutant Message: Down Under.* New York: HarperCollins Publishers, 1991.

Morse, Melvin with Paul Perry. *Where God Lives: The Science of the Paranormal And How Our Brains Are Linked to the Universe.* New York: HarperCollinsPublishers, 2000.

———. *Parting Visions: Uses and Meanings of Pre-Death, Psychic, and Spiritual Experiences.* New York: Bantam, 1994.

———. *Transformed by the Light: The Powerful Effect of Near-Death Experiences on People's Lives.* New York: Villard Books, 1992.

———. *Closer to the Light: Learning from the Near-Death Experiences of Children.* New York: Ivy Books, 1990.

Myss, Caroline. *Sacred Contracts: Awakening Your Divine Potential.* New York: Three Rivers Press, 2002

———. *Anatomy of an Illness: The Seven Stages of Power and Healing.* New York: Random House, 1997.

————. *Energy Anatomy: The Science of Personal Power, Spirituality, and Health.* Boulder, Colorado: Sounds True Audio, 1996.

McElroy, Susan Chernak. *Animals as Teachers & Healers: True Stories and Reflections.* New York: Ballantine Books, 1996.

Nachman, Rebbe. *The Empty Chair: Finding Hope and Joy.* Woodstock, Vermont: Jewish Lights Publishing, 2001.

Naparstek, Belleruth. *Your Sixth Sense: Unlocking the Power of Your Intuition.* San Francisco: HarperCollins, Publishers, 1997.

Orloff, Judith. *Positive Energy: 10 Extraordinary Prescriptions for Transforming Fatigue, Stress & Fear into Vibrance, Strength & Love.* New York: Harmony Books, 2004.

————. *Dr. Judith Orloff's Guide to Intuitive Healing: 5 Steps to Physical, Emotional, and Sexual Wellness.* New York: Times Books, Random House, 2000.

————. *Second Sight.* New York: Warner Books, 1996.

Pearsall, Paul. *Miracle in Maui: Let Miracles Happen in Your Life.* Makawao, Hawaii: Inner Ocean Publishing Co., 2001.

————. *Making Miracles: A Scientist's Journey to Death and Back Reveals the Powerful Hidden Order Behind Chaos, Crises and Coincidences.* New York: Prentice Hall Press, 1991.

Pert, Candace B. *Molecules of Emotion.* New York: Scribner, 1997.

Price, Jan. *The Other Side of Death.* New York: Fawcette Columbine, 1996.

Raud, Paul. *Making Miracles: An Exploration into the Dynamics of Self-Healing.* New York: Warner Books, 1990.

Radin, Dean. *The Conscious Universe: The Scientific Truth of Psychic Phenomena.* San Francisco: HarperEdge, 1997.

Remen, Rachel Naomi. *My Grandfather's Blessings: Stories of Strength, Refuge, and Belonging.* New York: Riverhead Books, 2000.

————. *Kitchen Table Wisdom: Stories That Heal.* Riverhead Books, 1996

Ring, Kenneth. *Heading Toward Omega: In Search of the Meaning of the Near-Death Experience.* New York: William Morrow, 1985.

Rinpoche, Sogyal. *The Tibetan Book of Living and Dying.* New York: Harper Collins, 1993.

Rocha, Adriana and Kristi Jorde. *A Child of Eternity: An Extraordinary Young Girl's Message from the World Beyond.* New York: Ballantine Books, 1995.

Rodegast, Pat and Judith Stanton. *Emmanuel's Book III. What Is an Angel Doing Here?* New York: Bantam Books, 1989.

————. *Emmanuel's Book II: The Choice for Love.* New York: Bantam Books, 1989.

————. *Emmanuel's Book: A Manual for Living Comfortably in the Cosmos.* New York: Bantam Books, 1987.

Ruiz, Don Miguel. *The Mastery of Love: A Practical Guide to the Art of Relationship*. San Raphael, California: Amber-Allen Publishing Co., 1999.

———. *The Four Agreements: A Practical Guide to Personal Freedom*. SanRaphael, California: Amber-Allen Publishing Co., 1997.

Sabom, Michael B. *Recollections of Death: A Medical Investigation*. New York: Harper and Row, 1982.

Sams, Jamie and David Carson. *Medicine Cards*. New York: St. Martin's Press, 1988.

Samuels, Michael and Mary Rockwood Lane. *The Path of the Feather: A Handbook and Kit for Making Medicine Wheels and Calling in the Spirit Animals*. New York: G.P. Putnam's Sons, 2000.

Sanders, Catherine. *Surviving Grief and Learning to Live Again*. New York: John Wiley & Sons, 1992.

Schulz, Mona Lisa. *Awakening Intuition*. New York: Three Rivers Press, 1998.

Sheldrake, Rupert. *Dogs That Know When Their Owners Are Coming Home*. New York: Three Rivers Press, 1999.

Smith, Penelope. *Animal Talk: Interspecies Telepathic Communication*. Hillsboro, Oregon: Beyond Words Publishing, Inc., 1999.

———. *Interspecies Telepathic Communication Tape Series*. Point Reyes, California: Pegasus Publications, 1994

———. *Telepathic Communication with Animals*. Crestone, Colorado: Hartworks, Inc., 1990.

Siegel, Bernie. *Love, Medicine, and Miracles*. New York: Harper and Row, 1986.

Stearn, Jess. *The Sleeping Prophet*. New York: Bantam Books, 1968.

Stevenson, Ian. *Children Who Remember Previous Lives*. Charlottesville, Virginia: University Press of Virginia, 1987.

Targ, Elisabeth. "Distant Healing." *IONS Review,* August–November, Number 49, 1999, pp. 24–29.

Targ, Russell and Jane Katra. *Miracles of Mind: Exploring Nonlocal Mind and Spiritual Healing*. Novato, California: New World Library, 1998.

Tolle, Eckhart. *The Power of Now: A Guide to Spiritual Enlightenment*. Novato, California: New World Library, 1999.

Thayer, Steven J. *Interview with an Angel: Our World, Our Selves, Our Destiny*. Gillette, New Jersey: Edin Books, Inc, 1997.

Van Praagh, James. *Heaven and Earth: Making the Psychic Connection.* New York: Simon & Schuster Source, 2001.

———. *Talking to Heaven: A Medium's Message of Life After Death.* New York: Penguin Putnam, 1997.

———. *Reaching to Heaven: A Spiritual Journey Through Life and Death.* New York: Penguin Books, 1999.

Vincent, Ken R. *Visions of God. Burdette,* New York: Larson Publications, 1994.

Virtue, Doreen. *Divine Guidance: How to Have a Dialogue with God and Your Guardian Angel.* Los Angeles, California: Renaissance Books. 1998.

———. *Healing with the Angels: How Angels Can Assist You in Every Area of Your Life.* Carlsbad, California: Hay House, 1999.

Wakefield, Dan. *Expect a Miracle: The Miraculous Things That Happen to Ordinary People.* San Francisco: HarperCollins, 1995.

Walsch, Neale Donald. *The Little Soul and the Sun: A Children's Parable Adapted from Conversations with God.* Charlottesville, Virginia: Hampton Roads Publishing Company, 1998.

———. *Conversations with God: an uncommon dialogue, Book 2.* *Charlottesville, Virginia: Hampton Roads Publishing Company, Inc., 1997.*

———. *Conversations with God: an uncommon dialogue, Book 1.* New York: G.P. Putnam's Sons, 1996.

Weil, Andrew. *Breathing: The Master Key to Self-Healing—The Self-Healing Series.* Boulder, Colorado: Sounds True Audio, 1999.

Weiss, Brian. *Messages from the Masters: Tapping into the Power of Love.* New York: Simon & Schuster, 1988

———. *Through Time into Healing.* New York: Simon and Schuster, 1992.

———. *Many Lives, Many Masters.* New York: Simon and Schuster, 1988.

Woolger, Roger J. *Other Lives, Other Selves: A Jungian Psychotherapist Discovers Past Lives.* New York: Bantam Books, 1988.

Yogananda, Paramahansa. *Autobiography of a Yogi.* Los Angeles: Self Realization Fellowship, 1946 & 1972.

Zaleski, Carol. *Other World Visions.* Oxford: Oxford University Press, 1987.

Zukav, Gary. *Soul Stories.* New York: Simon & Schuster, 2000.

———. *The Seat of the Soul.* New York: John Wiley and Sons, Inc. 1992.

——— and Linda Francis. *Heart of the Soul: Emotional Awareness.* New York: Simon & Schuster, 2001.

Index

About the Author

For close to 20 years, Susan Apollon has worked as a psychotherapist, psychologist and healer, treating children and adults who are traumatized, diagnosed with cancer or other life-threatening illnesses, dealing with death and dying, and those who are grieving. She brings to her patients a gentle blend of warmth, compassion and wisdom gained from surviving her own illnesses and losses; her expertise and training as a wife, mom, teacher, psychologist, researcher and student of energy, mind and consciousness; and finally, her own intuitive development.

Coming from a family of physicians (father, brothers, aunts and uncles, and daughter Rebecca), Susan's intent is to heal (emotionally, mentally, physically and spiritually), but at the level of the soul—and always with love and compassion. Focusing on the many blessings each of us has, she guides her patients to the recognition that we are here to live life in joy and peace (to be happy) and that the resources for this are within each of us. "Intention is everything," she often tells her patients. "With love, clear intent and choice, transformation, healing, and very often, spiritual awakening, become our reality. And when this occurs, everything feels wonderful."

Among Susan's most treasured blessings are her husband, best friend, and partner, Warren, a practicing orthodontist in Langhorne, PA, whom she has known and loved for more than forty years, and her two grown children whom she respects, honors and adores—David, a marketing consultant—and Rebecca, a second year resident in emergency medicine. She has been in private practice in Yardley, PA since 1991.

Bonus Offer

In appreciation of your reading this book,
you are invited to receive an additional
special report online for free.

Visit my website:
www.touched-by-the-extraordinary.com/specialreport

register your name and
enter the password:

TBTEBook

How to Contact the Author

If you have experienced a unique inspirational
and/or extraordinary story that you would like to share
with Susan, please contact her at:

Matters of the Soul, LLC
PO Box 403
Yardley, PA 19067

PHONE: (215) 321–0632
FAX: (215) 321–3830
EMAIL: susan@touched-by-the-extraordinary.com

or visit her website:
www.touched-by-the-extraordinary.com

Order Form

ONLINE ORDERS:	www.touched-by-the-extraordinary.com
TELEPHONE ORDERS:	Call 1–888–768–8353
	(have your credit card ready.)
FAX ORDERS:	215–321–3830
POSTAL ORDERS:	Matters of the Soul, LLC
	PO Box 403
	Yardley, PA 19067
	Telephone 215–321–0632

TITLE	PRODUCT	PRICE	QUANTITY	SUBTOTAL
Touched by the Extraordinary	Book	$19.95	_____	_____
		Sales Tax*		_____
		Shipping**		_____
		TOTAL		_____

*Sales Tax: Please add 6% tax for products shipped to Pennsylvania addresses.

**Please add $3.50 for first product and $0.50 for each additional product. Please add $5.50 for priority mail.

Sold to

Name: _____

Address: _____

City, State Zip: _____

Telephone: _____

E-mail address: _____

Send to

Name: _____

Address: _____

City, State Zip: _____

Telephone: _____

Payment

❏ Check enclosed   ❏ VISA   ❏ MasterCard

Card Number _____

Security Code* _____

*Three digit number on the back of card after card number

Exp. Date _____

Name on card _____

Signature _____